1006065146

CONVERGENCE AND COLLABORATION OF CAMPUS INFORMATION SERVICES

EDITED BY PETER HERNON
AND RONALD R. POWELL

WESTPORT, CONNECTICUT • LONDON

Library of Congress Cataloging-in-Publication Data

Convergence and collaboration of campus information services / edited by Peter Hernon and Ronald R. Powell.
  p. cm.
  Includes bibliographical references and index.
  ISBN 978–1–59158–603–6 (alk. paper)
  1. Libraries and colleges. 2. Academic libraries—United States—Case studies. I. Hernon, Peter. II. Powell, Ronald R.
  Z718.C858 2008
  027.70973—dc22   2008029356

British Library Cataloguing in Publication Data is available.

Copyright © 2008 by Peter Hernon and Ronald R. Powell

All rights reserved. No portion of this book may be reproduced, by any process or technique, without the express written consent of the publisher.

Library of Congress Catalog Card Number: 2008029356
ISBN: 978–1–59158–603–6

First published in 2008

Libraries Unlimited, 88 Post Road West, Westport, CT 06881
A Member of the Greenwood Publishing Group, Inc.
www.lu.com

Printed in the United States of America

The paper used in this book complies with the Permanent Paper Standard issued by the National Information Standards Organization (Z39.48–1984).

10 9 8 7 6 5 4 3 2 1

CONTENTS

Illustrations	ix
Preface	xi

1 Introduction 1
Peter Hernon and Ronald R. Powell

Literature Review	2
Study Objectives	3
Procedures	3
Questionnaire Findings	5
Site Visits	12
Conclusion	12
Notes	14
Appendix: The Eleven Case Studies	16

CASE STUDIES

2 Innovation Is an Ongoing Process: Collaboration
   at the University of California–Irvine 35
Carol Ann Hughes

Convergence	37
Technological Convergence	38
Programmatic Convergence	44
Conclusion	47
Notes	47

CONTENTS

3 Sowing an Old Field with a New Crop: Collaborative
   Services of Libraries and Other Campus Units   49
   Richard W. Meyer and Tyler O. Walters

   Part I: Recognizing Motivators   50
   Part II: Reshaping Facilities   52
   Part III: Refocusing Services   57
   Conclusion   61

4 From Isolation to Engagement: Strategy,
   Structure, and Process   63
   Barbara J. Krügel and Timothy F. Richards

   Creating the Conditions for Success   63
   Changes in Organizational Structure   66
   Organizational/Staff Development   70
   Campus Outreach Programs   72
   Conclusion   77
   Appendix: University of Michigan–Dearborn, Mardigian Library   78

5 Convergence and Collaboration in Information
   Services at the University of Calgary   81
   Darlene Warren

   Convergence of Library, Museum, Archives, and Press   82
   Collaborations   84
   Planning and Strategic Transformation   91
   Building for the Future, from Information Commons
     to Learning Commons   97
   Conclusion   98
   Notes   98

6 The Library as Model of Integrated Student-centered
   Academic Support Enterprise   101
   Jay Schafer and Anne C. Moore

   Creating the Learning Commons: Collaboration across
     the Campus Organization   102
   Other Campus Agencies Have Been Integral to the
     Creation and Success of the Learning Commons   104
   Pedagogy and Faculty   107
   Student and Academic Support   114
   Internal Library Operations   120
   Future Initiatives   123
   Conclusion   123
   Note   124

7	The University of Georgia Student Learning Center *Florence E. King, Carla Wilson Buss, Nadine Cohen,* *Deborah Stanley, and Elizabeth White*	125
	History and Development of the SLC	127
	The Future	137
	Conclusion	138
	Notes	139
8	From Faction to Fusion: The Columbia University Libraries as Information Services Enterprise *James Neal*	141
	Organizational Context	141
	Converging Units	143
	Compelling Trends	145
	Conclusion	149
9	Libraries and Convergence at Yale *Alice Prochaska*	151
	Curriculum Reform and the Growth of Interdisciplinary Studies	152
	Research Support and the Exposure of Collections	155
	Changing Configurations of Space	157
	Conclusion: The University and Its Communities	159
	Notes	160
10	The Poetry Center at Suffolk University *Fred Marchant and Robert E. Dugan*	163
	The Gift	163
	Convergence	167
	Strategies	170
	The Results	171
	Intentio Dilato (Convergence Expanded)	173
	Conclusion	174
	Notes	175
11	Collaborative Initiatives to Deliver Agricultural Information *Barbara S. Hutchinson, Jeanne L. Pfander, and George B. Ruyle*	177
	The Agriculture Network Information Center: A Model Alliance	180
	The University of Arizona AgNIC Experience: A Collaborative Web Site for Rangeland Management	185

　　　　Conclusion: Lessons Learned from the AgNIC and
　　　　　　Western Rangelands Collaborations　　　　　　　　192
　　　　Notes　　　　　　　　　　　　　　　　　　　　　　　194

CONCLUSION

12　Other Perspectives and Concluding Thoughts　　　　201
　　Peter Hernon, Ronald R. Powell, and Amy F. Fyn

　　　　Perspectives of Non-librarians　　　　　　　　　　　202
　　　　Conclusion　　　　　　　　　　　　　　　　　　　209
　　　　Notes　　　　　　　　　　　　　　　　　　　　　　211

Bibliography　　　　　　　　　　　　　　　　　　　　　　213

Index　　　　　　　　　　　　　　　　　　　　　　　　　　223

About the Editors and Contributors　　　　　　　　　　　　233

ILLUSTRATIONS

Figures

3.1	Educational Technologies Preliminary Organization Chart	60
7.1	Collaboration in the SLC	126

Tables

7.1	What Do You Do in the SLC?	135
12.1	Selected Readings on Convergence and Collaboration	210

Photographs

3.1	Library West Commons (long view from above)	54
3.2	Library East Commons study cluster (one study cluster with four students)	56
5.1	Students Can Book Collaborative Workrooms through an Online Booking System	85
5.2	a–d: The Information Commons	86
5.3	Student Navigator Assisting a Student	87
6.1	Procrastination Station Café	105
6.2	Third Floor Quiet Study Area	108

6.3	Writing Center	116
6.4	Academic Advising Link and Career Services Desk	119
6.5	Glass Study Room and "Pods"	121
6.6	Students with Laptops at a "Pod"	121
10.1	The Poetry Center Arranged as Lecture Space	172
10.2	The Poetry Center Arranged into Three Group Study Rooms	172
10.3	The Poetry Center Arranged as Creative Writing Space with the Zieman Poetry Collection in the Background	173
10.4	The Zieman Poetry Collection	175

PREFACE

Convergence and collaboration enable an academic library to be more fully engaged with its campus and perhaps beyond—on a local, state, regional, or national level—and to better achieve the educational mission of the library and its parent institution. In its simplest form, convergence is defined as joint activities of a campus's units (e.g., academic departments, information technology (IT), food services, and educational development services) to further their shared mission of supporting teaching, learning, and inquiry. Convergence, which can involve collaboration and even merging of both organizational structures and service delivery, leads to users' benefiting from contact with all individuals who have relevant expertise. Collaboration also may lead to convergence of collections, thereby enhancing library resources available to an institution's constituents.

Convergence is not limited to renovation projects or joint service units within the library; collaborative spaces might exist elsewhere—either physically or virtually—and involve partnerships between libraries and IT or instructional technology departments; academic departments; campus centers for learning, teaching, or writing; and student and food services. Specific examples of convergence include centers for teaching excellence, tutor and writing centers, information arcades, facilities for multi-media production and delivery, information and learning commons, cafés, photocopying centers; centers for distance education, participation in the use of course management software (e.g., Blackboard) to make library resources available to classes digitally and to make students more information literate, publishing (e.g., university presses and digital collections, including institutional repositories), counseling and career centers, and services for students for whom English is a secondary language (mostly in community colleges).

The purpose of *Convergence and Collaboration of Campus Information Services* is to give those practicing different types of convergence and campus collaboration an opportunity to give first-hand accounts of their experiences. Chapter 11 serves as a reminder that this phenomenon may involve players outside the immediate campus and involve partnerships with other universities and stakeholders. This book underscores that libraries are actively involved within their campuses and play a central, redefined role in the educational process. Clearly, the old definition of a library centered on its collection is no longer applicable, and thus this book should be of interest to students in graduate schools of library and information science regardless of their area of specialization, the stakeholders libraries serve and deal with, academic librarians trying to describe to others the services that they want to adopt, and anyone wanting to learn more about the new directions in which some leading libraries are going.

Peter Hernon
Ronald R. Powell

1

INTRODUCTION

Peter Hernon and Ronald R. Powell

As Jerry D. Campbell writes, "academic libraries today are complex institutions with multiple roles and a host of related operations and services developed over the years. Yet their fundamental purpose has remained the same: to provide access to trustworthy, authoritative knowledge."[1] The educational role that academic libraries assume, however, actually involves more than access. Campbell, for example, thinks that,

Over the next decade, colleges and universities will have to make critically important practical and policy decisions about the function of libraries, about the space devoted to libraries, and about the roles of librarians. If these decisions are made wisely, the academy may be able to maintain much of the ineffable, inspiration value associated with academic libraries while retaining their practical value through altogether transformed activities and functions built upon a new mission designed for a more digital world.[2]

Convergence, which enables a library to be more fully engaged with its campus, helps to address the types of issues that Campbell raised. The word *convergence*, which was first used in the sciences in 1713,[3] has become a "buzzword" that "describe[s] everything from corporate strategies to technological developments to job descriptions."[4] Convergence is not limited to renovation projects or joint service units within the library; collaborative spaces might exist elsewhere—either physically or virtually—and involve partnerships between libraries and information technology (IT) or instructional technology departments; academic departments; campus centers for learning, teaching, or writing;[5] and student and food services. Convergence as a consequence involves, but is not limited to, the integration of information, communications, and computing resources and services that seamlessly traverse multiple infrastructures and deliver content to multiple platforms or appliances. That integration, which supports learning and meets the information needs of the constituencies served, includes collaboration that is effective and mutually advantageous to the parties involved.

Specific examples of convergence include centers for teaching excellence, tutor and writing centers, information arcades, facilities for multimedia production and delivery, information and learning commons, cafés, photocopying centers, centers for distance education, participation in the use of course management software (e.g., Blackboard) to make library resources available to classes digitally and to make students more information literate, publishing (e.g., university presses and digital collections), counseling and career centers, and services for students for whom English is a secondary language (mostly in community colleges).

Some types of convergence (e.g., information commons, digital repositories, and cafés housed in libraries) have received extensive coverage in the literature of academic librarianship. However, the literature has not thoroughly covered the full array of collaborative efforts, including the extent to which libraries cooperate with other institutional units, the reasons for engaging in convergence activities, and the direction in which those partnerships might go in the near future. The purpose of this chapter is to help address that gap in the literature and to set the stage for subsequent chapters that delve more fully into convergence activities at individual libraries. In doing so, this chapter and book reinforce Campbell's thesis that the academic library of today and tomorrow is not easily characterized. This chapter, however, only examines convergence activities within the institution and not with other institutions such as cultural institutions in the immediate area.

LITERATURE REVIEW

Joan K. Lippincott helps set the stage for a discussion of convergence by stating that "as academic libraries renovate or build new spaces that provide services to users they should consider opportunities to collaborate with other units on campus to develop collaborative services in the new space."[6] "Planning collaborative facilities," she explains, "requires an institution-wide vision and a willingness to think beyond the confines of administrative structures."[7] In 2004, a combined issue of *Resource Sharing & Information Networks,* which provides an excellent introduction to convergence, notes, "It is the rare library that exists in a vacuum; most are part of a system, such as a university or a municipality, and all libraries exist in a broader societal context which requires interaction and cooperative activity. In order to best serve those who need them, libraries must cooperate widely with entities other than themselves."[8]

Gordon Brewer identifies the "common drivers" for convergence as

managerial—to provide a unified and effective management structure; **operational**—to ensure efficient working practices, including if possible seamless service at the point of delivery; **financial**—to reduce costs and achieve efficiency savings through economies of scale; **technological**—to realize an effective institutional information strategy, optimizing the benefit of investment in IT applications; [and] **pedagogic**—to enhance and maximize access to resources for student delivery.[9]

Nancy F. Campbell and Threasa L. Wesley view a "collaborative dialogue" with teaching faculty as a way for "repositioning the academy library... as the heart of the university."[10] Convergence might represent a partnership between the library and teaching faculty in advancing information literacy pedagogy and helping students to learn how to use and cite material in digital collections.[11] Gerald V. Holmes and Charna K. Howson discuss a partnership between the Office of Research Services and the library's reference department at the University of North Carolina at Greensboro to purchase information resources for use in grant workshops that they jointly offered.[12]

The purpose of partnerships with centers for teaching excellence is to help faculty members improve their teaching skills,[13] and with writing centers to assist students in developing their written communication skills and in gaining experience in creative writing and writing poetry.[14] Shirley Ricker and Isabel Kaplan conducted a nationwide survey of the types of library-writing collaborations, their impact on students and staff, any benefits, and any barriers encountered.[15] Terry Hanson reported that convergence is well established in academic libraries in Britain and the United States but appears infrequently elsewhere in Europe, except for Germany and Finland.[16]

STUDY OBJECTIVES

The objectives for the study that provided the information for this chapter were: to identify, describe, and categorize the types of convergence common to a number of academic libraries; to determine the rationale for the development of those programs and services; to discover any advantages and disadvantages of such convergence; and to identify any plans for future development or refinement.

PROCEDURES

The researchers wanted to examine activities representing the many types of convergence between academic libraries and other campus units. However, as there is no comprehensive listing of such activities, there was no population list from which to select a sample for a study. As a result, the researchers used a nonprobabilty, self-selected sample, namely those libraries responding to queries placed on four discussion lists in April and May 2006:

1. CJC-L (community and junior colleges)
2. COLLIB-L (college libraries)
3. ULS-L (university libraries)
4. ARL Directors Discussion List

These queries announced the study as one of all types of academic libraries, physical as well as virtual convergence, and fully merged services as well as merely collaborative activities. Readers of those discussion lists were asked to contact the researchers if they were involved in such convergence and were willing to share information about their activities. In addition, the literature was reviewed for examples of convergence in other libraries and their directors were asked to participate.

The calls for participation resulted in responses from libraries at four community colleges, 11 colleges, and 35 universities in both Canada and the United States. In reviewing the activities described in these initial responses, it was decided that some instances did not represent convergence or were too situation-specific. The revised sample included one community college, nine colleges, and 27 universities, whose enrollment ranged from small to large. The 37 institutions varied in size, type, geographical location (in North America), and prestige; there was no attempt to align the selections to *The Carnegie Classification of Institutions of Higher Education*.[17]

In April and May 2006, responses to the call-for-participation were gathered and a questionnaire was developed. In May and June, the questionnaire was distributed electronically to a contact person at the 37 libraries. The respondents were asked to answer eight open-ended questions regarding the nature of their libraries' convergence with other campus services. Two questions asked participants to identify themselves and their institution and to list other individuals in the library or on the campus who might be contacted regarding this matter. The final questionnaire item requested copies of any documents that were related to convergence. By the end of September, completed questionnaires had been received from 27 of the libraries, for a response rate of 73 percent.

The next phase of the study involved site visits to some of the responding libraries. Based on a review of the responses and the geographic proximity of participating libraries to either investigator, 11 libraries were selected for more in-depth coverage. Conducted from July through October 2006, these visits complemented questionnaire responses. The investigators interviewed librarians and other interested partners involved with convergence, reviewed the typology depicted in that figure with them, examined relevant documents, and observed converged services (see the Chapter appendix).

INTRODUCTION 5

QUESTIONNAIRE FINDINGS

The activities that survey respondents described fit within 12 broad categories:

1. Add new reporting lines. For example, the library director is responsible for the university archives or university press.
2. Cooperate with auxiliary services. This category covers publishing, bookstores (e.g., coordination of author book-signing events), cafés, and copy centers. Academic advising and career counseling might also be considered as part of auxiliary services.
3. Help departments or campus centers in organizing special collections and making them accessible. Examples include librarians work with faculty or a center to catalog (or train staff to catalog) special collections. The library at the University of Michigan-Dearborn received a donation of children's books published from the 1700s to mid-1900s. The library organized the books and made them available to students in the School of Education.
4. House an information commons, learning commons, or cyber/computer center. For example, "The Commons [at the University of Tennessee, Knoxville] is a collaborative partnership between the Office of Information Technology and the University Libraries to connect students and faculty with the tools and information they need to be successful learners and teachers in the 21st century." Its services include "material retrieval and checkout; printing, copying, scanning; use of the media center & studio; reference & research services; study area with group & individual work spaces; computer help desk services; quiet study space after midnight; digital media services faculty drop-off; and computer area with wireless, standard software & hardware, and loaner laptops."
5. Maintain institutional repositories. Examples include overseeing the university archives and, in cooperation with faculty, developing digital archival collections of materials that faculty gathered and offered to their students. The repositories have as their mission to collect and disseminate "all intellectual output from the campus, starting with dissertations" (Georgia Institute of Technology).[18]
6. Offer media production services. Such services might be available as part of an information commons or integrated with the information literacy program or other services. Media production services might involve audio and video dubbing, lamination, and so forth, as well as video production for faculty and researchers, the Web, and collaboration with the university television station (The University of Michigan-Dearborn).
7. Offer satellite help services aimed at improving student academic skills by providing space in the library, budgeting to purchase relevant material, and/or sponsoring workshops. Examples include quantitative skills centers, speaking centers, tutoring centers, writing centers, career centers, and teaching and learning centers.
8. Provide students with physical space in the library to work on particular classroom activities. An example is the University of Rochester library, which houses a special collection of medieval literature and history and provides offices for graduate students affiliated with the Chaucer Bibliographies Project and the TEAMS Middle English Texts Project (see http://www.lib.rochester.edu/camelot).
9. Serve as chair or participate on campus committees and teams. Examples are advising the institution about academic integrity or copyright, working with legal

officers on contracts, or having librarians serve on the faculty senate or other university committees.
10. Support disability services by making equipment, materials, and services available. For instance, helping the institution meet the information needs of students with disabilities and honor the requirements of the Americans with Disabilities Act.
11. Support university activities. Examples include providing meeting or office space in the library; offering kiosks for students to assess their accounts or making cash withdrawals; overseeing Web site design for all campus units; participating in orientation of new students or an undergraduate seminar focused on student presentations on research (Albion College); holding campus conferences and meetings in the library; letting the registrar schedule classes in the library; interacting with prospective students and their families (Florida Institute of Technology); and participating in first-year and other student programs. Libraries might also collaborate on exhibits placed around campus.
12. Tailor course management software to meet classroom needs. For instance, libraries assisting faculty to develop and maintain their course sites on Blackboard.

These 12 categories are not mutually exclusive; some activities occur in more than one category. For example, a learning commons might represent a collaborative partnership among the library, the office of information technology, a center for teaching and learning, an office of career counseling, and a central office for student tutoring that includes advising and writing support. A common purpose of the varied services, however, is to support the academic success of students and to make it easier for them to receive assistance at the point of need.

The most prevalent categories are:

- House an information commons, learning commons, or cyber/computer center
- Maintain institutional repositories
- Offer satellite help services aimed at improving student academic skills by providing space in the library, budgeting to purchase relevant material, and/or sponsoring workshops
- Tailor course management software to meet classroom needs

Examples

University of Calgary

Convergence might result in a new organizational structure that allows new digital initiatives to emerge and for the physical library to strengthen its position as the heart of the campus. For example, the library at the University of Calgary is part of Libraries and Cultural Resources, an organizational structure that includes the library, archives and special collections, the image center, the university press, and the university museum. A collaborative learning space between the library and information technologies enables students "to find out about, access and use scholarly information and [to utilize] productivity tools needed to complete their scholarly work."

St. Bonaventure University

St. Bonaventure University has a director of technology services and a director of the library, both of whom report to the same vice president. Technology Services has two computer laboratories in the library and the library has a digital media center and a video-conferencing center funded through a grant from Verizon. As Ann M. Tenglund of that university explained,

> Technology Services pays for the equipment and student lab assistant help, and the library staff also contribute to the functioning of the labs and serve as a higher-end technical help presence when a student lab assistant cannot answer something or is not present. We also partner with Technology Services to offer a wireless laptop lending service. In addition, Technology Services maintains our networks and assists with the maintenance of library staff computers. The library maintains its own servers for the library information system.

Indiana University–Purdue University Columbus

In summer 2005, the libraries for Indiana University-Purdue University Columbus (IUPUC) and Ivy Tech Community College of Columbus merged. The library, which IUPUC manages, resides "in a shared space with the Center for Teaching and Learning (CTL), which is an institution-neutral organization that supports the needs of all teachers and learners in the Columbus community." The CTL features tutoring facilities for both institutions.

The University of California, Irvine (UCI)

The UCI Libraries is an example of multifaceted convergence; they are active in multiple categories and have eight different activities:

1. Electronic Educational Environment (EEE), http://eee.uci.edu/about/: It "is a collaborative effort that brings together four units from across campus to make educational technology available and effective....EEE partners include The Office of the Registrar/SAIS, The Division of Undergraduate Education, The UCI Libraries, and Network & Academic Computing Service. One major component of this collaboration is the EEE Web site, which is a home-grown course management system build to serve instructors and students at UCI."
2. Library Web site design: The Libraries "worked with a campus wide initiative to redesign the look and feel of campus Web sites. The Libraries' Web site was the first to implement the new design."
3. UCI Historical Records Project, http://www.lib.uci.edu/ucihistory/: It "provided much of the background and materials for exhibits, publications, and other events related to the 40th anniversary celebration of the founding of the campus."
4. Network and Academic Computing Services (NACS), http://www.nacs.uci.edu/: "One of the Libraries' study centers houses a computer lab that is managed in partnership with the campus-wide Network and Academic Computing Services. NACS

also collaborates with the Libraries' Systems department on a variety of technology related projects and services."
5. Libraries' Information Literacy Initiative (e.g., see http://www.lib.uci.edu/services/workshops/writing.html): The goal of this initiative "is to partner with faculty in order to teach information literacy as an integrated part of the course curriculum."
6. Writing and Library Research Peer Tutor Program: "Developed under the auspices of Student Housing's First-Year Initiatives program, the program provides academic support to students who need help making the transition from high school to the university. The program placed five Peer Tutors, who were trained by library staff in research skills, in freshman housing communities on weekday evenings. Peer Tutors will also be located in the main library during summer term."
7. Teaching in HumaniTech®, http://www.humanities.uci.edu/humanitech/: The "Libraries staff teach and cosponsor conferences in the HumaniTech program, which helps Humanities faculty learn about new technology and incorporate technology into their teaching and research."
8. Undergraduate Research Opportunity Program (UROP): The "Libraries, in partnership with the Division of Undergraduate Education, promotes a dynamic and student-centered research environment for...undergraduates that encourages inquiry, critical thinking and creativity."

The University of Kansas

The Libraries, according to Scott Walter, Assistant Dean of Libraries,

is committed to the idea that collaboration across campus is vital to the place of library service in a digital age. As the physical structures of the academic library encompass an increasingly narrow range of our full resources and services, it is critical that we foster substantive and sustainable collaborations with campus units that share our core mission of supporting teaching, research, and services through the discovery, access, evaluation, management, and presentation of information.

The programs related to convergence focus on common goals, such as "supporting student success by assuring access to information about campus life, [and] improving faculty teaching through the integration of information literacy instruction across the curriculum." Four examples of such programs are:

1. KU Info, http://www.kuinfo.ku.edu/: It is "a campus-wide approach to meeting student and community information needs related to the university. Jointly funded and managed by Information Services and Student Success, it involves close communication with the 20 departments in Student Success."
2. Collaborative Learning Environment (CLC), http://hdl.handle.net/1808/612: As a "'next-generation' approach to the information commons idea, the CLE was designed collaboratively by the Libraries, Information Technology, Instructional Development & Support, and Center for Teaching Excellence as a technology-enhanced teaching space that facilitates the use of collaborative learning techniques, team-teaching, and teaching with technology."

3. BudigOne, http://kudiglib.ku.edu/budig/index.shtml: This "digital media lab [is] designed and managed jointly by the Libraries and Instructional Development & Support." BudigOne supports "advanced graduate student and faculty use of digital media in their teaching and research."
4. Instructional Services, http://www.lib.ku.edu/instruction/: Housed in the Libraries and staffed by members of the Libraries and Information Technology, the unit represents "an integration of traditional library instruction and IT training."

Vanderbilt University

Paul Gherman noted that the Vanderbilt library works closely with the teaching, writing, and learning centers; jointly publishes several e-journals; hosts an institutional repository; manages the campus course management system; and "may take on e-portfolios." A Center for Academic Life is in the early planning stage. "We are hopeful that a remodeled and expanded central library building will eventually house...[the teaching, writing, and learning centers, and possibly the university press]. Prior to this building being created, our intention is to create a virtual organization to offer these services. Our intent is to offer a suite of academic support services that allow faculty and students to succeed in their teaching and research."

Advantages to Convergence

Respondents view convergence as a way for libraries to meet their missions (supporting teaching, learning, and inquiry), serve the entire institution, create new services, promote and improve existing ones, be involved in student learning and the life of the campus, reduce overlap with other campus services, gain more support from administration, share space and perhaps staff, create multiple points of service (more effective service provision), and increase campus visibility. In effect, convergence creates new opportunities for the library, increases the number of campus players working with the library, and is a logical extension of library services. Some respondents view stimulating and supporting student learning, creativity, and productivity as essential to student success at their institutions.

Scott E. Kennedy of the University of Connecticut-Storrs sees the advantages as offering "a more comfortable and convenient learning environment for library users," bringing "learning support services for general education skill sets together in one location," enhancing "student learning and student success," "seeking synergies and efficiencies in operations," developing "ties with other academic and support services on campus," improving "user access to information and computer-based resources on campus," and fostering "change in scholarly communication."

As Nancy L. Eaton of Pennsylvania State University (PSU) explains, "technology is driving the convergence or [at least] facilitating it." Collaboration integrates "library resources into the teaching and learning construct" and at

PSU facilitates "the library as a partner with the [university] press in new modes of scholarly communications." John P. Kondelik of Albion College adds,

We also believe that proximity is an important factor to encourage collaboration and that convergence happens as a stage in the process of collaboration. Proximity seems to be critical because of the possibility of informational interactions taking place. One of the most important advantages to convergence is the sharing of knowledge and insights about the interface between learning and technology.

Gherman makes an important observation: "For years now we have been forming partnerships with other libraries at the state and regional level to enhance our academic community's access to information. It logically follows that we should do the same thing on campus to strengthen our offerings of services." The library, he notes, "needs to build relationships on campus with other academic service providers if we are to maintain our significance to campus and not be marginalized as technology makes us more transparent. Being involved in those collaborative programs is central to our strategic plan."

Carol Ann Hughes of the University of California-Irvine (UCI) offers another reason for the involvement of libraries; "We continually search for new ways of engaging the 'just me' generation with customized content, library based and distributed services, and with tools students need most to succeed. They expect integrated services and that requires convergence."

Barbara I. Dewey of the University of Tennessee, Knoxville, indicates that "by leveraging expertise" from various places, the library "can provide more, not less, service and increase exponentially the excitement of our students. The administration is excited too and sees our work as helpful in recruiting and retaining the best and brightest. We are also reallocating resources (space, staff, and funding) to high-priority areas." She is not alone in her belief that convergence aids student retention—an issue of institution-wide importance. Richard Meyer of the Georgia Institute of Technology views improved student retention as a "measurable outcome."

Several respondents see convergence as beneficial to library users in that it provides "one-stop shopping" in a 24-hour environment. Faculty and students can go to one place without having to seek out different services. One-stop shopping better supports customer or client focused services, and the library in working with other campus partners reaches more students and faculty than it otherwise might. Meyer adds, a one-stop entity multiplies "the effectiveness of...[partnering] entities over what can be achieved in stand-alone operations."

Disadvantages to Convergence

Few respondents identified any disadvantages. Eaton regards convergence as "much harder to manage" because it crosses budgets and supervisory lines; it "requires a different type of coordination than [exists] in-house."

Beth Lindsay of Washington State University considers the disadvantages associated with communication and planning that involve more people who have a stake in the outcome as "minor and manageable." Kennedy comments on "some loss of flexibility." Kondelik notes a perception among institutional leaders that the primary purpose of such convergence is "cost savings" and an unwillingness "to invest in the development of merging and collaborative programs." "This is a concern because for convergence to work we need to bring the people together, and we need to provide shared space that encourages collaboration across programs." A few respondents express minor concerns about the time required for collaborative activities. For example, Carla Brooks of the University of Michigan–Dearborn comments that time would be the biggest disadvantage of convergence "if a collaborative project took too many hours from one's 'regular' work."

Sandra Yee of Wayne State University indicates that "there are often political issues in the convergence of programs and services, such as the feeling on the part of some that we are 'giving away space' rather than building a collaborative or cooperative venture. It is important that librarians think in terms of campus partners and that they meet their campus partners where they are as well as in our own house." The respondents view achieving convergence as a gradual process. Because it focuses on campus priorities, time is an unimportant barrier.

Yale University Librarian Alice Prochaska comments,

Sometimes, proposals or negotiations do not work out, and then of course all parties regret the expenditure of time and effort. There can be occasions when, from a library perspective, our contribution is not adequately acknowledged, which make the use of scarce library resources a little frustrating. A large part of the effort is directed to educating our colleagues on campus in the many ways in which the library can and should be useful to them.

She continues, "Our challenge is to maintain the position of the library at the heart of the educational enterprise, at a time when libraries are in some ways rendered less visible."

Areas for Possible Future Convergence

Two respondents express interest in a café, though one notes a physical barrier related to a lack of a water supply in any suitable public area.[19] The other (Tenglund) mentions that due to a lack of space in the library, the library would like to establish a "relationship marketing" venture with campus food services. Students could bring their drinks into the library and the library would like "to get travel mugs with library information printed on them, and then ask campus food services if they would give us coupons to put into the mugs, as well as hand out the mugs at library events."

The University of Connecticut-Storrs is currently negotiating the cooperative development of university-wide copyright policies; the cooperative licensing of room-scheduling software; and the inclusion of bibliographic records for books, video, and other materials housed in the university cultural centers (e.g., the Women's Center) into the library's online catalog.

The UCI Libraries "are on the cusp of being involved in the development of a student portal on campus which will be a new level of seamless integration into the natural 'workflow' of students. It will bring our services to them 'where they are' instead of requiring...[them] to come (even virtually) to the library." Some other respondents want to create an institutional repository. The most important point is that the libraries are willing to forge new partnerships or to expand existing ones.

SITE VISITS

The Appendix summarizes each site visit, whereas chapters 2 through 11 build on those visits. Suffice it to say, some of the librarians interviewed see convergence as a way for libraries to contribute (and be seen contributing) to student success and for libraries to gain recognition as a campus social center. However, Harriette Hemmasi of Brown University does not see the activities in which the university library is engaged as representing a new role; rather, the role builds on the traditional abilities of librarians to organize and make collections accessible. For example, e-reserves build on the purpose of a reserve collection. The ability of catalogers to understand and apply metadata affords opportunities for a library to develop new applications, such as the availability of digital resources for one course to be available throughout the institution. Students as a consequence may be unaware that they are in fact using library resources and services.

The library at the University of Connecticut–Storrs, which has an early version of an information commons, is planning to create a learning commons similar to the one at the University of Massachusetts, Amherst. Staff at both of these libraries looked at the learning commons of Indiana University–Bloomington and the University of Arizona while planning their learning commons. Librarians from the three universities visited Emory University, the Georgia Institute of Technology, and the University of Georgia, which have noteworthy examples of information/learning/library commons.

CONCLUSION

Of the types of convergence discussed in this chapter, most represent a continuation of the types of services that libraries have traditionally offered. A number of libraries have expanded their role in ensuring that course management software meets classroom needs. Information commons comprise an educational technology facility that, for example, offers high-end multimedia development workstations, electronic classrooms, and information research workstations for searching databases. Learning commons and cyber/computer centers represent an expansion of the concept of an information commons. Among other things, institutional repositories, which build on the archival role that various libraries have played, represent an effort to capture and preserve the intellectual output of one or more university communities. Such repositories continue to evolve.

At least for this study, the rationale for academic libraries' deciding to collaborate and converge with other campus units and services is not always as well articulated as the activities themselves. A number of respondents could not recall who took the initiative to develop specific convergence activities. There was, however, a consensus that such activities enable the library and campus to accomplish their mission of supporting teaching, learning, and inquiry.

Respondents are also hard-pressed to identify many disadvantages of convergence and collaboration with other campus units. Other than a few institution-specific issues, most of the concerns deal with time, money, and the administration of joint programs. As noted in a presentation about the new Student Learning Center at the University of Georgia, specific challenges that must be met by those involved in that joint facility include common training modules for all staff, student orientation to a building that has no books, changing identities/roles for staff, building and staffing hours, technical problems, and integration of student life activities into staff work.[20] The "Memo of Understanding" for the new library commons at the Georgia Institute of Technology discusses several issues for which the parties are responsible if the commons is to be a success. They include teamwork and governance, partner responsibilities, development of new partnerships, public relations, and evaluation and assessment.[21]

As was noted above, the most oft-stated general advantage of collaboration and convergence is the enhanced ability to meet the institution's mission. Other advantages identified by respondents include the opportunity to create new services and opportunities, increase the library's involvement in student learning and campus life, gain more support from the campus administration, consolidate learning support services, develop ties with other campus services, integrate learning and technology, and re-allocate resources. Outcomes identified as representing success for the University of Georgia Student Learning Center, for instance, include significant increase in use, increased response to client requests, adaptation to a new service environment for the partners, positive feedback from every constituent group, quick integration into the culture of the campus, the addition of new services, integration of student life activities, collaboration on building security and event support, and successful cooperation and working relationships among partners.[22] According to Crit Stuart of the Georgia Institute of Technology, the success of the partnership resulting in the new learning commons is characterized by exceptional popularity with students, faculty enthusiasm for student multimedia creation, the emergence of an influential library and student advisory council, various tutoring and support services seeking space in the dynamic setting, and the realization that students benefit from a writing center. The beneficiaries of such partnerships are students, faculty, library and other campus staff, and the entire campus.[23]

The quantity, variety, and quality of the convergent and collaborative ventures that academic libraries of all types and sizes are undertaking are most impressive. Among the themes that stand out are the provision of comprehensive, one-stop services available in and through libraries; the integration of information services into campus and student life; the expanding role of academic libraries and their partners; and the enthusiasm evidenced by the study's respondents. As Stuart concludes regarding the learning commons at the Georgia Institute of Technology, "partnerships across department lines can actually increase the prestige of each player, rather than weaken one's position on campus."[24]

NOTES

The authors would like to thank John Gantt for assisting with the collection of some of the interview responses and the many study participants, especially those who hosted site visits.

1. Jerry D. Campbell, "Changing a Cultural Icon: The Academic Library as a Virtual Destination," *EDUCAUSE Review* 41 (January/February 2006), 16.

2. Ibid., 30.

3. "Convergence," *Oxford English Dictionary*. Available at http://0-dictionary.oed.com.library.simmons.edu/cgi/entry/50049149?single=1&query_type=word&queryword=convergence&first=1&max_to_show=10 (accessed June 21, 2006).

4. University of Southern California, Annenberg School for Communication, "Convergence," in *USC Annenberg Online Journalism Review*. Available at http://www.ojr.org/ojr/business/1068686368.php (accessed June 21, 2006).

5. See James K. Elmborg and Sheril Hook (ed.), *Centers for Learning: Writing Centers and Libraries*, ACRL Publications in Librarianship no. 58 (Chicago: Association of College and Research Libraries, 2005).

6. Joan K. Lippincott, "New Library Facilities: Opportunities for Collaboration," *Resource Sharing & Information Networks* 17, nos. 1/2 (2004), 147. See also her dissertation, *Collaboration between Librarians and Information Technologists: A Case Study Employing Kolb's Experiential Learning Theory* (College Park, MD: University of Maryland, Department of Education Policy, Planning, and Administration, 1999), and her homepage, http://www.cni.org/staff/joan_publications.html (accessed June 21, 2006).

7. Lippincott, "New Library Facilities," 155.

8. William Miller, "Introduction: Cooperation within Institutions," *Resource Sharing & Information Networks* 17, nos. 1/2 (2004), 1.

9. Gordon Brewer, "Convergence for the Right Reasons," *Multimedia Information and Technology* 29 (November 2003): 107–109.

10. Nancy F. Campbell and Threasa L. Wesley, "Collaborative Dialogue: Repositioning the Academic Library," *portal: Libraries and the Academy* 6, no. 1 (2006), 93.

11. See, for example, Danuta A. Nitecki and William Rando, "Evolving an Assessment of the Impact on Pedagogy, Learning, and Library Support of Teaching with

Digital Images," in *Outcomes Assessment in Higher Education: Views and Perspectives*, edited by Peter Hernon and Robert E. Dugan (Westport, CT: Libraries Unlimited, 2004), 175–96; Denise L. Hattwig, "The UW Image Bank: A Libraries and Visual Resources Digital Image Collaboration at the University of Washington, Part I," *Visual Resources Association Bulletin* 31, no.3 (*Spring 2005*): 31–4.

12. Gerald V. Holmes and Charna K. Howson, "Grants: Interdepartmental Collaboration to Teach Grantsmanship Skills," *The Bottom Line: Managing Library Finances* 13 (2000): 146–49.

13. Trudi E. Jacobson, "Partnerships between Library Instruction Units and Campus Teaching Centers," *The Journal of Academic Librarianship* 27 (July 2001): 311–16.

14. See Elmborg and Hook, *Centers for Learning;* Susan Fliss, "Collaborative Creativity: Supporting Teaching and Learning on Campus," *College & Research Libraries News* 66 (May 2005): 378–80; Barbara I. Dewey, "The Embedded Librarian: Strategic Campus Collaborations," *Resource Sharing & Information Networks* 17, nos. 1/2 (2004): 5–17; Charles Kratz, "Transforming the Delivery of Service: The Joint-use Library and Information Commons," *College & Research Libraries News* 64 (February 2003), available at http://www.ala.org/ala/acrl/acrlpubs/crlnews/backissues2003/february1/transforming.htm (accessed June 21, 2006); Debra Shapiro, *E-Scholarship,* A LITA [Library & Information Technology Association] Guide No. 12 (Chicago: American Library Association, 2005); *ARL Bimonthly Report* 222 (June 2002), available at http://www.arl.org/newsltr/222/ (accessed June 21, 2006); "Collaborative Facilities" (Hanover, NH: Dartmouth College), available at http://www.dartmouth.edu/~collab/ (accessed June 21, 2006); "Library Teaching & Learning Experimental Space" (New Haven, CT: Yale University), available at http://www.library.yale.edu/cclexp/ (accessed June 21, 2006); "Collaborative Learning Spaces" (Lawrence, KS: University of Kansas), available at http://www.ku.edu/~hvc2/colloblearning.shtml (accessed June 21, 2006). Additional materials are available at "*Collections of Materials on Collaborative Spaces,*" Planning Collaborative Spaces in Libraries: An ACRL/CNI Preconference, June 20, 2003. Available at http://www.cni.org/regconfs/acrlcni2003/resources.html (accessed June 21, 2006).

15. Shirley Ricker and Isabel Kaplan, "Are We Crossing the Line? A Survey of Library and Writing Program Collaboration," PowerPoint presentation available at http://docushare.lib.rochester.edu/docushare/dsweb/Get/Document-22020 (accessed June 23, 2006).

16. Terry Hanson (Ed.), *Managing Academic Support Services in Universities: The Convergence Experience* (London: Facet, 2005).

17. *The Carnegie Classification of Institutions of Higher Education* (Stanford, CA: The Carnegie Foundation for the Advancement of Teaching, 2006). Available at http://www.carnegiefoundation.org/classifications/ (accessed August 21, 2006).

18. See also Association of Research Libraries, SPEC Kit 292: *Institutional Repositories* (Washington, DC: ARL, 2006); Tyler O. Walters, "Reinventing the Library—How Repositories Are Causing Librarians to Rethink Their Professional Roles," *portal: Libraries and the Academy* 7, no. 2 (2007): 213–25.

19. It merits mention that the café at the University of Massachusetts—Amherst relies on bottled water to make coffee and some other drinks.

20. "Georgia's Five Little Acres: The Student Learning Center at the University of Georgia." A PowerPoint presentation by William Gray Potter, presented at the

Coalition of Networked Information Meeting, Spring 2004. Available at http://www.cni/tfms/2004a.spring/abstracts/PB-georgia-potter.html (accessed July 31, 2008).

21. "Library Commons; Memo of Understanding" (Atlanta: Library and Information Center, Georgia Institute of Technology, n.d.)

22. "Georgia's Five Little Acres."

23. Crit Stuart, "Collaborative Learning Space: A Partnership between Information Technology and the Library" (Atlanta: Library and Information Center, Georgia Institute of Technology, 2005).

24. Ibid., 2.

APPENDIX: THE ELEVEN CASE STUDIES
ALBION COLLEGE (ALBION, MI)

The visit to Albion College provided an excellent opportunity to gain the perspectives of campus personnel and library staff. The researchers met with the Executive Vice President who is also the Vice President for Information Technology and Chief Information Officer and responsible for Instructional Technology, an Instructional Technologist, the Director of [computer] User Services, the Director of the Academic Skills Center, and the Vice President for Academic Affairs, as well as the library director and two librarians.

Much of the library's collaboration with other campus units began with instructional technology (IT). The college received a grant for integrating IT into the college and the local community. That provided an opportunity to integrate the library more fully into academic programs in an efficient manner. The Instructional Technology Department, which used to be in the library building but is now in a separate building, interacts with the library on instructional technology matters, including faculty development and student instruction. The level of collaboration between the two units varies, but typically involves consulting with one or two librarians. The collaboration tends to be informal.

The Academic Skills Center, which includes the Writing Center but is not part of the library administratively, is housed in the library building. The director of the Academic Skills Center believes that it is advantageous for the Center to be in the library. He notes that he and the library director are in philosophical agreement regarding the college's mission. The Center's collaboration with the library includes sharing the costs of books-on-tape, sharing a secretarial position, working with reference librarians on the design of assignments, and providing workshops on plagiarism and teaching and writing.

Most of the interviewees indicate that the impetus for collaboration came from the library and other campus units on a roughly equal basis although some believe that the library director is somewhat more active in this regard. Specific factors cited as motivating collaboration include the limited availability of some facilities, the ability to improve campus services, financial constraints or need for cost efficiency, the increased ability to work with others in key positions that have similar concerns ("helps to provide all of the necessary pieces"), the reduction of overlap or duplication of effort (sometimes resulting in merged positions), and the users' desire to be able to go to the library for instructional technology resources. Most of the participants do not believe that politics is a major factor, although one individual notes that outside bodies such as accrediting organizations encourage collaboration.

Future plans regarding library collaboration with other campus services include a possible information commons. Such an endeavor might well involve all of the services mentioned above and could involve more formal convergence administratively and budgetarily. However, more than one person notes that the campus is being careful not to do too much too quickly on this possible project. The college is more concerned with undertaking such a project in a manner that will ensure its success. The Instructional Technology Department wants to collaborate more with the library and is developing plans for a Digital Assets project that will "span IT and the library." The current Vice President for Academic Affairs regularly meets with the library director, and they often discuss collaboration; however, other more formal cooperative projects may have to await the appointments of a new college president and academic provost.

BROWN UNIVERSITY (PROVIDENCE, RI)

Because the university is decentralized, different groups collaborate in order to limit duplication of services, work from a shared expertise, and advance the "collaborative university-college model" set forth in the "Plan for Academic Enrichment," http://www.brown.edu/web/pae/. The library collaborates with Computing and Information Services (CIS) on curricular support related to:

- Course reserves and WebCT. This collaboration also involves faculty members who want resources (audio, visual, and text) placed on e-reserve. The Library's course reserve system passes code to WebCT for every course with reserves. When launched, this code displays a course's reserves in all formats within a single WebCT window. Library staff and CIS Instructional Technologists use library-developed administrative interfaces to manage digitization and file upload tasks.
- Computing cluster support. The library has different clusters of personal computers available for student and faculty use and makes student support available to provide help for identifying and retrieving source material. Other clusters exist around campus and are managed by CIS. They might cover statistical analysis or other software.
- Digitization services. The Center for Digital Initiatives focuses on the "production of digital materials for use in scholarship and teaching efforts at Brown;" the "digitization of 'signature collections' from Brown's world renowned Special Collections;" the "development of databases, programs, and applications to enhance access to and use of these materials;" and "consultative services for library and

academic units undertaking digital projects" (see http://dl.lib.brown.edu/index.html). The *Napoleonic Satires* is a good example of a collaborative project (see: http://dl.lib.brown.edu/napoleon/about.html). For a list of cooperative projects with faculty, see http://dl.lib.brown.edu/repository/projects.php.

The Center for Digital Initiatives collaborates with different campus technology groups, including the Scholarly Technology Group on faculty research projects. At this time, the library collaborates with 15–20 faculty members on various digital library projects. Many of these projects are done in a collaborative fashion with the faculty member and may make use of students to assist in the preparation of metadata records, historical research, or other activities.

The Center jointly manages (with the Music Library) Brown EARS (Electronic Audio Reserve System), "a joint Library and CIS project that streams required listening assignments to students registered in Brown University classes" (see http://dl.lib.brown.edu/databases.html). Among other programs of the Center are:

- Instructional technology support in the classroom. The library provides the equipment for classroom use. The library's department of media services delivers equipment to and from the classroom and instructs faculty in the use of that equipment as needed. Campus classrooms need modernization, and the university is moving toward wireless classrooms.
- Student technology experience group. The library works with several groups on campus, beyond CIS, on this activity (e.g., the Dean of Student Life, individual academic departments). The group considers what students use and need once they come to campus and interacts with students to understand the student culture and, for instance, student use of the Facebook, an online directory that connects people through social networks.
- Technology training. Such training involves library instruction and searching of library databases.

The library also works with Public Affairs and Alumni Relations (PAUR) to support campus speakers. On a small scale, the library partners with the Sheridan Center to support faculty seeking improvement in their teaching.

There are plans underway to collaborate with the Graduate School, the Vice President for Research, and individual academic departments to make dissertations available digitally; and with the Vice President for Research and the Dean of the Faculty to create an institutional digital archive. Dissertation and other campus assets would be placed in that repository. The library director does not see the activities described above as necessarily representing new roles for the library; rather, the opportunities build on the traditional abilities of libraries to organize and make collections accessible. For example, e-reserves and the availability of e-resources beyond an immediate class build on the traditional function of a reserve collection.

Likewise, the ability of catalogers to understand and apply metadata is not so distant from the skills and concepts that they have honed as MARC catalogers. Clearly, there are many opportunities for the library to be involved in both visible and invisible services and partnerships across the campus. The challenge is to identify and respond to those opportunities in a timely and appropriate fashion.

COLUMBIA UNIVERSITY

James G. Neal, the Vice President for Information Services and the University Librarian, maintains that the study reported here focuses on "3Cs:" convergence, collaboration, and competition. Competition, he maintains, is a "fundamental value" as libraries compete within the institution and with other libraries. Convergence is clearly represented in the organizational chart for Columbia University. Among the many responsibilities of the Deputy University Librarian are area studies and the libraries' digital program, both of which involve working with the faculty, course management software, and the institutional repository. The libraries are creating a portfolio of faculty and researcher publications and patents, which may be merged into the institutional repository.

Some of the direct reports to the University Librarian are a Copyright Advisory Office for the entire university and Columbia's Center for New Media Teaching and Learning (CCNMTL). CCNMTL is engaged in externally funded projects, and these projects significantly increase its resources each year.

Examples of other activities include the Electronic Text Center and the Electronic Data Service (EDS), which is operated jointly by the Columbia University Libraries and Columbia University Information Technology (CUIT) and which supports instruction and research that involve numeric and geo-spatial data resources. EDS provides consulting services for faculty. DigitalCommons@Columbia is a pilot project for building a university institutional repository and is a service of the university libraries.

EMORY UNIVERSITY (ATLANTA, GA)

As is stated in one of its brochures, Emory University's libraries provide integrated services in an innovative, inviting environment for scholarly inquiry, research, and teaching. Its converged and collaborative activities include the following programs, services, and campus departments that it provides, houses, or cooperates with:

- Information commons. It is located on parts of four floors of the main library and includes more than 150 networked computer workstations, three electronic

classrooms for instruction in the use of library resources, and electronic and print course reserves.
- Academic and administrative information technology. It maintains and coordinates centralized computing service on campus as well as supports academic and administrative departments in technology use.
- Emory Center for Interactive Teaching (ECIT). As the name suggests, this unit focuses on faculty services.
- Emory College Language Center. It is the university's main language laboratory.
- Cox Hall Computing Center. It is a state-of-the-art computer and media center in a separate building that houses the Center for Educational Technology (CET), a student-focused service.
- Library instruction. Some of the library instruction is provided in collaboration with academic departments.
- Coffee shop. This service is housed in the main library but managed by the campus food services.
- Copy center. This is another service that is housed in the main library but managed by an outside agency. Students, however, tend to view it as a library service.
- Blackboard. The library does some interfacing with the university's course management system.
- Student research award. The library provides this award, and a faculty jury selects the award winner.
- Freshman Advising and Mentoring (FAME). Freshmen advising groups meet once per week for six weeks. Each group includes librarians, faculty, university staff, and student leaders.

The library's director of planning noted that two previous vice provosts had encouraged the library to collaborate with other campus units but most of the collaboration noted above had been internally motivated. He also mentioned that people do not collaborate unless they have a reason to do so and that it is important to maintain a balance of library-only services and collaborative services. In the future, the library would like to be involved more with an institutional repository, with a career center, and with Emory College, including its research fair.

GEORGIA INSTITUTE OF TECHNOLOGY (ATLANTA, GA)

The Library and Information Center of Georgia Institute of Technology is involved in a number of collaborative activities similar to those of other libraries included in this chapter. These activities include involvement with the Center for Enhancement of Teaching and Learning (CETL), which recently moved its annual poster session and faculty training sessions to the library; Undergraduate Academic Advising; the Office for Information Technology

(OIT), which has moved all of its walk-in help service to the library; the Graduate Fellowship and Scholarship Office; the Counseling Center; and Auxiliary Services (it provides a café in the library). The Library and Information Center also provides space for campus tutoring, manages the university's rapidly expanding institutional repository, and provides new e-publishing services focusing on journal and conference output production.

Particularly noteworthy among the activities above is the library's new learning commons, which is located in two recently renovated areas of the main library. The West Commons provides 105 computer workstations located in either the general productivity area or the multimedia studio and a presentation practice space. The East Commons provides 30 high-end team workstations, a study zone that transforms into a presentation theater, and displays of student art and outstanding research. Digital forms of the student research and creative output are also deposited in the institutional repository. Planning for the first learning commons involved the library director and an associate director from OIT, with programming developed by a team from the library and OIT. Programming for the East Commons was drawn exclusively from student focus groups. Architectural design was developed in house. The library and OIT created a "Memo of Understanding" stating that administrative responsibility for the commons is to be shared, with OIT having primary responsibility for equipment, server, and productivity software support. Both East and West Commons are administered jointly by the head of library Information Services and an OIT person and supported by a mix of OIT and library staff and student assistants who have both technology and information skills. These facilities are guided by an advisory council consisting of three OIT staff members and two library staff members. The council meets monthly. Monies for these installations were provided by the library with support from OIT, the Provost, Facilities, and external foundations. There was no real pressure from the university administration to develop a learning commons.

What stood out the most during the visit to Georgia Tech, however, was the success that the library has enjoyed in building student support for and involvement in its programs and services. As stated by the library's Associate Director for Public Services, students want their library to be the "replete box." To that end, the library has created a Student Advisory Council consisting of eight to 10 student leaders. This council has obtained a $250,000 grant for the library, advised on the design of the East Commons, asked the library to sponsor a summer reading program, and made a supportive presentation to the university's Executive Board. The Council is cofacilitated by library and OIT administrators. What follows are some relevant passages from the charge to the Student Advisory Council:

> With other Campus partners, principally OIT, we are developing services, resources and physical spaces to have a positive impact on student learning, in step with changes

in pedagogy.... The primary focus for the Student Advisory Council is to assist with the evolution and renovation of Library spaces to facilitate student learning and productivity, and to revitalize "Library as indispensable place" for student success. The Council assists with capturing, evaluating and interpreting the feedback, opinions and wisdom of GT students regarding Library improvements.

Additionally, the library provides a meeting room for certain student groups, works with the student newspaper, conducts student focus groups, and may host a major alumni group that will include student groups as well. A recent issue of the campus student newspaper, which has a Web version produced with technologies hosted by the library and OIT, had a positive front-page article about the library's new East Commons. Such activities and publicity reflect an unusually high degree of student involvement in a university library and indicate that the students are not only library users but also stakeholders.

UNIVERSITY OF CONNECTICUT (STORRS)

The library collaborates with University Dining Services (a café and a sandwich shop that also contains e-mail stations, a television lounge, and fax machines), the University Coop (a newsstand that offers stationery, supplies, cosmetics, snacks, pain killers, newspapers, and magazines), the Bursar and Accounts payable (direct billing), University One (a university debit card cash deposit machine), the General Education Oversight Committee and the freshman English Program (information literacy education for first-year students), the Institute for Teaching & Learning (a Learning Resource Center for student technology training, a Writing Center satellite for tutoring in writing skills, and a Q Center satellite for tutoring in math and statistics), and various departments on campus (collaborative programming). In addition, the library uses WebCT, the university's course management service (referred to as a learning management system), to deliver electronic course reserves and facilitate access to other library resources (e.g., databases); offers exhibit space, tables, and display boards for student activities; and public meeting and conference spaces. The library computer laboratories host university licenses software for general use, the library provides office space for centers of research and learning (Human Rights, Oral History, and Geographic Information & Analysis), and the library has developed and manages the university's institutional repository (http://digitalcommons.uconn.edu), which, among other things, will provide access to theses and dissertations produced on campus.

Regarding future plans, the library wants to convert its information commons into a learning commons patterned after the one at the University of Massachusetts–Amherst. The goal is to redesign the first floor over time as monies become available. The first floor will house the commons, which includes two classrooms, the Q Center, a writing center, the learning resource center, the existing information cafés, the reference area and the reference collection, and other services. There are plans to construct five group study spaces (istudios), and the Institute for Teaching and Learning currently manages a high tech learning center on the first floor that offers student training with the Microsoft office suite, the development of e-portfolios, and other applications.

The library will support the above-mentioned centers by providing space and furniture. The centers then make staff and other resources available to the students. An advantage for these centers is that they are placed in areas of high traffic and visibility.

The various activities described in this section support the library and university missions by providing additional resources and support services to the university community and by fostering research and improved scholarly communication. The university has developed a new general education program based on literacy related to writing; quantitative reasoning; information retrieval, evaluation, and use; information technology; and foreign languages. Through its collaborative spaces, the library is involved in all these activities, except for foreign language literacy. Convergence leads to new forms of collaboration as well as facilitates and fosters communication and information sharing among academic and service units.

UNIVERSITY OF GEORGIA (ATHENS)

The visit to the University of Georgia focused exclusively on its new classroom and library building—the Student Learning Center (SLC). The idea for what became the SLC grew out of perceived needs for more campus classrooms and more library seating. The SLC project was coordinated by the Office of the University Architects and representatives of the university libraries, the Center for Teaching and Learning (CTL), and the computing center (EITS). The SLC is aimed at undergraduate students and provides classroom space, an electronic library, and computing functions (information commons). In other words, it is intended to integrate instruction, library and information resources, and computing into "one-stop shopping."

The three partners report to the Provost and Senior Vice President for Academic Affairs. They continue to maintain their individual administrative distinctions, but the heads of the units meet on a regular basis. The three units form the "SLC Support Partnership" and have an agreement on specific and joint areas of responsibility for operations and services in the SLC. The university libraries are responsible for the facility, security, reference services, programming for special events, copy services, and coordination with outside groups such as the Coffee Shop, Writing Center, and various tutoring centers, among others. The computing center is responsible for the maintenance and repair of all workstations and related technology, the wireless network, software, etc. The Center for Teaching and Learning is responsible for the classrooms (including their equipment and supplies), faculty preparation rooms, and the loading dock. The campus reservations office is responsible for scheduling the classrooms. The libraries, EITS, and CTL share responsibilities for some items such as staffing information desks and training and supervising staff. There is no separate budget for the SLC building.

The combined services of the SLC include the following:

- 4,800 seats
- 96 group study rooms
- coffee shop
- one reference/computer help desk
- five computer help desks
- 500 computer workstations
- electronic resources including productivity and graphics tools, citation and full-text databases, Electronic Journal Locator, and guides to electronic resources in subject areas
- wireless network
- printing services
- four computer labs
- classroom support

Regarding the staffing of the SLC, each area has supervisory responsibility for its staff. Cross training between the libraries and EITS for provision of service at the reference/computing help desks is shared, and all three areas keep strong lines of communication open to evaluate services, building needs, training, security, and other issues that need group input. The current staff includes ten librarians and library staff (with additional support from the Main and Science libraries), five classroom support staff, and two EITS staff, plus approximately 60 student assistants for the entire building.

Successes that have been attributed to the new SLC at the University of Georgia include significant use (1.75 million people entered the library space in the building in 2006), positive feedback from all constituents, a new digital media wing and lab, an enhanced culture on campus, new services, more integration of student life activities (use by student groups has been quite high), collaboration on building security and event support, and more cooperation among campus partners. Since the SLC opened, the Writing Center and math tutoring have scheduled hours for their services in the facility; and Freshman College, an intensive two-week program for selected new students, has used the SLC almost exclusively for classes and other programs. As was eloquently stated by the University President Michael F. Adams, on January 15, 2004:

The opening of the Student Learning Center may have had the greatest impact on the intellectual climate of this institution since Old College was constructed (in

1806)...Every time I am there the place is alive with academic activity....I do not know of another facility on this or any other campus where design so fully meshes with function....For decades to come, the Student Learning Center, with its combination of Electronic Library and classroom spaces, will be a defining experience for almost all UGA students.

UNIVERSITY OF MASSACHUSETTS (AMHERST)

W.E.B. DuBois Library is engaged in collaborative activities such as a café called Procrastination Station, developing an institutional repository, and working with faculty to integrate library resources and services into the curriculum through the academic liaison program. The Learning Commons (LC), which opened in October 2005, is a broad, cooperative venture among the library, the provost, the Learning Resource Center, interested faculty, the office of information technologies, and the information technology minor (an undergraduate academic program). The LC, located on the renovated main floor of the library, has multiple service points: library reference service (staffed by professional librarians), technology support (provided by library staff and personnel from two departments of the office of information technologies), a writing center, career services, and academic advising. There is a separate room for students needing to use assistive technology; most of the software, however, is also available on the personal computers available throughout the LC. The Learning Resource Center provides tutoring and supplemental instruction for students enrolled in barrier or challenging courses in a range of disciplines from chemistry to journalism. Custodial services maintains nearly 24/7 upkeep of the LC and the 26-story building. The library also has separate quiet study areas for students who find the commons too noisy as well as over 350 private study carrels.

The staff at the multiple service points work together and are familiar with what the others do. Joint training translates into a minimum of running around regardless of where a student asks a question. The goal, a seamless, self-contained environment that supports student socialization, learning, and scholarship 24/5, focuses on inclusiveness or "one-stop" service (academic support) within the building—not one-stop service available through a single service point. Students might purchase food from the café or order its delivery from an area restaurant; however, if they do so, they must go outside the building to pick it up. The LC has vending machines, even one from the bookstore that sells office supplies (e.g., notebooks, pencils, headsets for computers, jump drives, and post-its). Students use their university debit cards to pay for their purchases, and they also have access to photocopy machines, printers, scanners, and a fax machine.

It is important to note that the declining gate count that the library experienced before the opening of the LC has been reversed. The library and the other academic support services are now recognized across campus for their contribution to student *success*—defined in terms of academic achievement—and student retention. The image of the library on campus has changed to one of an open, inviting environment—one that students embrace as their own space—that does not depict a rigid organization with a rigid set of rules by which students must abide.

The LC is part of any tour for prospective students and occasionally prospective faculty, and commons staff might serve on a hiring committee for university staff, thereby creating a broader awareness of the LC's mission. A strength of the LC is that the furniture is movable and formal receptions can be held there. On the negative side, there is limited space to expand services. Nonetheless, there is a base of service from which the library and its campus partners can build. As space permits, other academic support services might expand their physical presence and services in the LC.

The campus is discussing the possibility and implications of establishing additional "learning commons" type spaces in other buildings, including how this expansion would impact provision of library, technology, and academic support services. There may, however, be some confusion among students about the difference between the two and the services offered. Learning Commons could become a campus buzzword and not reflect the array of services currently available through the library housed LC.

UNIVERSITY OF MICHIGAN (DEARBORN)

The collaborative activities of the library of the University of Michigan (UM)–Dearborn represent a wide range of activities:

- Voice/Vision Holocaust Survivor Oral History Archive. This project essentially started when the library took responsibility for the campus TV studio. The original goal was to make transcripts of audio and video tapes, catalog them, and make them available for checkout and interlibrary loan. Two librarians volunteered to manage the project as time permitted during their normal work activities. The archive is funded by grant monies, but the library director administers its budget. Library staff are involved with programming and so forth. In short, the library sees its role as one of facilitating.

- May G. Quigley Collection. As a result of the library director's networking with colleagues throughout the state, approximately 4000 children's books were donated to UM–Dearborn by the Grand Rapids (Michigan) public library. It is a resource for the School of Education, but the library has full budgetary and administrative responsibility.

- Armenian Research Center (ARC). Another collection and resource with which the library collaborates. Library catalogers trained ARC staff to catalog materials for the Center's collection and to add the records to the library's public catalog and to OCLC.

- Henry Ford Estate Collection. Library catalogers trained Archives staff to catalog materials at the Henry Ford Estate and to add the records to the library's public catalog and to OCLC.

- University Archives. The library has full responsibility for campus archives. A librarian assumed the position of University Archivist. The library director collaborated with the Vice Chancellor for Business and Finance to incorporate care for the Henry Ford Estate's book collection and archives as part of the University Archivist's responsibilities.
- Course management system (CMS). Library staff are working with other campus units to develop a comprehensive set of criteria needed in a CMS for the campus and the library expects to participate more fully in any future system.
- Student information system implementation. A librarian cochaired the campus interdepartmental team charged with selecting and implementing a new student information system implemented in the mid-1990s. "This four-year project helped create many connections with other campus units and staff members."
- Campus focus action group. This takes the form of informal participation with a campus committee focused on student recruitment, retention, and life.
- Orientation and Welcome Week. The library staff participates with committees and activities related to orientation and Welcome Week in the fall term.
- Campus techs group. The library director noted that it is crucial for the library to be involved with this activity and indeed library systems staff are contributing members of this group.
- Faculty Senate Scholarship Committee. A library staff member participates with faculty and staff from all of the colleges and some campus support units to oversee the various scholarships available to current students.
- First-year seminars. The library director chaired a campus committee that investigated options and opportunities for reshaping the general education program. The Liberal Arts College now offers first-year seminars that are partly designed by a librarian.
- Distance-learning classroom. The library collaborates with ITS and Internet2 and media providers to support this facility.
- Academic integrity. Library staff work with the faculty senate to support student academic integrity.
- Campus media services. This service began as the TV studio but is now a converged service that is essentially a department of the library.
- Institutional repository. This repository is being developed in conjunction with University of Michigan–Ann Arbor.
- Faculty salon. The library brings faculty together to encourage collaborative research. The library director sees this as "an ideal example of convergence."
- The library director chaired a faculty senate appointed committee charged with investigating "issues involving academic integrity including prevention, detection, and sanctions." The campus has since adopted many of the committee's recommendations.

These activities reflect a university library that is well integrated into the activities and mission of its parent institution. Indeed, throughout the site visit, the library director stressed the importance of the library's being involved (engaged) with the campus. Librarians, in fact, must be involved in campus activities outside the library in order to be promoted. The director also noted the political importance of the library's collaborating with other campus units. He stated that it is "our job" to do so. He commented that working with faculty is a fundamental task of the library. The director was not able to cite any examples of convergence and collaboration saving the library money, but he noted that such activities do result in more university support for requested budget increases. The director commented that the library's being viewed as neutral turf facilitates its campus-wide activities; the associate director added that it is easier to be turf neutral in collaboration than in full convergence. The library's mission statement and current strategic plan stress the importance of collaboration, working with faculty, communication, and engagement with the campus community.

WAYNE STATE UNIVERSITY (DETROIT, MI)

The Wayne State University (WSU) Library System is actively engaged in a number of collaborative activities and programs. The variety, depth, and scope of these projects is a testament to the Libraries' commitment to take an increasingly proactive, influential role in the university's future. Following is a sample of the collaborative activities being pursued and the units with whom the Libraries are collaborating:

- The Technology Resource Center (TRC)—TRC is the primary face of collaboration between Computing & Information Technology (C&IT) and the Libraries, but the collaboration is much more extensive, including mutual support for computer labs in the libraries, the 24-Hour Extended Study Center, and so on. TRC is an example of both virtual and physical convergence.
- Office for Teaching and Learning (OTL)—As part of the Library Computing & Media Services, OTL collaborates extensively with other campus units, including but not limited to the full gamut of instructional departments.
- Student life—Participation in all new student and parent orientations; recently developed a new Web site for the First-year Experience.
- English department—Extensive collaboration with regard to instruction.
- Graduate school—Collaboration on the electronic submission of WSU dissertations to the WSU digital repository, among other things.
- Provost's office—Convergence projects have focused on recruitment and retention, academic integrity.
- Math and computer science departments—Physical collaboration in terms of space sharing, but also higher-level collaboration with respect to WSU's status as one of 20 finalists in the National Center for Academic Transformation's "Road Map to Redesign" process, aimed at securing grant funding for mathematics lab development. The Road Map entails collaboration on instructional design, and WSU librarians are actively lending their expertise to this effort.

- Honors program—The Libraries help to extend computer support services to the Honors Program through a cooperative arrangement. This represents another example of physical and virtual collaboration.
- Auxiliary Services—Collaboration has taken a number of forms, including the forthcoming addition of a coffee shop to the Undergraduate Library.
- Academic Success Center—Some collaboration with the Academic Success Center has been pursued.
- Reuther Labor Archives—Collaboration on digitization projects, including an Institute of Museum and Library Services (IMLS)-funded project to digitize the photo archives of the *Detroit News;* and continue to work together to make the archival collections more accessible.
- Housing Services—Collaboration on the establishment of Learning Communities in campus housing.
- Distance education services—The Libraries have collaborated with the Office for Metropolitan Programs and Summer Sessions in the provision of distance education services.

The extent of the Library System's current collaborative activities is impressive, and is reflective of the Libraries' commitment to take a proactive role in shaping the continued transformation of learning modalities and instructional design on campus. As the Dean of Libraries noted, "The Libraries can no longer wait for people to come to us. As part of the "Just for You" service model, the Libraries are committed to actively pursuing opportunities to collaborate and take a leading role in designing new ways to integrate technology into instruction." The Dean cited the following as the principal advantages to convergence/collaboration: "Sharing resources, sharing expertise, shared marketing, and access to relationships not possible without collaboration and convergence." She pointed out that, in some cases, collaboration permits the sharing of expenses, which can result in fiscal savings. For instance, the Honors Program's cooperative agreement to gain access to the Libraries' Computer Support Team, as mentioned above, is a win-win situation for both the Library System, which receives a bit of money, and for the Honors Program, which thereby obtains more access to Computer Support than would otherwise be possible.

On the downside, the Dean noted that campus politics can make collaboration a tricky proposition at times: "Collaboration is a skill, and you have to understand the politics that are at play. Often, the group that has control of the money has the control. You have to understand these issues and work together as part of the collaborative process...Occasionally, convergence turns to control and that is something that we would find a disadvantage, especially if the controller does not meet our goals for serving our customers. Depending on how the convergence is determined, it may not be possible to adequately cover or share costs in a meaningful way. Finances are always an issue, as are personnel and other resources."

The Dean concluded that the advantages of collaboration far outweigh any disadvantages: "Some services would not be possible without these collaborations, such as the support for the Blackboard CMS and the funding for equipment that comes from our work with C&IT.... All of the groups with whom we collaborate share a common mission of providing access to the best information resources that we can find, providing assistance for our customers when and where they need or want it, and providing cost effective services both on campus and virtually. We work together to fulfill that mission."

YALE UNIVERSITY (NEW HAVEN, CT)

According to Alice Prochaska, each collaborative program "has its own rationale. Overall, the library serves the entire campus and wishes to partner with other parts of the university to the maximum extent possible. Collaborations enrich our own work, help to make the library visible and valued, encourage optimal use of scarce resources, share expertise, and bring many other benefits."

Inspired by Cornell University's DCAPS (see http://dcaps.library.cornell.edu/), Yale's Digital Production and Integration Program (DPIP) is currently under development. Its goal is to be the "underpinning" for the library's campus-wide partnership related to digitalization; it views campus-wide convergence "as a whole and not piece-meal." Among the activities currently available through DPIP are:

- Classics Department Digital Collection: DPIP provides project management, technical infrastructure, metadata recommendations and quality assurance services for the digitization of the Classics Department Slide Collection (35,000 35-mm slides and 10,000 lantern slides).
- Hellenic Studies Byzantine Collection conversion: DPIP provides project management and metadata services for the cataloging of 6,000 images.
- *Yale Daily News* Digitization Project: DPIP and the Preservation Department work in close partnership to accomplish the digitization of a portion of the *Yale Daily News* back file (8,000 out of a total of 160,000 pages). DPIP staff assist with RFP preparation, vendor evaluation, project management, and repository development. Preservation serves as primary contact with vendors, and DPIP provides technical advice, manages the implementation of a public interface to the collection, and conducts usability studies.
- Library E-reserves Prototype: DPIP provides project management and research services for the Library's prototype e-reserves project (see http://www.library.yale.edu/iac/dpip/).

Other collaborative efforts in which the library engages are wide-ranging and include, for instance, work with the School of Forestry and Environmental

Studies to supply free online access to environmental research for developing countries, the Whitney Humanities Center to provide postdoctoral fellowships, and academic departments to archive resources and to provide other support for programs of oral history (see http://library.yale.edu/lhr/jobs/intern/scfellow.html). Four collaborations are highlighted here:

1. Teaching and Learning Portal. The Sakai-based, open-source enterprise was designed jointly by Yale's Information Technology Services (ITS), Student Financial and Administrative Services (SFAS), and the library. Precipitated by the need to replace an old-course-management service, this portal provides greatly enhanced capability and will increasingly include library content.
2. Electronic Library Initiatives (ELI) program. Supported by a grant from the Davis Educational Foundation, it facilitates and studies "the use of digital images and other materials in teaching, learning, and scholarship" (http://www.library.yale.edu/eli/). Joining in the collaboration are interested faculty, the graduate school, and ITS.
3. Collections Collaborative. Supported by a grant from the Mellon Foundation, the program provides re-grant support to initiatives that bring together collections and users in different ways from across the campus (including museums, galleries, and libraries). For example, one project—unlocking digital data collections across the sciences—will develop a collaborative initiative to formulate a common workflow and generate a cost model for metadata production for digital data collections in two discrete scientific domains at Yale University. Another project—the World War I experience—will select and digitize a range of pamphlets, broadsides, posters, prints, and sound recordings that provide primary source documentation on the war's impact in Britain and the United States. The goal is to develop a prototype for improving description and access to nonstandard published materials.
4. Programs in International Educational Resources (PIER) program. This example of collaboration with the MacMillan Center for International and Area Studies at Yale provides guided access to the university's international educational and study resources for competitively selected fellows from Connecticut community colleges (see http://www.yale.edu/ycias/).

"Yale University libraries and librarians regularly participate in a wide range of initiatives that are international in scope and cooperative in nature" (see http://www.library.yale.edu/international/).

CASE STUDIES

2

INNOVATION IS AN ONGOING PROCESS: COLLABORATION AT THE UNIVERSITY OF CALIFORNIA–IRVINE

Carol Ann Hughes

In an editorial, Rush Miller, university librarian and director of the university library system at the University of Pittsburgh, stated,

> It would be very useful to me, and I believe to others, as we think about our future to understand better the relationship of the digital content we create and the methods of discovery of it by our users. *We must particularly keep in mind that the purpose of knowing these things is not to better "educate" our users to the superiority of the traditional library approach and tools, but to create better integration with the actual tools of choice now and in the future used by our students and faculty.* I expect we will likely learn that innovation is an ongoing process and that earlier successes such as the decades-old MARC format are no longer the best format for current and future systems preferred by our users.[1]

Although this statement could easily be expanded to include all information, not just digital content that librarians create, Miller's voice is but one of the many now heard who are promoting totally rethinking library services and the spaces in which they are provided. The landscape of what is considered the purview of the library is changing rapidly toward Library 2.0, which emphasizes interactivity between users and library information;[2] NetWorkflows, the discussion of building services around users' work and learning flows;[3] and explorations of re-embedding library information in other contexts, commercial and otherwise.[4]

Librarians are being called upon to take a larger and more dynamic role than that of collectors and information mediators. They are reexamining the role of metadata and requiring that it be more flexible and sustain a variety of uses beyond reflecting local collections to a geographically limited clientele. Information offered through the library is now open to the world and the task of how to scale up the impact of librarians' work for the global community is one of the key issues of the day.

The "Top Ten Assumptions for the Future of Academic Libraries and Librarians," developed in 2007 by the Association of College and Research Libraries (ACRL) Research Committee, has indirectly acknowledged this trend in noting that "the demand for technology-related services will grow...[and] students will increasingly view themselves as customers and consumers, expecting high-quality facilities and services."[5] *What Haven't You Noticed Lately?*, the OCLC environmental scan from 2003, outlines the sea changes that confront the profession daily.[6] It describes a landscape in which "the future of libraries is inherently integrated with the future of a larger context: economics, technologies, social developments."[7]

Few library organizations, however, have commented lately on how librarians are going to achieve this brave new world. The Library Information Technology Association (LITA), American Library Association, outlined one path to success in its list of top technology trends when it identified "convergence" as one of the top strategies to succeed in the future. "There is no longer a clear line between what 'we' do with technology and what 'they' do with technology."[8] Jim Duncan took the analysis of convergence as a strategy for success deeper with his white paper for the EDUCAUSE Evolving Technologies Committee. He defined convergence as "the evolution of multiple systems and multiple services into a single, holistic environment, one completely accessible from the friendly neighborhood Web browser."[9]

The conceptualization of "convergence" specifically does not mean the merger or administrative alignment of campus units. In the late twentieth century there was much interest in either the merger of libraries and computing centers or changing the institution's organizational hierarchy so that both units reported to the same administrative position. In a review of the literature on this topic, Mary Bolin notes that the earliest discussions of the relationship between campus computing centers and libraries was conducted among academic librarians who were beginning to explore the implications of rapidly proliferating digital formats. Later in the 1990s university administrators revived the conversation as the rise of the Internet led to a demand for ubiquitous computing and the belief of some administrators that electronic information would render physical libraries obsolete.[10]

As the library-computing center debate has matured, the "urge to merge" has dissipated and, according to Bolin, the model of a merged unit on campus is rarely found in larger institutions, at least among her study population of land-grant universities. Perhaps the achievement of a new user service paradigm through adjusting the university's internal organizational structure was an exercise that was doomed to failure anyway. Indeed, as early as 1988, Cyril C. H. Feng and Frieda Weise noted that users want information and services and are agnostic about which organizational structure provides them.[11] When Feng and Weise were writing, however, librarianship was still far from the current emphasis on user-driven innovation. Librarians were the architects of innovation. Librarians would provide the expertise and keep users in mind as services were developed within the framework of technologies designed and deployed by libraries.

Defining and offering services with users merely "in mind" is not sufficient for true innovation and impact to occur. Libraries need to provide services that integrate into the users' workflow and social landscape. Personalization, customization, and interoperability with other campus "common services" are required. In order to accomplish the shift from offering services to being interwoven into the fabric of people's work lives will require more than re-organization. It requires convergence.

CONVERGENCE

"It has become clear," as Brian L. Hawkins and Patricia Battin note, "that traditional notions of libraries and information technology organizations are no longer intellectually and economically sustainable...[N]ew interrelationships and organizational structures will be necessary to manage, finance and coordinate the choices and opportunities made possible by digital information resources."[12] Yet, the fundamental role of librarians has not changed significantly in the midst of technological upheaval. Ranganathan's five laws still apply:

1. Books are for use,
2. Every reader his or her book,
3. Every book its reader,
4. Save the time of the reader, and
5. The library is a growing organism.[13]

The challenge is how best to actualize these five laws and ensure that the library, as a growing organism, can most effectively operate for users who live "on the network." One of the organizational processes available in the university setting to support users in the full context of their scholarly work life is that of convergence, as Duncan defines it above.

In his think-piece, Duncan, who takes a user-oriented perspective, proposes that institutional service planners consider how to make investments that provide seamless user experiences between "silos" of administrative units. Some of the questions presented as worthy of exploration as one approaches "convergence" among stakeholders on any given project are:

- "Is there trust between the...stakeholder groups?
- Do the members of the stakeholder groups speak the same language and understand the terminology, priorities, and goals of the other? What are their respective roles with regard to their respective systems?
- Logistically, how can the staff members for these two organizations begin to work together to support an integrated offering?
- Does an environment exist where experimentation and failure are possible?
- Does a collaborative effort between two stakeholders overtly align with direction from the executive leadership of the institution?"[14]

It is rare that librarians and computing staff have the leisure to ponder questions such as these prior to launching a new project or service. It is more often the case that opportunities for making progress on a project suddenly appear, partnerships form and lurch forward. Such opportunism has been the case at the University of California–Irvine (UCI), although the joint projects undertaken here have indeed built trust, a shared understanding of each others' priorities, and an environment in which the executive leadership is supportive of innovation and risk taking. The next section of the chapter will discuss several examples of cross-campus convergence in which UCI Libraries has taken an active role.

TECHNOLOGICAL CONVERGENCE

The University of California–Irvine, a relatively new institution of higher education, was founded in 1965. True to the spirit of the time, the culture of the university welcomed individuality and decentralization of academic programs and the services that supported them. The campus has continued its tradition of decentralization. Yet, when cross-campus collaborations occur, they are dynamic and long lasting.

Electronic Education Environment

The Electronic Education Environment (EEE) was an early collaboration on the campus. Begun in 1995, the collaboration involved the Division of Undergraduate Education, Network & Academic Computing Services (NACS), the UCI Libraries, and the Office of the Registrar. The initiative grew out of the Chancellor's statement "Growing into the 21st Century: UCI's Opportunities," which included the goal of preparing UCI students to acquire twenty-first-century electronic information skills. This "manifesto" was fully supported by the Chancellor's Educational Technology Task Force in 1996 which gave this project the framework within which EEE could align its goals with the vision of the campus executive leadership.[15]

EEE was launched in 1996 with 10 Web sites that instructors had created in this homegrown course management system, the first in the University of California system. William Parker, then Director of the Office of Academic Computing, named the initiative "Electronic Education Environment." The order of words in the title was to emphasize "that the university's existing Educational Environment was being extended and enhanced electronically, as opposed to any attempt to take an Electronic Environment and fit educational efforts to it."[16]

Faculty interest in harnessing the flexibility of the Web technology of the mid-1990s was a driving force in the founding of EEE. Faculty wanted to use multimedia and new learning tools that the Web offered as well as moving into an environment where they could more easily manage the details and logistics of teaching courses with large enrollment. According to Stephen Franklin, one of the founding creators of EEE, the motivations on the part of the libraries, NACS, and others was a realization that they all served this common constituency. The UCI Libraries leadership was well connected within the faculty community and this contributed to the ease with which the libraries aligned its objectives with the other partners. An Executive Committee was formed to refine the vision which was soon followed by an operational group to manage the details of implementing and enhancing the original system.

The libraries have continued to be an active partner in the collaboration over the last decade. Catherine Palmer, Head of Education and Outreach in the UC Irvine libraries, has served continuously in the Operational Group, including as chair, since its founding days. Her leadership has helped the libraries integrate resources and tools related to twenty-first-century electronic information skills into the fabric of the course management system.

EEE continued to thrive through the early 2000s. "MY EEE" functionality was added which allowed students to use the site to drop off coursework, chat with classmates, manage a personal calendar, take quizzes, submit course evaluations, and get their grades.

In 2002, the Academic Web Technologies group of Network & Academic Computing Services was honored for developing the EEE by the Larry L. Sautter Award for Innovation in Information Technology. The Sautter Award honors projects developed by faculty and staff in any department at the ten UC campuses for "innovative deployment of information technology." Since this time, the technology (and the partnership) has reached a comfortable "middle age." Adoption on campus has been widespread and faculty who are by no means "early adopters" are largely satisfied with the functionality. The innovative energy of the partners has turned to other projects.

In 2003, the Operational Group wrote a memo that expressed its belief that EEE has "for the most part...achieved our original goal of presenting a unified and responsive environment to faculty and students despite the fact that services are provided by several different UCI organizations."[17] The collaboration is mature now and, although a new vision of growth for EEE may need to be developed, with over 10 years of close operational collaboration, EEE partners have achieved a type of convergence which will stand them in good stead for the next "new thing" that may require joint resources.

Content Management System

Early in 2003, it became clear that the processes and infrastructure behind the UC Irvine libraries Web site needed to be enhanced if the UCI Libraries was to be able to handle its growth effectively in the future. The initial vision had been a decentralized model of Web development, with staff in different parts of the organization building Web pages in Dreamweaver that added to the store of "content." Dreamweaver templates, however, were more difficult to set up and less flexible than anticipated. Many staff in units outside of Web Services were not interested in Web page production or able to dedicate time to keeping Web pages up to date. There was also a lack of coordination which led to confusion and difficulties in keeping track of versions.

Anticipating continued growth prompted a serious consideration of how scalable were the current processes and how well suited the processes would be for a site that was growing steadily larger. The answer to achieving scalabilty was to centralize Web production services, to standardize the graphic style of pages, and formalize the process of publishing content. Web Services needed to develop a widely shared vision of the purpose of the libraries' Web site, the reason behind architecture and global navigation choices, and so on, but assign the work of designing and approving Web pages in a more centralized manner.

A subcommittee of staff who had interest and some experience in supporting the current Web site was convened within the Web Advisory Committee. This group identified the set of criteria and required functionality for content management system (CMS) software. Various products were reviewed and a top product was selected. However, before the purchase decision was made the libraries hired a new Webmaster who was interested in open source software solutions. Consequently, the purchase of commercial software by the libraries was deferred.

Over the course of the next 18 months, the libraries struggled with development of an open source solution for content management system software. During this time, in a totally separate effort, the UCI Libraries Design Services staff worked with the newly appointed campus Director of Web Communications to establish a new "look and feel" for the campus Web site, which the libraries was the first unit on campus to adopt. This smaller project provided the first platform for developing the trust necessary to launch into future partnerships to accomplish more complex and larger projects.

Simultaneously Webmasters within other campus units were beginning to realize that they also had a need for a more scalable solution to their own Web production issues. The campus Director of Web Communications knew that the libraries were working on a CMS installation. She also knew that Advancement, University of California, Irvine Healthcare, Administrative Computing, Student Affairs, and University Communications were all interested in developing a robust Web infrastructure. The Web sites managed by these units ranged from the Chancellor's Web site, to the staff portal, to all student services, including the Registrar, to the combined Web site for the School of Medicine and the UC Irvine Medical Center in Orange, California. Added to this grassroots interest was the appointment of a new Chancellor for the campus who was interested in developing a more consistent campus identity through Web design across campus.

Over the course of 2005–2006, the Director of Web Communications cultivated this group of Web operations administrators. The libraries' struggle to build a system on its own with an open source solution was time-consuming and taxing. Joining forces with the group of leading campus Web administrators seemed a way to leverage valuable expertise and provide partnerships for building the technical infrastructure for this sophisticated software system. By the end of 2006, the units were ready to join forces, develop a request for proposal, and make a commitment to adopting a common infrastructure, with the assurance that the individual "look and feel" of each Web site would be maintained through independently customized templates.

The breadth of this collaboration is somewhat rare at UCI. Campus executives have been deeply impressed with the willingness of diverse units to come together at the grassroots level to solve a common problem. In analyzing the success-to-date of this project through the guidelines mentioned above by Duncan, trust has been built through the process of sharing needs and requirements for the CMS functionality. Certainly the stakeholders in this group were peers who had the right level of authority to make commitments and judgments about strategic directions such as this. And, the Chancellor's executive leadership has set the tone for encouraging more shared initiatives.

Although implementing a CMS is not really innovative, this collaborative infrastructure will allow UCI Libraries to more easily create a flexible Web environment in which user needs can be quickly addressed and in which innovative Web-delivered services can be more easily managed. It will also bring together two other independent systems, the staff administrative portal and the student portal, in an interrelated environment that will make both systems stronger and more flexible. From that perspective, the CMS project has brought together various campus "silos" in a new convergence that will leverage the institution's resources to address current challenges and new opportunities. And, the libraries have found new allies with whom to build partnerships for new ventures. One such new venture is the development of a UCI student portal.

Student Portal

Late in 2003, UCI Administrative Computing launched planning for the development of a student portal. Planning was initiated through a steering committee which included Network and Academic Computing in order to leverage the functionality of the EEE course management system for the portal. Because of the libraries' strong relationship with NACS and several of the other partners through EEE, the libraries were invited to participate in the early planning.

UCI Administrative Computing, however, had already implemented a successful staff portal based on uPortal software so it was natural that the discussions soon centered on the use of uPortal as a basis for the student portal implementation.[18] Over the course of the next two years, action was delayed because of personnel changes and other matters, until late in 2005 when the project emerged into a funded development phase, led by the director of Student Housing Information Technology (Administrative Computing) and Director of Web Communications (University Communications) rather than by the EEE partners.

Between 2003 and 2005, the senior leadership in Administrative Computing and in Communications made the key decision to decouple control of the project from the provision of staffing and expertise to the project. In other words, there was a commitment by Administrative Computing and University Communications to open up the project to cross-campus partnerships which would allow participating units input into the shape of the project and autonomy in how they participated even though programming resources were being supplied solely through Administrative Computing and University Communications. This was a pivotal decision that represented a shift in campus culture which had heretofore equated the provision of programming support with control of the definition and implementation of a project.

Similar to and simultaneous with the grassroots partnerships that were emerging around the content management system, several campus units expressed interest in being able to develop portlets and provide data to the tools within the student portal. The libraries eagerly embraced this opportunity which coincided with discussions about Web 2.0 technologies and how to provide services to users who reside "on the network" and who may never enter the libraries' buildings.

Librarians brainstormed what possible services the libraries could provide. Some obvious choices were to offer electronic reference, RSS (Really Simple Syndication) feeds of new resources, polling functionality, and library hours. Other services, which are dependent upon single sign-on capabilities for the libraries' online catalog, include embedding due dates for checked out materials within the student calendar and e-reserves links tailored for students enrolled in specific courses. The strategy of working with a campus-wide portal rather than enhancing the libraries' Web site is based upon the premise that the libraries should be putting its best functionality where the students are already working and then draw them into specialized functions on the libraries' Web site as they need them, rather than trying to drive them to the libraries' Web site which operates as a silo, disconnected from their natural workflow. In this way, "convergence" on behalf of users is achieved and the libraries help to create a vital campus-wide site with critical mass of functionality that benefits all the development partners.

Institutional Repository

Many institutions worldwide are currently engaged in creating institutional repositories to assist in the collection, management, and preservation of scholarly communication in partnership with faculty.[19] "While institutional repositories centralize, preserve, and make accessible an institution's intellectual capital, at the same time they will form part of a global system of distributed, interoperable repositories that provides the foundation for a new disaggregated model of scholarly publishing."[20]

The University of California eScholarship Repository is the system-wide answer to the need for UC faculty to have an "institutional" repository. Begun early in 2002, the eScholarship Repository is a free, open-access infrastructure that offers all UC departments, centers, and research units direct control over the creation and dissemination of the full range of their scholarship, including prepublication materials, journals and peer-reviewed series, postprints, and seminar papers. These materials are freely available to the public online.[21]

Also during 2002, NACS staff approached UCI Libraries when they learned that the libraries were beginning to build a local programmatic initiative in support of scholarly communication. Establishing workshops and programs about such topics as copyright and open access took precedence over considering the need for a local repository for quite a while. Building content for eScholarship contributed by UCI faculty was also a priority that delayed the work on a local repository.

With the development of a system-wide repository in support of the advancement of scholarship, UCI Libraries had not needed to develop a local instance of repository software quickly. Eventually, however, NACS raised the question again in early 2007 and the time was right for UCI Libraries to step up to a partnership around building local repository services. Over the course of the last several months, the notion of developing a local repository that complements eScholarship by emphasizing information of primarily local importance has grown stronger.

Projects that encompass both preservation and access are being considered. For instance, UCI Libraries are interested in developing preservation for digital copies of the campus newspaper and materials from other local digitization projects. Another repository project focuses on the NSF funded

ADVANCE program. UCI was one of the first awardees of an institutional transformation grant from that program (http://research.cs.vt.edu/advance/index.htm). The development of this program to promote gender equity by increasing the representation and advancement of women faculty in academic science and engineering careers is of importance in campus life and the program's documents need to be preserved and disseminated to a wider audience. Other possibilities include collection research and scholarly materials from local faculty that do not qualify for or which are not yet ready as a contribution to eScholarship. All of these types of materials could benefit from curatorship that is provided nowhere else on campus.

At the time of this writing, the partnership is based on NACS contributing server support and backup services, while UCI Libraries takes responsibility for supplying the server and is soliciting content. While this is not a transformational convergence, it is a solid collaboration that will evolve as the needs of the campus repository evolve.

PROGRAMMATIC CONVERGENCE

All the examples above are technology-based collaborations. "The evolution of multiple systems and multiple services into a single, holistic environment" for the user, however, does not necessarily have to be technology based. The UCI Libraries have a history of developing strong programmatic partnerships. All of these projects further the library's mission of supporting teaching, learning, and inquiry. All of them leverage professional expertise and integrate librarians more seamlessly across the campus. All of them contribute to building services around users' work and learning flows.

Undergraduate Research Opportunity Program

The UCI Undergraduate Research Opportunity Program (UROP) encourages and facilitates faculty-mentored research and creative activities by undergraduates from all schools and academic disciplines on campus. Although the libraries had long been a supporter of the UROP program through providing extended loan privileges, free copy cards, and access to a special study room for undergraduate honors students, our support took a giant step toward "convergence" in 2005 when the decision was made to direct libraries endowment monies into a monetary award for qualified UROP fellows.

Prior to 2005, the libraries supported a student essay writing contest on a topic related to reading or books and awarded cash prizes to winning entries. However, the work involved in soliciting and judging the essays was considerable and the quality of the essays was highly variable. UCI Libraries wanted to develop an award program that was easier to administer, would highlight the libraries' support for research to a broad campus audience, and would bring increased visibility to students who make unique, creative, or extensive use of library resources in their research projects. Rather than make an award after the research project is over, the libraries needed to be an initial part of the student's research experience. The libraries needed to become an integrated part of the student's workflow.

The Head of Education and Outreach proposed that students have the opportunity to apply for a Library-UROP Research Fellowship when they submit their original research proposal. In order to be considered, students would have to submit a 500–750 word essay explaining their project and why they think it might qualify for the Library Research Fellowship. The proposals would then be reviewed by the UROP Faculty Board which, in addition to selecting the proposals that would qualify for UROP, would consider and select those that applied for the Research Fellowships. Once the proposal was accepted for a fellowship award, the student would be assigned to the Research Librarian who is a subject expert in their field and who would assist them with their project. The monies formerly dedicated to the essay contest winner were used to fund the new awards.

Students who receive the Library–UROP Research Fellowship award are required to participate in the campus research symposium and to write a paper summarizing their project. Their presentations and their papers are clearly identified as supported by the Libraries Research Fellowship, posters from their presentations are displayed in the libraries buildings, and the paper is guaranteed publication in the *UCI Undergraduate Research Journal*. With this shift in focus, UCI Libraries strengthened its visibility with faculty across campus as to librarians' role in cultivating research skills for young scholars and "converged" with the UROP program, a vital and respected part of the educational scene at UCI.

Peer Tutoring Program

The UCI Libraries Education and Outreach Department has long had a deep partnership with the Campus Writing Coordinator. The libraries are fully integrated in the sequence of required freshman writing courses (Writing 39A, 39B, and 39C) and all librarians participate in providing instruction during these courses to students and the teaching assistants who conduct the classes. The goals for these classes are to: teach information literacy concepts as part of the W39C library orientation curriculum, incorporate active learning activities into the class session, and teach students the research skills they will need in order to succeed in W39C.

It was not possible during the time devoted to course-related instruction for the libraries to address as many topics as early career students needed to be successful researchers. Another solution was needed, so a pilot project was developed to offer "Ask a Librarian" services to the freshman dorms in the evening in collaboration with the new Director of Housing, but attendance was very low. Meanwhile, the Writing Coordinator was offering additional workshops that address the process of writing and peer review, research skills, and policies about plagiarism, while looking for a way to make them more effective.

In 2005, the Head of Education and Outreach, UCI Housing, and the Writing Coordinator took a step toward "convergence." A Writing and Library Research Peer Tutoring pilot program was proposed. This proposal was developed initially by UCI Housing in connection with its "First Year Initiative," which is dedicated to integrating academics into the residential communities for first-year students. The proposal cited the need for help to first-year students encountering the greater demands of college writing courses and was developed in accordance with the large body of pedagogical theory about the efficacy of peer assistance in writing. Both librarians and peer tutors knew that students often can not distinguish problems with the research writing process from problems caused by poor sources or inadequate research methods. Therefore working through the peer tutors was a chance to assist students who would never have approached a reference desk or the electronic Ask a Librarian service.

The peer tutoring program begins with excellent tutors: juniors, seniors, and graduate students from various majors with proven writing skill and good judgment. Tutors have undergone a training course and meet weekly with a professional coordinator for consultation. The Head of Education and Outreach is a full partner in the tutor training, meeting once per week for 30 minutes with all the tutors and meeting all the lower-division writing course staff to inform the instructors about the tutoring service. Peer tutors get a thorough grounding from librarians in good research techniques which they can pass along to the students and use for their own benefit as well.

An evaluation of the program was done in Spring 2007 by the Division of Undergraduate Education. The 459 students who participated in the tutoring program over the entire academic year self-reported their learning outcomes. Results of the assessment indicated that, although students were more likely to seek assistance for writing versus research, they were more likely to agree that they developed new research strategies as opposed to new writing strategies. Similarly, students were more likely to agree that they were more confident in their research skills versus their writing skills as a result of their tutoring both in the Winter and Spring Quarters.

As a three-way collaboration, the Writing and Library Research Peer Tutoring Program has been a great success. Undergraduates at any level may bring writing-in-progress from any course to a peer tutor for consultation at either of the freshman dorms and at the two major libraries on campus. The libraries provide tutors with a meeting room dedicated to their private consultation needs, complete with a laptop for wireless access, and salary support. Now the libraries have gotten into the work flow of lower division students, working through their preferred source of information (their peers) and in their preferred work locations (both the dorm and the library).

CONCLUSION

Integration with users' tools and information gathering strategies of choice, now and in the future, is the key to success for libraries. Librarians should focus less on further enhancement of library-based services and take note of how users are actually working. As John Seely Brown notes, "The key to predicting how we should move forward is paradoxically to look not ahead, but to look around."[22]

If one looks around at how users are working and where they find their information, it becomes clear that convergence with other campus services is essential to allow librarians to continue to develop systems that fulfill the profession's fundamental service and organizational philosophy according to Ranganathan's Five Laws. Convergence is difficult. Building trust with other campus units may take time; establishing an environment that allows experimentation and possible failure certainly will be a challenge; the logistics of sharing staff, money, and time will be difficult. However, both technologically and programmatically, supporting users within a natural workflow is the only way to serve their needs effectively and ensure the continued relevance of library services to the educational enterprise.

NOTES

1. Rush Miller, "What Difference Do We Make?" *The Journal of Academic Librarianship* 33, no. 2 (2007): 2.

2. Michael E. Casey and Laura C. Savastinuk, "Library 2.0: Service for the Next-generation Library," *Library Journal.com* (September 1, 2006). Available at http://www.libraryjournal.com/article/CA6365200.html (accessed September 1, 2006).

3. Lorcan Dempsey, "Networkflows," *Lorcan Dempsey's blog*. Available at http://orWeblog.oclc.org/archives/000933.html (accessed January 28, 2006).

4. Lorcan Dempsey, "Lifting out the Catalog Discovery Experience." *Lorcan Dempsey's blog*. Available from http://orweblog.oclc.org/archives/001021.html (accessed May 14, 2006).

5. James L. Mullins, Frank R. Allen, and Jon R. Hufford, "Top Ten Assumptions for the Future of Academic Libraries and Librarians: A Report from the ACRL Research Committee," *College & Research Libraries News* 68, no. 4 (2007): 241.

6. "The 2003 OCLC Environmental Scan: Pattern Recognition: What Haven't You Noticed Lately?" (Dublin, OH: OCLC, Inc., 2003). Available from http://www.oclc.org/reports/escan/toc.htm (accessed August 18, 2007).

7. Karen Coyle, "The Future of Library Systems, Seen from The Past," *The Journal of Academic Librarianship* 33, no. 1 (2007): 140.

8. "Top Technology Trends for Libraries: Y2K" (Chicago, Library Information Technology Association, 2000). Available at http://www.ala.org/ala/lita/litaresources/toptechtrends/midwinter2000.cfm (accessed August 18, 2007).

9. Jim Duncan, "Convergence of Libraries, Digital Repositories & Management of Web Content" (October 11, 2004). Available at http://connect.educause.edu/library/abstract/convergenceoflibrari/37263 (accessed August 18, 2007).

10. Mary Bolin, "The Library and the Computer Center: Organizational Patterns at Land Grant Universities," *The Journal of Academic Librarianship* 31, no. 1 (2005): 3–11.

11. Cyril C.H. Feng and Frieda O. Weise, "Library/Computer Center Partnership," *Journal of the American Society for Information Science* 39, no. 2 (1988): 126–130.

12. Brian L. Hawkins and Patricia Battin (eds.), *The Mirage of Continuity: Reconfiguring Academic Information Resources for the 21st Century* (Washington, DC: Council on Library and Information Resources and Association of American Universities, 1998), 7–9.

13. Michele V. Cloonan and John G. Dove, "Ranganathan Online: Do Digital Libraries Violate the Third Law?" *Library Journal.com* (April 1, 2005). Available at http://www.libraryjournal.com/article/CA512179.html (accessed August 17, 2007).

14. Duncan, "Convergence of Libraries, Digital Repositories & Management of Web Content."

15. *Final Report of the Chancellor's Educational Technology Task Force* (University of California, Irvine, 1996). Available at http://eee.uci.edu/about/_assets/EdTechTF.FR.html (accessed August 18, 2007).

16. Stephen D. Franklin and Ellen Stenski, *Building University Electronic Educational Environments* (Norwell, MA: Kulwer Academic Publishers, 1999), xiv.

17. Catherine Palmer, "EEE Operational Group Report," e-mail message to Carol Ann Hughes (December 1, 2003).

18. Mark Askren and Marina Arseniev, "Combating Stovepipes: Implementing Workflow in uPortal," *EDUCAUSE Quarterly* 27, no. 2 (2004). Available at http://www.educause.edu/pub/eq/eqm04/eqm0429.asp (accessed August 17, 2007).

19. Gerhard van Westrienen and Clifford A. Lynch, "Academic Institutional Repositories: Deployment Status in 13 Nations as of mid 2005," *D-LIB Magazine* 11, no. 9 (2005). Available at http://www.dlib.org/dlib/september05/westrienen/09westrienen.html (accessed August 17, 2007).

20. Richard K. Johnson, "Institutional Repositories: Partnering with Faculty to Enhance Scholarly Communication," *D-LIB Magazine* 8, no. 11 (2002). Available at http://www.dlib.org/dlib/november02/johnson/11johnson.html (accessed August 17, 2007).

21. "eScholarship Repository" (California Digital Library, 2007). Available at http://repositories.cdlib.org/escholarship/more_about.html (accessed August 17, 2007).

22. John Seely Brown and Paul Duguid, *The Social Life of Information* (Boston: Harvard Business School Press, 2000), 8.

3

SOWING AN OLD FIELD WITH A NEW CROP: COLLABORATIVE SERVICES OF LIBRARIES AND OTHER CAMPUS UNITS

Richard W. Meyer and Tyler O. Walters

As the title of this chapter suggests, finding a metaphor that captures the transition from the linear tradition of libraries to a new collaboration does not fully capture the profound changes in this environment. The old tradition focused on buying books, cataloging them, and then helping users find the content they need in the books. The older world was one of silos and linear work flow that started with acquisitions and ended with reference. Special collections, archives, records management, and art and music collections tended to be the purview of adjunct operations. They usually played a non-critical role in the academic mission of the library, but this is no longer true. Over the past several years, many academic libraries shifted to an interlinked cross-silo world with many other campus components and especially with a robust engagement of special collections and archives.

Today's library relies extensively on collaborations with other campus units. Usually collaboration includes the computing center, which is called Office of Information Technology (OIT) at the Georgia Institute of Technology (hereafter called Georgia Tech). Many other campus services, however, gain synergistically by collaborating with the library. Not only does putting in a course management system require collaborative effort among academic support, computer services, distance learning, and libraries, but usually includes support from teaching and learning units on campus as well. In our building, provision of support for undergraduates requires simultaneous access to computing, along with library services.

Looking at this transition from the standpoint of motivation demonstrates how accommodating this shift has affected our operations. Putting changes in place to effect this transition seems to have expressed itself at Georgia Tech by means of a three-part process as described in parts I through III below. To do so, we had to recognize motivators, reshape facilities, and refocus services. Additionally, it is important to recognize what motivators emerge from a social environment deeply affected by Internet-driven opportunities built upon easy information sharing and ubiquitous linkage capabilities.

Technology advances provided the opportunity for more collaboration among parties at all levels. That collaboration capacity helped drive pedagogical shifts toward multiparty exercises. At the same time, technology offered students opportunities to respond to class assignments using Web pages, PowerPoint presentations, full motion video materials, and a variety of other media. In turn, these opportunities drive student's need to command expertise with many more software applications than just Word and Excel. Try teaching math without *MatLab*.

PART I: RECOGNIZING MOTIVATORS

Various motivators are fundamentally important to the library's strategic mission and agenda. Although the list is not in any particular order other than that imposed by emotional reactions to the factors affecting us, it includes the consolidation of journal publishing; escalating journal prices; online delivery of research output; collaboration needs of students; increasing emphasis on undergraduates along with collaborative problem solving; students' simultaneous need for information technology (IT) and bibliographic resources; the overlap of library roles with information technology, advising, tutoring, and writing; along with the impact of a flattening and interconnected world.

The library collaborates with three other universities to acquire the entire portfolio of publishers, including Elsevier. The continued increasing expense of these resources combined with the magnifying opportunity for self-publishing in the Internet, however, motivate us toward repository development. Similar collaboration motivators have shifted pedagogy almost completely from individual exercises completed outside class to collaborative projects.

The flattening world affects us directly as well. Georgia Tech delivers access to some of its resources to students in China, Ireland, France, Brazil, and other countries. Providing those resources requires close collaboration with distance learning faculty and staff and common support of course management technology. Much of what follows in this chapter focuses on the impact of that collaboration on library facilities. The change made in those facilities empowers library staff to meet the collaborative needs of users.

The shift from a print-dominated world to digital-dominated world brings with it a transition from a linear environment to an interactive environment. In the traditional library, activity tended to be concentrated in three separate sequential activities. Acquisitions engaged in buying books and journals from vendors item by item. Following their receipt, cataloging units produced cards or some form of static catalog. The library's public services components then subsequently pointed users to the right print tools/sources. In contrast, in the modern library, particularly with collaborators, our efforts focus differently.

Today, libraries are shifting rapidly toward managing the internal intellectual assets of the campus as well as nurturing the engagements needed to foster student success. For acquisitions everything comes online in a package. For cataloging added metadata comes with the package. Public services mixes library and computer user support environment. To these basics we must add digital initiatives, which is the campus repository for intellectual and informational delivery. Furthermore, the special collections service is no longer a sidebar. It is now a very important host to campus history and societal definition, which refers to dissertations, campus news, administrative speeches, radio, public relations, and preservation of identity of the campus. They have emerged to shape the intellectual agenda of the campus.

Georgia Tech currently acquires nearly 26,000 subscriptions online, digitally. Cataloging sort of occurs, but it is likely not needed. The reason is that user access occurs directly from online indexes and the full-text digital articles, without the need to query an online catalog in the middle. Actually, the library does communicate links via SFX software, but no check-in clerk is required. Such an activity engages a wide circle of library operations, including systems, acquisitions, collection development, reference, and licensing.

Somewhat similarly, the public services involve a cooperative relationship with the Office of Information Technology. Their mutual efforts engage a panoply of components collaborating to offer joint support of users, namely collection development, licensing, instruction, and user instruction. The library, however, has added some functionality. For example, the digital initiatives efforts at Georgia Tech have extended to much of the output of faculty and student research as well as general campus information sources.

It is interesting to note that the Internet and related operations are making special collections a mainstream part of the library's services. Imagine if we reached a day when no one published in a commercial or society venue, but simply posted his or her scholarly endeavors to a robust campus Web support system like digital initiatives and special collections. The whole process of scholarly communications would be turned upside down. Of course, some publishers do not think that will happen. Still, who has ever seen full motion video or manipulatable datasets offered through a paper journal? The opportunity to augment scholarship delivery via campus-managed digital services is profound.

PART II: RESHAPING FACILITIES

Observations of what occurs on other campuses influence the Georgia Tech Library and how we conduct experiments intended to shape the undergraduate learning center. Staff reallocation and job revision coupled with partnerships with OIT and others have embedded a coordinated management arrangement into an infrastructure of technology support. This section focuses largely on the collaborative efforts at Georgia Tech to create a facility and support system that optimizes student success. Retention is a concern on any campus, even here where it is respectable. The public services venue here seeks to provide a point of interaction where all the right people are in place to intervene when a student finds himself or herself unable to determine an appropriate course of action, for example when confronted with an assignment to use unfamiliar software to write a paper or create some form of digital artifact.

This convergence helps when a student needs to write a paper, but does not know how to get access to the information resources or how to move content from those resources into the application being used. To create a set of overheads for a class presentation, it is relatively easy to use Microsoft Picture Manager to manipulate a store of images into slides. Likewise, composing the associated text via a word processor is easy. If students, however, want to link a full motion segment into a PowerPoint presentation, they may need to learn more. They would benefit from the collocated support system described here.

Currently, the Georgia Tech Library occupies two buildings well connected at five levels. They are maxed to capacity with collections and offices. The library has seats for only 7 percent of the student body. By any standard known to the profession, this is inadequate. A new building is planned and funding support is being sought. It will be much more multipurpose—accommodating campus functions that complement the library, because they represent pedagogically logical collaborators. In order to plan better, the library and OIT decided to implement some modest changes in facilities to learn what would be needed in a new building complex.

Georgia Tech's long-range plans include adding an addition to the library that will approximately double the space from 230,000 to 460,000 square feet. The new building focuses on undergraduate success with a multipurpose facility. During the planning phase, several experiments were conducted to determine the best collaboration partners as well as the physical arrangements of those partners that best support undergraduate success. Some offices for the OIT and advising services were imbedded in the library. Some hotel space for tutoring, writing support, and general advising augments the service areas.

The primary collaborative management team includes librarians from public services and OIT staff who carry responsibility for student academic support. This includes office technology support as well as services helping the campus understand and implement the digital environment. For example, making WebCT or Sakai work with the libraries' online resources requires some facilities adjustments and co-location of the right collection of people. Pushing this support forward required some experiments, which have taken shape in the form of two modest renovations.

Georgia Tech's experimental "Library West Commons" (LWC) opened in August 2002 with complete renovation of approximately 6,000 square feet, nearly immediately inside the front door to the library. The LWC contains 100 networked desktop computers clustered fairly tightly into stations with a single user orientation. Staff from OIT occupy offices in this area immediately next to reference.

In August 2006, the library opened a second phase of renovation called the Library East Commons (LEC). This renovation focuses on the collaborative work agenda of today's students. This area of the library, which can be entered from near the main entrance, occupies 9,000 square feet. It contains 30 group study computers, configured in multiple user orientation workstations. The LEC operates with guidance as needed from special library staff who were selected for their technical skills and academic backgrounds, but they are not librarians.

Those experiments have moved forward in three stages. The two described above were engineered largely by the library. The third is a basement level user support facility staffed by OIT that includes a help station for computer technical problems, password control, purchasing hardware, and related issues. It also houses meeting spaces for students to meet with general academic advisors and tutors in freshman standard courses (e.g., calculus).

These two main experiments described above are very successful. They are packed with students from mid morning until 3:00 A.M. every day. The crowd in the library tapers off to a few hundred by 3:00 or 4:00 A.M. Students have access to 130 high-end computer workstations, which are heavily used from 10:00 A.M. until the middle of the night. This is true even though students are required to bring their own computer to campus, and over half of them bring two.

A couple of images help to convey some sense of the operation and what is available to users. But, without getting hung up in the facility issue, this is even more about the collaboration of library services with other academic support services. The first image (Photo 3.1—north view at the top) is a photograph of the first implementation that moved the circulation desk away from the front door to another area of the library, and replaced it with a "reference" counter supported by the library and OIT. If the quality of the photograph was better, the main library entrance would show in the top middle where building security support stations itself. The intention is in part

Photo 3.1: Library West Commons (long view from above).

to put those individuals best equipped to help students right up front where the students could find staff as soon as they enter. This arrangement works and eliminates the need to place circulation immediately next to the exit.

The view in this photograph is from the northwest corner of the main floor with the north face on the left. (It is a window wall facing directly north, so it is a well-lit, pleasant environment.) The second floor is effectively a balcony over part of the first level. Early in 2003, library and OIT leaders evaluated extending the LWC to that level, but abandoned that plan in favor of a lateral extension for reasons related to scale and access. The facility gives students plenty of workspace even with the PCs hanging on the backs of the flat panel monitors. What became very apparent early on, however, is that the spaces work poorly in support of student collaboration. This is important since instruction requires joint work by students. Also, one segment of the floor focuses the technology on multimedia support. Faculty increasingly expect student project output to be in the form of joint presentations, Web pages, full motion video projects, and a variety of media forms that facilitate the delivery of the ideas students are trying to express. Collaboration is more critical in this pedagogical setting than in earlier periods where student projects amounted to writing a paper.

The proximity of reference librarians and OIT staff within literally 15 feet of these services has proven helpful to gaining instructional synergies. Students fail at their efforts far less in this arrangement than in the common situation where computer rooms are remote from library staff. Again, this facility does not lend itself to joint work by students. LWC is single-user oriented and has limited capability for students to shape their area of workspace for collaboration. The LEC is multiuser oriented and highly flexible for user arrangements and collaborative work. It also has macro spaces for theatre, café, and student displays.

In order to address the shortcoming in support of collaborative student work, the LEC was developed to improve opportunities for student engagement. The planning included input from students to overcome the shortcomings of the LWC described above. Space planning was guided by collaboration, this time from the library and OIT as well as student leadership. Library management now has a student-selected team of eight advisors who permanently comprise a board of advisors with the library and OIT. They meet with library and OIT management at least eight times each semester during a campus dead hour at 11:00 A.M. on Tuesdays or Thursdays. The library gives them lunch and they provide ideas, support, and advice in return. This group of students started with several who are campus leaders and they have agreed to sign on for the full time they are undergraduates and to select their successors from student leaders they identify. The library holds itself accountable to this group for undergraduate support.

Library and OIT management has been positively impacted by this group. The management team gains an understanding of undergraduates and vets nearly every agenda relating to instruction through this group of students. It is important to note that this space focuses on providing students with a flexible learning environment. It takes what was learned in the Library West Commons and extends it. Much of the extension focuses on creating student adjustable spaces for collaboration. It includes facilities such as lighting color control to push the margins of engagement with students in a robust manner.

Furthermore, the LEC extends library collaboration with OIT to include some research faculty who now use the space as a laboratory for studying the interactions of students engaged in the curricula and the effects of the surroundings on their success. Furthermore, it is a point of focus for the library team to interact collaboratively with undergraduates. A selected team of eight undergraduates serves as a permanent advisory committee helping us to adjust our agenda to meet the needs of matriculation better. Finally, for the first time the library is working for those who benefit from our efforts, not for an administrator in the campus tower.

It is not useful to dwell on the importance of physical infrastructure, but understanding that infrastructure helps explain the overall progress of the library to improve undergraduate support. Some steel framing running along the ceiling from the center top toward the left side is visible in the next photograph (Photo 3.2). Although that is part of a system designed by Hermann Miller company for retail, it provides an infinite grid of contact points for lighting, power, and IT access. It is used to advantage to create a malleable space suitable to rearrangement by students into collaborative work centers.

Photo 3.2: Library East Commons study cluster (one study cluster with four students).

In the photograph, the point of focus is a unit of fixed workstations designed for multiuser access. It works very well for up to four people. Other stations are available that will handle up to six, but groups of more than four needing to work together on a computer occurs only occasionally. When groups larger than four require use of technology, there are break-out rooms for groups that simulate a classroom environment in the LWC and in the OIT center downstairs.

These spaces are within the library, but owned and operated by the library and OIT. The equipment provided is all refreshed as needed by OIT with student fee support. Services are collaboratively supported by the library, OIT, and campus's center for teaching and learning.

The renovations and service enhancements described above can be summarized as follows:

- The library wanted to improve support of undergraduate retention. Retention appears to have increased by 6 or 7 percentage points. Since other changes were introduced in the campus roughly at the same time the first component was built, it can not be proven statistically that retention was positively impacted, but the suggestion is getting stronger. In particular, survey results from LibQUAL+™ support this premise.
- The library wanted to test collaboration with other components of the campus to see which ones are important. It appears that undergraduate education is yielding to pressures on faculty time such that faculty are off-loading advising, out of

class contact, and related functions of the old days to support operators trained to accommodate them (e.g., full-time nondiscipline advisors).
- Staff wanted to evaluate several kinds of facilities resources and their juxstapositioning in order to know better what would work in a new building.

Since these renovations and changes occurred, the library's door count has nearly doubled from just over 500,000 to 1.0 million. This suggests the program to restructure is on the right track.

PART III: REFOCUSING SERVICES

In addition to making changes in library spaces to accommodate contemporary learning models, libraries are also changing their services. The emphasis of many of these new services are digital in nature, and they focus on areas such as the production of campus-born digital information resources, the integration of scholarly content into virtual learning environments, and the digital capture of live scholarly and student events. At Georgia Tech, these activities have given rise to the SMARTech institutional repository service, the EPAGE suite of services (Electronic Press at Georgia Tech), and the arrival of Sakai as the chosen collaboration and learning environment for Georgia Tech courses. They have led to much collaboration with campus units and have provided students with new services, alongside their new learning spaces hosted in the library. The following elaborates on two points of focus.

SMARTech Repository and EPAGE Services

The SMARTech repository service supports student production of scholarly works and live events being created through the library's EPAGE publishing and capture services. SMARTech (Scholarly Materials and Research @ Georgia Tech) is a repository for the intellectual output of Georgia Tech in support of its teaching and research missions. Based upon the DSpace software, it opened in August 2004. Today it holds nearly 12,000 items in over 160 collections. Usage has increased precipitously with 1,000,791 item records viewed, 489,292 items downloaded, and 50,434 searches between July 2005 and June 2006. This activity makes SMARTech one of the largest and most used institutional repositories in the world. The EPAGE suite of services provides technical support in publishing eBooks, eJournals, and eConference proceedings, capturing instructional materials and other multimedia resources, and hosting online versions of conferences, symposia, and lecture series. Together, SMARTech and EPAGE have fostered many partnerships among the library, faculty, students and student groups, and campus units with the hope of many more joint efforts in the future.

One of the services most used currently is EPAGE's digital capture of live student and scholarly events. The main thrust of the service is to capture speakers' oral presentations that are part of a Georgia Tech distinguished lectures series or a Georgia Tech-hosted symposium. Examples of these are the History of Women's Health symposium (2006), hosted by the School of Literature, Culture, and Communication, the library-hosted Faculty Tuesday Talks lecture series, and various presentations such as those given by the president of Georgia Tech, Dr. Wayne Clough. There has also been a productive congruence between the library's development of its learning spaces and EPAGE services. The LEC with its instant theatre is host to many student presentations and informal speaking events. The library also uses the walls of the LEC to display students' creative activity or their research products. Library staff digitally record or capture these, which then become objects maintained and made accessible through the SMARTech repository.

The EPAGE services also provide technical support for more traditional publications, such as scholarly journals and student theses and newspapers. The scholarly journal being supported currently is *Information Technologies and International Development (ITID)*. This collaboration involves the MIT Press, the Georgia Tech Library, and the two journal editors who are faculty at the University of Maryland and in Georgia Tech's Sam Nunn School of International Affairs. *ITID* originated as a print and subscription-based journal with the MIT Press. Today it is an open access electronic journal with financial support from various sponsors and continues to be published by the MIT Press. Librarians and technologists support its technical production using the Open Journal System software (OJS), an open source software tool. They have also been involved in the joint ARL/ACRL Scholarly Communications Institute, held at Duke University during December 2006. This has been a most fruitful collaboration among the four parties and the library plans to assist in initiating more journal projects in the future.

Student publishing is another active area. Georgia Tech launched *The Tower: Georgia Tech's Journal of Undergraduate Research* in fall 2007. This electronic journal is a collaboration among the library, the Office of Undergraduate Research, the School of Literature, Culture, and Communication, and the Student Publications Board. The library also collaborates with the Office of Information Technology and students to produce *The Technique*, Georgia Tech's student newspaper. The library's archives department coordinated this new electronic workflow when the newspaper's editorial staff learned they no longer had enough server space to operate and when the archives was simultaneously expressing its interest in preserving the newspaper digitally. Today the live production version is produced on OIT servers while the newspaper's text and images are maintained in SMARTech. Through these two projects, the library is thoroughly ensconced in the major publishing initiatives of Georgia Tech students.

Undergraduate research is another source of library–campus unit collaboration. There has been increasing growth of undergraduate research at

Georgia Tech, in terms of the number and robustness of undergraduate research programs, scholarships, awards, and international research support. While there are many others (over 30 programs), a few examples of these programs are:

- The President's Undergraduate Research Award (PURA)
- Summer Undergraduate Research Experience (SURE)
- Undergraduate Research Opportunities Program, ECE (UROP)
- Undergraduate Research Opportunities in Computing (UROC)
- Summer Undergraduate Research Fellowship Program (SURF)
- International Research Experience in Southeast Asia (IREP-SEA)
- Undergraduate Research Scholars Program (URS)
- Facilitating Academic Careers in Engineering and Sciences (FACES)

In addition, the new Undergraduate Research Option (URO), managed by the Undergraduate Research Office, produces undergraduate student theses. In a partnership between the library and the Undergraduate Research Office, the library is adapting the Virginia Tech-created ETD-db software to facilitate the submission of URO theses into SMARTech. This approach also gives the students experience in electronic processing of their writings as well as some experience with and understanding of the electronic publishing they may be doing in their future careers.

Learning Technology Collaborations

One of the more "cutting edge" areas of library–campus unit collaboration has been the continuing discussions surrounding technology-enhanced learning and the management of digital learning objects and other related multimedia. This content management need is an outgrowth of the proliferating number of student multimedia projects associated with coursework as well as the faculty's self-designed learning objects and digitally captured courses. Discussions about erecting a media and learning object repository have been ongoing, with the main partners involved in conversation being the library, the School of Electrical and Computer Engineering's (ECE) Digital Media Lab, and Distance Learning and Professional Education (DLPE). The ECE Digital Media Lab is building easy-to-use learning object authoring tools over Macromedia Flash for faculty interested in creating their own instructional materials in digital form. The library is interested in building a repository to manage and provide access to these learning objects. Lastly, DLPE is a major distributor of courses and educational content for Georgia Tech and is looking into how it can best encourage faculty to create online courses, maintain instructional content over time, and distribute their courses in whole, or in part, online. Together these three units form the continuum of learning content creation, management, and distribution that may serve as the core of technology-enhanced learning at Georgia Tech.

Several other noteworthy planning initiatives and projects have taken place in regards to digital learning environments and library participation. One major project is the Tegrity Course Capture Software Pilot Team, a collaboration among DLPE, OIT, and the library. The Tegrity software allows faculty to capture all aspects of their classroom teaching (lecturing, audio, video, computer-projected, and written notes) for digital playback by students. The students' notes taken during class using a Tegrity-supplied digital pen and board are time synched to the faculty member's presentation. Students can click on their digital notes, go to that time in the professor's presentation, and can then review the audio and video on their computers. The library collaborates in the planning of Tegrity's deployment and provides student training classes on how to use the software system in Tegrity-enabled courses. The library also has participated in the GT Academic Technologies Advisory Committee, the Virtual Learning Strategy Group led by the CTO, and the Campus Portal Steering Committee. All of these groups and projects have had heavy library involvement and representation in them.

The latest project to continue the successes of the digital learning environment collaborations is Georgia Tech's move to use Sakai, an open source collaboration and learning environment, for virtual learning support in courses. This has been the culmination of the many discussions, committees, and projects mentioned above. Adopting Sakai has led to creating a new Educational Technologies unit, reporting to the Vice Provost for Academic Affairs (see Figure 3.1). There has not been a "learning technologies" unit before at Georgia Tech. Library leaders serve on the Education Technologies Program Board, responsible for Sakai's implementation, as well as on the Educational Technologies Governing Board, responsible for the overall direction of these technologies and their application. Specifically, the library has dedicated staff working on integrating library technologies, content, and services into Sakai.

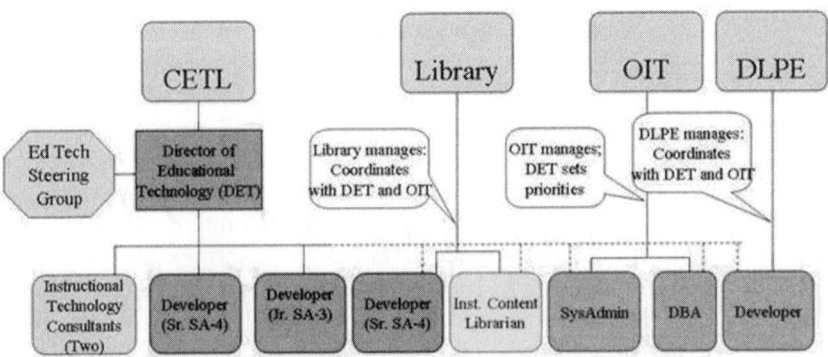

Figure 3.1: Educational Technologies Preliminary Organization Chart.

It also has librarians assisting the instructional designers of the Center for the Enhancement of Teaching and Learning (CETL) with training faculty and students to use Sakai effectively.

CONCLUSION

The library has been a robust partner and collaborator in planning and executing virtual learning initiatives. The efforts described here to re-engineer library services from a unit-based approach to one based on collaboration seems in retrospect to be a change in the correct direction. Silos separating campus components of the academic agenda lose synergy and effectiveness when collaboration, communication, and joint effort do not occur. Students engaged in out-of-classroom work today depend heavily on joint effort and on support that converges from several points. Since this phenomenon emerged and facilities were renovated here to accommodate it, the Georgia Tech Library has entertained visits numbering in the hundreds per year from all over the United States and even as far away as India. Those visits offer evidence that the experiments developed show substantial promise. In fact, since 2002, nearly every library serving in the Association of Research Libraries now provides a service point engaging more than simply library staff. The future portends opportunity for even more robust academic engagement to benefit student effort.

4

FROM ISOLATION TO ENGAGEMENT: STRATEGY, STRUCTURE, AND PROCESS

Barbara J. Kriigel and Timothy F. Richards

The Mardigian Library at the University of Michigan–Dearborn seeks to be an engaged entity within the university. Over time it has developed a mission statement, a set of values and principles, and a statement of strategic direction. A key theme that runs through these various statements is campus engagement. The library's leadership arrived at this theme out of the conviction that the work the library does is important, indeed vital, to the education of students and that the knowledge and skills of library staff members, both librarians and non-librarians, are valuable to the larger institution. The responsibility for accomplishing the mission of the university lies with all members of the university community, including library staff members, and the library has the responsibility of contributing its talent and energy to the larger purposes of the institution. This chapter describes the journey that the Mardigian Library traveled over the last 18 years in an effort to create a library that is a fully engaged, active participant in the life of the campus. When the library embarked on this journey, no one had in mind the terms "convergence" and "collaboration" or the definitions of those terms as they are used in this volume. Nevertheless, the library set out from the beginning to create the conditions within the library that would enable the library and its staff to be effective, active participants.

CREATING THE CONDITIONS FOR SUCCESS

When we arrived at the Mardigian Library in our roles as director (Richards) and head of technical services (Kriigel) in mid-1989, there were numerous opportunities to improve the operational effectiveness of the library, and an essential first step was to position the library as a visible and effective agent on campus. It is the responsibility of senior management to provide the leadership to create the conditions so that the library and its staff members can be successful in becoming active, engaged participants in the life of the campus. In retrospect, some basic routes that we pursued over the years, at times simultaneously and at times sequentially, to move the library toward this goal include:

- changes in organizational structure and process
- organizational/staff development
- development of campus outreach programs

Richards interviewed for the library director position late in 1988. During the interviews, several library staff members expressed their awareness and frustration that the library was on the sidelines and not an active "player" on campus. It was clear they hoped the library's new director would take action to position the library so that it could play a visible role at the University of Michigan—Dearborn. At that time, virtually the only involvement outside the library by library staff was selectors' communication with faculty members concerning selection of books and journals.

Partly because of this clearly stated sense of frustration, Richards made it a condition for accepting the director's position that the library director would be a member of the Provost's Council of Deans. Until this time, the library director had not been included in this body. The purpose of this requirement was to begin positioning the library as a "player" on campus. From there, it was easy for the director to become engaged in a variety of campus-wide groups, giving increased exposure to the library. These opportunities included the director's membership on a campus-wide Policy Council and participation in campus-wide committees, including the Goals for the Undergraduate Experience Task Force and the Distributed Learning Task Force, which established a set of principles to govern campus efforts in distributed learning. More recently, Richards chaired the Working Group on General Education/Distribution Requirements (2002), a group appointed by the Provost, and a Faculty Senate-appointed task force on academic integrity (2003). These kinds of experiences outside the library have given the library director the opportunity to network, to gain an understanding of the organizational topography, and to establish relationships with deans, associate deans, department chairs and senior faculty members across campus.

Mission, Vision, and Goals

During the first year, library staff worked to establish department and library goals. In 1994, a retreat was held for all library staff where a consultant helped us develop the library's formal mission and vision statements. The purpose of having the whole group create the statements was to develop an understanding among staff members that a library is more than the sum of its parts; that, while each unit may have specific goals to achieve and tasks to perform, the unit is part of a larger entity, which has a purpose that transcends unit-specific goals. Library staff regularly review and update this document.

Librarian Promotion

In 1989, librarian promotion appeared to be an *ad hoc* process, without clear criteria or process. The only thing that was obvious was that the campus did not provide funding to support salary increases for librarians' promotions, requiring that resources come from within the library's existing budget. This, of course, created a huge disincentive to encourage promotion. Richards worked with the newly installed provost to create a promotion process that:

- requires that librarians provide evidence of increased levels of engagement both on campus and outside the library as a criterion for promotion
- provides salary increases from central university funds (as with teaching faculty)

The librarian promotion policy is the single most important component in our success in moving the library from being on the sidelines to being an involved player on campus. The reason is that it created the incentive for librarians to get out of their offices and to be involved, both on campus and professionally outside of the campus.

Library System and Campus Student Information System

The first major project, in 1989, was to conduct an intensive, comprehensive study of the options for replacing the library's increasingly inadequate GEAC-based circulation system and online public access catalog (OPAC). The work of the study team, led by Kriigel, was well received and the university leadership agreed to fund the acquisition of a new integrated library system.

Approximately one year after the new system was implemented, the provost indicated that the campus needed to investigate options for a new student information system (SIS) for the campus. Richards suggested, and the provost agreed, that based on her experience implementing the library's system, Kriigel should chair the selection committee to review and recommend a new SIS vendor and software. After completing this assignment, true to the principle that "no good deed goes unpunished," the provost asked Kriigel to co-chair the implementation committee, which, as it turned out, consumed most of her time for three more years. This experience was a watershed event in the library's effort to move into a more visible and active role on campus. For the first time, university administrators and staff members from a variety of units across campus had visible proof that a librarian had knowledge and skills that are not only transferable to other campus operations and services, but that the knowledge and skills that librarians possess could be of vital importance to the campus. The library continues to benefit to this day from the relationships created through this experience; library staff members serve on various advisory committees for the SIS, and the library has direct access to student data, enabling the library to better serve patrons. For example, library staff can create files of patron data on a timely basis to load into the library's automation system whenever needed, without assistance from ITS. Circulation staff are authorized to update a student's "hold" information in the campus system whenever a fine is paid or a temporary release is granted. Staff can easily verify a patron's status if there are problems with the patron's library account and resolve the issue immediately. Prior to the new system's implementation, library staff were never allowed to view, let alone update, student information; all requests had to go through ITS, a lengthy and time-consuming process. The library's participation on the implementation team helped prove that library staff could be trusted with access to data and that library staff could help resolve data issues affecting the entire campus. A common "joke" at the time was that Kriigel worked for four years just so student records would have library barcode information and circulation staff could release holds!

CHANGES IN ORGANIZATIONAL STRUCTURE

TV Studio

A relatively uncommon feature of the library is that it contains a fully functional video production facility. Originally called the TV Studio, it was part of a unit focused on continuing education with virtually no relationship with the library. In the early 1990s, the provost invited the library director to take responsibility for the TV Studio. At that time, more than 90 percent of the TV Studio's work was done for nonacademic purposes and the provost charged the library director with reversing the proportion of effort that the TV Studio devoted to academic support. This was the library's first foray into what is called "convergence" since the two units were merged, "forcing" everyone in the library (including the director) to work with staff from a separate unit who, ironically, worked in the same building but who were not viewed as colleagues.

Over the next few years the TV Studio's operations underwent several changes that facilitated and enhanced the library's ability to interact with other campus units. Most important, within two years, 90 percent of the TV Studio's production work was in support of academic programs on campus.

The head of the TV Studio taught classes as an adjunct instructor in the liberal arts college's communications program and the studio did all of the production work to create courses on videotape that students could take on their own schedule. The School of Management became the most important client during this period; its faculty members and students made heavy use of production facilities to create videos for marketing, advertising, and other student projects. The TV Studio, which continued to evolve over the years, is now called Campus Media Services (CMS). Its current charge includes working closely with campus academic units to deliver Internet-based services, including videoconferencing. CMS also provides distance-learning technology support for the liberal arts college in the event that courses taught on-site need to be delivered via distance-learning technology due to a pandemic or other disaster that might make it impossible to conduct face-to-face classes on campus.

Information Technology Services

About a year after Richards assumed responsibility for the TV Studio, the provost asked him to take on responsibility for overseeing Information Technology Services (ITS), the unit responsible for campus computing operations. This had a huge and not altogether positive impact on the effort to get the library more involved in the life of the campus. The principal positive consequence of this restructuring was that integrating ITS staff into the library's organizational structure helped everyone to take a broader view of campus support needs and to look for areas of collaboration. Negative consequences of this restructuring included diversion of the director's attention to an area in which he was not (and is not) deeply knowledgeable, and a diminution in the ability of the director to advocate for library resources when the need to boost funding for ITS was so self-evidently paramount for the campus at the time.

One tangible consequence of this arrangement was a general-purpose computer lab placed in the library and operated by ITS. The structural merger of the library and ITS lasted approximately five years (1992–1997). While this chapter cannot develop and discuss the favorable and unfavorable consequences of this formal merger, it may be sufficient to state that the major drawback to the formal organizational structure was that library funding issues always ranked lower than funding requests to support IT needs, putting the director in an untenable, or at least an uncomfortable, position. Ultimately, ITS was reestablished as a separate formal unit under the direction of a chief technology officer in 1997. Since that time, ITS and the library's systems staff have had a strong, collaborative relationship with reasonably clear domains of authority.

Under this new arrangement, the library enjoys ample opportunities to communicate productively with ITS staff. ITS maintains the campus network but does not administer library servers or workstations. Most technology problems in the library are handled by library systems staff personnel with assistance from ITS as needed. The Information Technology Advisory Committee, on which three librarians now serve, advises the campus chief technology officer of issues on campus that relate to the mission of ITS and fosters a free flow of information about technology issues. The library systems staff members are included in the campus-wide computer support personnel committee. Recent collaborations between the library and ITS include moving library staff to a new mail system and new login server.

Network Resources Librarian Position

It became clear that the combined interests of IT and the library could be served without detriment to either group's interests by increasing faculty awareness of the then-new phenomenon of networked campus information resources and by increasing faculty adeptness in the use of these resources. This led to the creation in 1994 of a position known as the network resources librarian. Our idea was to employ a librarian to bridge the gap between faculty members and IT staff, who had technical expertise but relatively poor "people skills," in order to help faculty use online resources effectively. The creation of this position enabled the library to have one librarian whose primary responsibility was working with faculty members.

Over time, the specific duties of this position have evolved. Today, while this librarian still does much faculty education and training for access to network resources, the position also plays a key role on campus in educating faculty members and university staff about copyright and intellectual property. The individual in this position also works closely with the Faculty Senate and the provost's office to administer and support the technologies that the university employs in addressing academic integrity on campus, serves as the campus "point person" in collaborating with the University of Michigan Ann Arbor campus on faculty members' use of the University of Michigan institutional repository, and is in the early stages of collaborating with faculty members on educating faculty on scholarly communication issues.

The network resources librarian was recently appointed to serve as head of Campus Media Services. Despite the evolving nature of the specific duties, responsibilities and title of this position over the years, the primary emphasis of the role is the same 13 years after its creation: work with faculty members to encourage and facilitate their use of online resources.

Archives

Shortly after arriving on campus, Richards recognized that the campus lacked an archival program. Over a period of nearly 10 years several small steps led to the creation of a university archive in 2001, staffed by a professional archivist. These steps included reallocating the duties of an existing librarian position and collaborating with the Bentley Historical Library on the Ann Arbor campus of the University of Michigan. While intended to focus on collecting, preserving, and making accessible records of the university, the existence of the archive has provided numerous opportunities to foster collaboration with units across campus, including the chancellor's and provost's offices, University Relations, student government, the student newspaper and other student organizations, deans' offices, and other administrative units across campus (e.g., the Women's Resource Center). The archivist has been extremely proactive in reaching out to a variety of academic programs, including Women's Studies and the Center for Arab-American Studies. Additionally, the archivist has been a participant in the NEH (National Endowment for the Humanities)-funded Science and Technology Studies interdisciplinary project, which includes collaboration with the nearby Henry Ford Museum, and has been deeply involved in the development of two interdisciplinary programs:

- The Center for the Study of Automotive Heritage, an interdisciplinary program of research and an active site for labor, business, and public policy discussions about the history of the automobile and the automotive industry
- The Science and Technology Studies project, which was established to provide undergraduate students with an opportunity to examine the relationship between science/technology and society with special attention to the impact of the automobile and automobile industry on American culture

Audiovisual Services

For many years the library delivered and supported audiovisual (AV) equipment for faculty use in the classrooms. With the explosion of technology and multimedia resources, faculty demand rose dramatically from year to year. Faculty members understandably wanted classrooms to be fully equipped with the latest and best computers and AV equipment for ease of use and to eliminate booking and delivery. Library audiovisual services staff and student assistants needed increased levels of training to be able to troubleshoot the problems that inevitably arose with the introduction of a wide range of new equipment, especially the computers. It became evident to us that a significant amount of money was needed to buy more equipment, upgrade classrooms, and provide adequate staffing. However, there was little support from the academic units to increase the library's budget for this purpose. The result was that a library service that had worked well for many years when faculty mostly wanted overhead projectors and a few video players, no longer worked well when everyone expected a computer, video player, and projector in every classroom. Since the library could not keep up with demand, some units began purchasing their own equipment for their faculty to use (an example of the decentralized campus culture). Eventually it only made sense to move this service away from the library's control; equipment was distributed to various units and one library staff member was transferred to the liberal arts college (CASL), which is the largest campus unit. Deans and their faculty now identify and fund their units' AV needs. Everyone is now better served and happier, and library efforts are better focused on meeting informational needs rather than equipment delivery.

Henry Ford Estate

As a result of negotiations with the University's Business Affairs Office, in 2003, the university archivist assumed formal responsibility for managing the archives of the Henry Ford Estate, the home of Henry Ford, a national historic landmark, which is located on campus. The thrust of this role is to develop and oversee projects to make archival material at the estate secure physically yet accessible intellectually.

ORGANIZATIONAL/STAFF DEVELOPMENT

The library needed to develop a strategic mind-set, with established and articulated mission, goals, and so on. During the 1990s, the library worked with several consultants who provided organizational and staff development training assistance and advice. Three of those experiences were particularly important in creating an outward-looking organization:

- *The Learning Organization:* In 1998, library staff worked closely with consultants Judy Sorum Brown and Peter Carlson on "learning organization" principles and practices. The key lesson learned from this work is that the library must constantly examine its own operations, adapting and adjusting behavior based on what is learned from that self-examination. Library staff realized that they did not know enough about what difference the library makes in the lives of students and faculty members; we needed to do a better job of acquiring this knowledge. Based on this experience, the library made a commitment to develop and articulate a coherent understanding of what the library does, what direction the library is taking, and what the library's priorities are.
- *RADAR:* Librarians worked with Richard M. Dougherty in 2002, to gather data from focus groups using a process called RADAR (Recognizing the Actual Desires And Requirements of users), which helped us understand how clientele see the library and what gaps exist between what we think they know (or should know) and what they do know. This was a real eye opener. Librarians learned that even the most active, committed faculty users and staunchest supporters were unaware of many library services or held inaccurate ideas about much of what the library had to offer. They realized that they had to communicate with and engage faculty members better. The key lesson learned from this experience was that we needed to reach out more effectively to the faculty.
- *FERA:* Library managers worked with Formative Evaluation Research Associates (FERA) in 2005 and 2006 to develop data collection processes and evaluation

instruments that could be used periodically to understand how students and faculty use the library and what they know about its resources and services. The principal goal was to obtain reliable data that library managers could use to make informed decisions about allocating resources in ways that would improve the quality of library service. The partnership with FERA has helped the library build the capacity to collect "actionable" data regularly and systematically. A key lesson confirmed by this work is that partnerships with faculty members are essential to success in encouraging and assisting students to use library resources.

Cultivation of Leadership

Cultivating strategic thinking within the library and its leadership is a crucial element in creating an organizational environment that fosters and supports collaboration with faculty and other members of the university community. To that end, the library endeavored to create an organization that provides ample opportunity for library staff members (librarian and non-librarian) to participate in groups, programs, and projects that have a strategic or external focus or that support the development of leadership skills and strategic thinking. On balance, the library has been fairly successful in achieving the convergence that was sought. Every member of the library's 25-person staff is involved in at least one of 14 standing library committees, which vary widely in focus and interest (e.g., campus relations, signage, and emergency readiness and response), and all librarians and support staff members are involved in at least one external collaboration, partnership, joint program, staff committee, faculty committee, or other projects on campus.

Among the most important efforts undertaken to develop leadership and cultivate this perspective are:

- *A-Team:* In April 1989, library decision making was focused on internal library operations; there was no library-wide group for interdepartmental communication, strategic thinking, or external relations. The "A-Team" was formed in the summer of 1989, to create a body that would facilitate sharing information across units, that could look at library-wide issues and opportunities, and that could help to identify external issues that might affect library operations. During the first two years of this group's existence, the major foci were to encourage members to share the challenges that they faced in their work with colleagues, to develop confidence in this body that it is was acceptable to disagree with the director, and to encourage members to propose ways of improving the library's effectiveness. After the group became comfortable with these approaches, the "A-Team" was expanded beyond director and department heads to include staff members nominated by staff and selected by the director for two-year terms. This body serves as a communications vehicle: a space to share ideas and information, to alert others to initiatives within departments or units, and to identify opportunities for collaboration within and outside the library. Key components of the twice-monthly meeting agendas are the "information, rumors and gossip" segment, in which we learn what is going on around campus that might affect the library and the "trends and issues" segment, where we discuss current articles pertaining to libraries and higher education. The intent of these discussions is to examine external ideas to help us see how the environment affects the library and what might be done to change, improve, or enhance service in the campus environment. Each year, the A-Team reviews the library's mission statement (see chapter appendix) to ensure that the mission, principles, and values contained in the document accurately reflect the library's direction and purpose.

- *COG:* The "Core Operations Group" (COG), created in 2003, comprises the library's four department heads. The charge is to work as a collaborative team that seeks, identifies, and acts on opportunities to advance, enhance, and improve library operational effectiveness in achieving the library's mission. The goal in creating this group was to encourage the library's middle managers to identify library-wide priorities and recommend the strategic direction that the library should take. COG has the authority to initiate discussion with the director regarding any action or issue they consider is likely to affect the library's relationship with the campus community.

- *Michigan Library Association Leadership Academy:* The Michigan Library Association (MLA) sponsors a Leadership Academy, which is described as "an intensive, experiential and focused program to prepare individuals for leadership roles within MLA, as well as prepare them for leadership roles within the library workplace." Over the last several years, the library has funded the cost of attendance by librarians who have applied to participate in this multiyear program. Attendees inform us that they have found the Leadership Academy to be an excellent opportunity for professional development and networking. The academy has been an important resource in developing library managers. After completing the program, librarians increase their level of engagement within the library, on campus and in the profession.

- Library Committees: A number of standing committees, *ad hoc* groups, and task forces were established to address issues, challenges, and opportunities. One purpose in offering opportunities for librarians and support staff to participate in these bodies is to encourage them to see the big picture and to realize that the library is part of an interdependent system, operating within the context of the campus. At last count there are 14 standing committees. Among those most directly involved in work with an outward focus are the Faculty Outreach Committee, the Campus Relations Committee, and the Library Events Committee.

CAMPUS OUTREACH PROGRAMS

Voice/Vision

The library houses the Voice/Vision Holocaust Survivor Oral Histories Archive, which is internationally known and which is an interdepartmental project to transcribe and provide online access to approximately 300 audio and video interviews with Holocaust survivors conducted by history professor Sidney Bolkosky. Library staff members collaborate with the project's curator, perform original cataloging for the interviews, and add the transcripts and audio portions of the interviews to the project's Web site. The library provides support to Bolkosky as he continues to interview survivors and teach classes on the Holocaust. The project is supported almost entirely through external funds; library staff members assist with events and other efforts to attain the goal of creating an endowment that will permanently fund the archive and a full-time curator.

Faculty Salons

The Library Events committee developed the idea of the Faculty Salon as a way to assist new tenure-track faculty members in identifying senior colleagues with whom to collaborate in research and grant writing. Librarians work with the provost's office and the director of research and sponsored programs to organize this event, which is held annually in the library.

Armenian Research Center Cataloging Project

The library initiated a project in 2004 with the Armenian Research Center (ARC) to make the Center's collection of approximately 8,000 volumes more accessible to scholars. Prior to this project, bibliographic records for the Center were not accessible online. The focus of this collaboration is to catalog the ARC collection in OCLC and add bibliographic records for the items into the library's OPAC. The head of technical services trained an ARC staff member to use OCLC and the library's automation system and continues to provide support (e.g., authority work) and advice to ARC staff.

Art Gallery Collaboration

G. Edward Wall, who was director of the library when the building opened in 1980, is an art aficionado who had a very important mission in mind for the library: to provide opportunities for University of Michigan—Dearborn students to, in his words, "encounter art."

In large part because of this intention, the library has been home to the university's collection of art glass since the building opened. For over 10 years, the library provided storage space for artifacts, a small display space, and office space for an art curator. A small portion of the collection was on display in cases throughout the library and occasional art receptions were organized by the art curator. In the mid-1990s, the university established the "Art Museum Project" to raise the funds necessary to build permanent accommodations for the collection. To support this purpose, Richards offered library space for conversion into a temporary art gallery so that the campus would have a way to increase the visibility of the university's art collection and to raise awareness of the project. The University funded the renovation, creating expanded office space and an art gallery, now named the Alfred Berkowitz Gallery.

The library and gallery collaborate in a number of ways. The gallery holds five to seven art exhibitions each year with opening receptions, bringing many visitors to the library, including artists, local dignitaries, and community residents. Visitors have the opportunity to see the library and the library in turn has the opportunity to market itself to these individuals. Library staff members have created several gallery exhibitions highlighting special collections such as the Juvenile Historic Collection and the Voice/Vision Holocaust Survivor Oral History Archive. The library also occasionally holds library events in the gallery while exhibitions are on display, creating a unique, interesting and appealing ambience for attendees. Both the library and the gallery have benefited from this collaboration. Students benefit as well. In keeping with Wall's original vision, they are exposed to art and culture they might not otherwise see, they have an opportunity to take a break from their studies in a peaceful atmosphere, and they are able to attend lectures and demonstrations by wonderful artists. It is definitely a win-win for everyone.

Juvenile Historic Collection

The library's Juvenile Historic Collection contains approximately 4,000 titles, some dating back to the early 1800s. Library staff worked closely with the faculty member who teaches children's literature to incorporate this rich collection of representative children's literature into the curriculum. The professor developed an extensive program to study the collection, including posting reviews written by students in the School of Education on the school's Web site. He was also deeply involved in the initial organization of this collection and we have worked closely with him to make items accessible and available to children's literature students.

Civic Engagement Project

The University initiated its Civic Engagement Project (CEP) in 2003 to foster active student participation in the communities served by the University of Michigan–Dearborn. (Richards has been a member of the project's steering committee since 2004.) A key component of the project involves engaging students and faculty members in academic service learning. The project recently moved into new office space provided by the library. Providing CEP a home in the library is a perfect fit: it is located in a building with a high volume of student traffic, is highly visible and easily accessible, is centrally located for students who are enrolled in all of the university's colleges and schools, and is consistent with the library's mission of being a student-centered campus resource.

Campus Web Strategy Team

Over the last few years, some library staff members have become knowledgeable and skilled in Web site usability testing. They have done a number

FROM ISOLATION TO ENGAGEMENT 75

of iterations of testing, which radically improved the library's Web site. The university formed the Web Strategy Team a few years ago to provide guidance, advice, and expertise to help develop the university's Web presence in a way that both promotes the university and assists the university's constituent groups in doing the things they need to do. The library has had representation on this group from its creation because the library was perceived to be a source of knowledge and expertise in Web design and Web usability testing. The librarian on the team made the library's usability testing station available to the group and provided guidance on conducting user tests so that data can be gathered from students, prospective students, alumni, faculty, and staff members on proposed redesigns of the university's home page.

Religious Music Project

The Pluralism Project at the University of Michigan–Dearborn has documented the diversity of the religious practices and customs among immigrant groups in the Detroit metropolitan area through photographs and case studies. The Campus Media Services unit collaborated with the director of this project to field record the music that is performed as part of religious services among immigrant groups.

Distinguished Faculty Friend

The library established the "Distinguished Faculty Friend" award as a way to recognize faculty members who make significant contributions to the library. The first award was given in 2003 and additional faculty members were recognized in 2005 and 2007. Each award was presented shortly after the retirement of a faculty member who was an extraordinary friend of the library, not necessarily in terms of giving money, but in being a supporter of and advocate for the library. The library hosts a luncheon and invites key donors and friends, and a small group of the honoree's choosing.

"Take a Faculty Member to Lunch"

The library has participated in the annual new faculty orientation at the beginning of each fall term for over 15 years. Although the format has varied, the orientation has always included an on-site presentation and some form of interaction between selected librarians and the new faculty members, typically 15 to 20. Over the years, librarians discovered that, despite their best intentions, the efforts to provide newly hired faculty members with pertinent information about the library during the orientation were not highly successful and were having a minimal impact on a strategically important target audience. Following a day of learning about registrar's requirements, tenure-track issues, and grant-writing expectations, many of the new faculty members were dulled by the mass of new information before they ever arrived in the library, if they made it to the library at all. The library's message was simply not being heard.

We came to realize that we could be far more effective in reaching new faculty members if librarians could get to know them on an individual basis, discover their interests and needs, and discuss ways the library can support their teaching, the learning of their students, and their research interests. From this awareness, we developed the idea of having librarians take each of the new faculty members out to lunch at a later time, during the latter half of their first semester.

Initially, some librarians were hesitant to lunch with a new instructor and worried about whether they could keep the conversation going, or how they would talk about services in the library with which they did not directly participate. To alleviate these concerns, we encouraged including two librarians at each lunch meeting and the library's *ad hoc* Faculty Outreach Committee developed a page of talking points for librarians who felt they needed some support. After about three years, most librarians viewed this as a very successful means of working with faculty members and were no longer diffident about having lunch with new faculty members. Now it is a yearly routine for library selectors to contact the new instructors in their discipline and some even lunch one-on-one!

Focus Action Committee

An *ad hoc* campus group called the Focus Action Committee has met irregularly for a number of years, discussing issues that affect recruitment and retention. The group consists of university staff members from such units as financial services, the registrar's office, student life, admissions, and financial aid. Kriigel was invited to join the group after she suggested to the vice chancellor for enrollment management and student life that the university should consider hiring admitted students in the summer before their freshmen year as a means of converting the students from admitted to registered. As a result, the library became a test site for the now-successful "Summer Pathways" program, which offers summer employment to admitted students.

The Focus Action Committee also has accomplished a number of cross-department projects, including improved communication with students and their parents, student e-mail accounts for admitted students, campus signage and maps, and recruitment and orientation events. Any issue is open for discussion and depending on the topic, staff members from other units are invited to attend meetings and lend their expertise. If necessary, budget proposals are written and submitted to the appropriate administrative units. Overall, an amazing amount of work has been accomplished at little or no cost. It is, in our view, an excellent example of one way in which the library is engaged with the campus community and offers an easy opportunity to reinforce the concept that library staff members have the knowledge and skills to help the university accomplish its mission.

CONCLUSION

Over the last 18 years, the library has experienced convergence and collaboration in terms of official structural changes (e.g., merging/unmerging with ITS) and "virtual" structural changes (e.g., helping implement the campus's student information system). In our experience, the "virtual" organization chart usually changes when significant collaborations are established with other campus units to accomplish long-term projects. These efforts are more than just normal committee participation; they represent a real time commitment on the part of library staff members with an acknowledgement from library administration that some normal work assignments may be affected. In a sense, it is like lending a staff member to another unit part time while maintaining the library's reporting and support structures for the staff member. Feedback from the other unit enables the library to perform meaningful evaluations and reviews.

Some projects have been both part of the library's official organization and its virtual organization. For example, the Voice/Vision Holocaust Survivor Oral History Archives started under the library's control but now reports to the College of Arts, Sciences, and Letters (CASL). The Archive is housed in the library and several library staff members work on the project and its fundraising efforts but the curator and budget are the responsibility of CASL and the professor who created the archival materials.

Other projects, such as work with the Armenian Research Center (ARC), have only been a virtual convergence. The head of technical services oversees the cataloging of the collection by ARC staff, organizes the outsourced cataloging process, and provides overall quality control, but she has never formally supervised the ARC staff.

Overall, there has been much success when the convergence and collaboration are "virtual" rather than "official." There are several reasons for this:

- *Decentralization:* The campus culture is highly decentralized. This sometimes leads to units focusing only on their needs rather than on those of the entire institution. It is easier to form unofficial alliances in a decentralized environment.
- *Competition for Resources:* When a project or collaboration is under the library's official reporting structure, it is our experience that it is viewed as "the library's problem" when issues arise or if there is a need for additional funding. The experience with obtaining appropriate funding and support for Audiovisual Services was an excellent example of this problem.
- *Budget Priorities:* When similar but unique departments are combined into one official reporting structure, setting priorities for budget requests to the university administration can be tricky. For example, when the library and ITS were merged,

in theory, the provost considered each group's annual budget requests separately. The reality, however, was a different matter. When each group had a significant budget request, the director usually faced the dilemma of having to prioritize them. Since technology upgrades were desperately needed across campus, the library's budget priorities typically received lower ranking. It was difficult for the director to champion more than one large budget request per year and if there is one cost that rises faster than academic serials, it is that of technology. As a result, the library collection was usually the loser in this process.

- *Reporting Structures:* Official organizational structures are not usually known for their flexibility and can be difficult to change, depending on the campus culture. Matters such as job titles, salaries, and who reports to whom take on a life of their own, requiring careful thought and time to create an efficient and effective organization. Virtual organizational structures, however, can come and go as needed. If they work, great; if not, dissolve them and try something else. The department of Human Resources is usually not involved since there are no permanent assignments or reporting lines involved.

The library's official organizational structure has changed many times over the last 18 years and only Campus Media Services (formerly the TV Studio) still remains as part of the official structure. There are various levels of virtual or collaborative connections with all the rest. Clearly, it is a win-win situation that has worked well for everyone—the library and its partners.

In 1989, the library was not a deeply engaged, active participant in the life of the campus. Over the years, a much different environment, one that fosters engagement within the campus community that it serves, has emerged. In the beginning, the strategic intent was that the library and its staff would be effective, active participants on campus. The standard things helped, namely the creation of a mission statement, a set of values and principles, and a statement of overall strategic direction. Most importantly, the library's leadership took seriously the responsibility to create the conditions so that the library and its staff members could be successful in becoming active, engaged participants in the life of the campus by focusing on three basic areas: changes in organizational structure and process, organizational staff development, and development of campus outreach programs. Whether called convergence or collaboration, the key lesson is that libraries need to be actively looking for and open to all opportunities to become engaged on their campuses. Only then will they be seen as integral and indispensable to the university.

APPENDIX: UNIVERSITY OF MICHIGAN–DEARBORN, MARDIGIAN LIBRARY

MISSION

The Mardigian Library will provide information resources and technologies to the University of Michigan–Dearborn community both on and off campus to create a positive learning environment enabling our students to develop the critical skills they need to achieve academic and career success.

BELIEFS

- We believe that our first priority is to support student learning.
- It is everyone's responsibility to ensure the end user has a positive experience.
- Teamwork and collaboration are essential to the success of the organization.
- Our essential characteristics are organizational integrity, quality, risk taking, proactivity, and flexibility.
- We must provide an environment that minimizes obstacles, complexities and stress factors.

OBJECTIVES

- The Mardigian Library will enable University of Michigan–Dearborn students to make effective and competent use of information and academic resources.
- Each staff member will make every effort to ensure that each use of library facilities, services and resources results in a positive experience for the end user.
- Library staff will be a motivated, productive, and satisfied team with a reputation for excellence.
- The library will collaborate with faculty and staff to provide communication and information resources that support the University's mission.

5

CONVERGENCE AND COLLABORATION IN INFORMATION SERVICES AT THE UNIVERSITY OF CALGARY

Darlene Warren

The University of Calgary is a comprehensive research university that, in its 41-year history, has grown to take its place among leading postsecondary institutions in Canada. The university aims to provide a research and scholarly foundation for students eager to acquire the knowledge and skills essential for a successful personal and professional life. The university is home to scholars in 16 faculties (offering more than 80 academic programs) and 36 research institutes and centers with some 2,600 teaching and research faculty and over 2,700 full-time equivalent support staff. Just over 28,000 full-time equivalent students, including over 1,200 international students from 87 countries, are enrolled in undergraduate, graduate, and professional degree programs.

There is a long history of convergence and collaboration in the delivery of information services at the University of Calgary. In identifying the most significant programs within the University Library that represent convergence and collaboration with other campus units and beginning to describe their conception and implementation, one quickly recognizes the significance of activities around 1988 and 1998 in the evolution of library and information services. In this chapter, the converged organization that is, in 2008, Libraries and Cultural Resources (LCR) will be described, as will the most successful services enabled by that convergence and collaborations with other units on campus. In addition, a snapshot will be provided of planning activities that took place in 1997–1999 creating the environment within which Libraries and Cultural Resources has evolved.

The library is part of Libraries and Cultural Resources along with the university's archives, museum, and press. This unit was formed in 1998 when two directors, one each for Information Resources (now called Libraries and Cultural Resources) and Information Technologies, were recruited to replace the outgoing Director of Information Services. The two new Directors, along with the Director of the Learning Commons (now called the Teaching and Learning Centre), reported directly to the Vice President (Academic) setting a solid base for collaborations in support of the academic enterprise.

This reporting structure stayed in effect until 2004 when the university filled the vacancy left by the departure of the Director of Information Technologies. At that time, the position was renamed Chief Information Officer (CIO) and reporting was transferred to the Vice President (Finance). This change was made in response to a review of the senior administrative structure in preparation for the recruitment of a new Provost and Vice President (Academic) and the recognition that the priority for Information Technologies over the first three to five years of the CIO's appointment would be the replacement of the university's legacy financial, staff, and student information systems with Peoplesoft. The newly appointed CIO came from within Information Technologies and had been a key manager in collaborations with the library and Information Resources. As CIO, he has continued to nurture those collaborations.

In October 2006, the Provost and Vice President (Academic) restructured his management team and announced the creation of three Vice Provost appointments, one of these appointments involved changing the title of the Director of Information Resources to Vice Provost (Libraries and Cultural Resources) and University Librarian. The components within Libraries and Cultural Resources were not changed from those included in Information Resources. At the same time the Provost announced that he would be initiating a search for a new Vice Provost (Students) who would "assume overall responsibility for student and academic services for both graduate and undergraduate students, and will play a key role in the promotion of student success and the further improvement of the student experience."[1]

CONVERGENCE OF LIBRARY, MUSEUM, ARCHIVES, AND PRESS

Until a few months ago, the Visual Resources Centre was one of the entities listed as comprising Libraries and Cultural Resources. In October 2007, the media library components of the Visual Resources Centre were merged with the Fine Arts Library to create a new unit, Fine Arts and Visual Resources. The retirement of the Director of the Visual Resources Centre provided an opportunity to change the reporting structure in preparation for planned service mergers in the new building. Over the past four months, the new Head of Performing Arts and Visual Resources has been working with staff to integrate processes, particularly acquisitions and description, with centralized Collections and Technical Services. Staff in the unit have been positively receptive to the merger which had been heralded during program planning for the new building. Providing access to digital media creates challenges and opportunities which apply equally to the two units brought together in the merger. Early in the program planning, the co-location of these units was identified as key to the ability to provide access to state-of-the-art technologies for access and manipulation of digital media. It was also clear to managers and staff in both units that the merger of service points would help increase and sustain staffed service hours. The organizational merger has taken place in advance of the physical merger, a positive step for the integration of processes and relationship building.

The reorganization of functions formerly managed within the Visual Resources Centre also saw some functions transferred to the Associate University Librarian for Technology and Scholarly Communication. This brings the digitization unit, and its management, within the purview of the leader responsible for digital initiatives.

Within the realm of scholarly communication and digital initiatives, the convergence of library, archives, museum, and press advantaged Libraries and Cultural Resources. The university press brought editorial expertise and imprint. The copyright officer brought expertise in the negotiation of rights for materials selected for digitization. Staff from the Visual Resources Centre brought imaging expertise. Librarians identified printed resources for inclusion in the various projects, curators identified artwork, and archivists identified archival collections. The library's Information Technology Services unit took leadership in the development of the supporting infrastructure and that unit's Associate University Librarian brought project management expertise, grantsmanship, and collaborative leadership ability. To obtain the funding to support our digitization initiatives, Libraries and Cultural Resources has often partnered with organizations outside of the university. Although external partnerships are outside of the scope of this chapter, the university's readiness to lead and pursue funding in these initiatives can be attributed to the merger of press, libraries, archives, and museums within Libraries and Cultural Resources.

With the expertise in place, the university was well positioned to obtain grants and become an early leader in digitizing Canadian materials. The first major digitization initiative was the Alberta Heritage Digitization Project. The project, initiated in September 2000, digitized Alberta local histories, local newspapers, and legal statutes and made them available through a Web site called Our Future Our Past. The content available through the project Web site continues to be expanded and now also includes art, air photos, medical history, a photographic collection from Grade Prairie, Calgary Stampede history, Kainai plants and culture, southern Alberta folklore, and, most recently, a collection of municipal bylaws. The success of this project was leveraged to create a collaborative which successfully sought funding from

Industry Canada and Canadian Heritage to create a national resource by digitizing and making local histories in both official languages freely available. Officially launched in October 2002, The Our Roots/Nos Racines project was jointly led by the University of Calgary and Université Laval.

Libraries and Cultural Resources continues to pursue opportunities to make Canadian content available online. The two most significant current digitization initiatives are the Multicultural Canada project (with Simon Fraser University)[2] and the recently funded Synergies: The Canadian Research Network for Research in the Social Sciences and Humanities. The Canadian Foundation for Innovation awarded $5.8 million to the Synergies project in November 2006 for the creation of "a national distributed platform with a wide range of tools to support the creation, distribution, access and archiving of digital objects such as journal articles."[3] This investment represents 40 percent of the four-year project budget, the remainder to be raised through provincial grants, participating institutions and vendors. The project will be executed by a consortium of 21 universities led overall by the Université de Montreal with the support of four regional lead institutions. The University of Calgary is the lead institution for the prairie region with responsibility for coordinating the digitization and online publication of Canadian journals in the prairie region and leading the development of a digital preservation strategy for the national network.

COLLABORATIONS

Libraries and Cultural Resources also collaborates with other information services units at the university. The success of the collaboration between the library and Information Technologies in the planning, implementation, and ongoing operations of the Information Commons is a testament to the value of working together to meet user needs. The Information Commons is a true representation of the facility envisaged in the original Concept Document, providing,

a focus for the provision of services and technology to support the effective identification, acquisition and use of information resources by members of the University Community. The facility provides all members of the University Community with timely access to the technology and expertise needed for the successful exploitation of information resources. The Hub staff have expertise in research consultation, information navigation, and technological support, and work in an integrated and open environment.[4]

The physical environment of the Information Hub accommodates many types of scholarly activity. The Hub serves as a central place for members of the University Community to meet and explore information and exchange ideas. The Hub includes group work areas, private study spaces, open consultation and service points, and adaptive workstations. Spaces are equipped to support the use of information technology. The space is also planned to support a high level of use.[5]

Photo 5.1: Students can book collaborative workrooms through an online booking system; here a group enjoys the amenities of one of the smaller workrooms.

The planning process will be discussed later in this chapter within the context of other planning initiatives that occurred in the late 1990s.

Now, more than eight years after opening, the Information Commons continues to satisfy the user goals identified in the concept document. The facility is fully subscribed and visitors often comment on the positive atmosphere as students collaborate with each other, with peer mentors, and with expert staff to complete their scholarly work. Both Libraries and Cultural Resources and Information Technologies view the Information Commons as our flagship service facility. The Information Commons was the recipient of the Canadian Library Association/Canadian Association for College and University Libraries 2000 Innovation Achievement Award and has been visited by librarians and university planners from across Canada, North America, and the world as they planned their own services and facilities.

The facility is collegially managed under the leadership of the Head, Information Commons (an academic staff position within the Client Services unit in Libraries and Cultural Resources). The Information Commons Service Desk is staffed by professional and support staff from both the library and Information Technologies. Two members of the Information Technologies

Photo 5.2 a, b, c & d: The Information Commons is a sunny welcoming environment with a variety of spaces. (a) Standup workstations provide a place to do quick look-ups or check e-mail before heading off to class; (b–c) The expanse of workstations is humanized by artwork donated and sited by faculty in the fine arts department. The lasagne design of the workstations provides six feet of work surface to each workstation while only taking four linear feet; and (d) Large oak worktables from the original library were originally planned as a place to consult paper reference materials located near the Information Commons Service Desk. They have become the most popular study tables in the library.

staff have full-time appointments within the facility and coordinate a crew of part-time student assistants (Navigators) to provide first level technology support. Information Technologies and Libraries and Cultural Resources contribute equally to the budget for Navigators' salaries. Librarians and paraprofessionals provide reference services. When a users' question cannot be answered at the desk, the staff will identify the appropriate expert and make a referral. The resident Information Technologies staff are a conduit to the appropriate experts within their organization in the same way that library staff can identify and broker connections with the appropriate experts in Libraries and Cultural Resources. If the question is not related to information resources or technologies and the answer cannot be easily accessed through the university's Web pages, the service policy of one-step referral still applies and the user will be referred to the appropriate individual or department office anywhere on campus. If they are unsure, staff will phone the receiving office to confirm that they are making an appropriate referral.

During the summer of 1999, in preparation for the fall opening of the Information Commons, all library staff slated to work there underwent an intense training program on all software loaded on public workstations. When the facility opened, planners had an expectation that all staff would be able to answer basic questions about the software and that more difficult questions would be referred to our IT partners. There was also an early expectation that, with appropriate training, Information Technologies staff would answer directional reference questions and refer any questions requiring more expertise to library staff on the desk. Rapid developments with technologies and electronic information resources made it difficult to sustain this model. Overzealous staff sometimes failed to recognize that more expert help was required for questions and the resulting failure to refer occasionally led to conflict. This early expectation was modified after the first year of service. Understanding that users don't differentiate their needs, service continues to be offered from a common service desk with library staff responding to reference questions and information technologists and student navigators providing assistance with technology questions. Library and Information Technologies staff respect and value each other's expertise and refer questions appropriately.

Photo 5.3: Student navigator assisting a student.

Continuous training and staff development is essential to convergence and collaborative service innovation. The Director of Information Resources modeled commitment to this principle through the sponsorship of a number of special conferences and an annual staff retreat/planning day. Colleagues from Information Technologies and the Teaching and Learning Centre are invited to participate in the retreat as are faculty and student representatives to the General Faculties Council Libraries and Cultural Resources Committee, the advisory committee charged with ensuring input from the academic enterprise. Each year, the retreat is focused on one theme and a team of interested staff from across Libraries and Cultural Resources works with the most relevant member of the management group to set the agenda, arrange for guest speakers, and coordinate all arrangements. The earliest of these retreats were focused on helping staff learn more about the work conducted in the component units of Libraries and Cultural Resources and two were focused on obtaining staff input to the business plan being developed to obtain funding for a new building. For other retreats, expert keynote speakers were brought in to focus on topics such as service quality, inquiry-based learning, and convergence of information services, all topics of broad interest to staff across Libraries and Cultural Resources and other information services units at the university.

In addition to the Information Commons Service Desk, there are two other service points within the Information Commons, one each for MADGIC (Maps, Academic Data, and Geographic Information Centre) and Document Delivery Services. There are also two smaller Information Commons facilities in the Health Sciences Library and the Law Library. The Head, Information Commons, has line authority for five full-time equivalent support staff (six individuals, two of whom work part time), one part-time reference librarian, and two night assistants and is the manager with direct responsibility for reference services offered at the main service desk. Librarians from Liaison Services, Collections and Technical Services, and Access Services also provide reference service at the Information Commons Service Desk. The Head, Information Commons must be an accomplished collaborator who is comfortable "managing the gray" as she must coordinate staff from across the organization to provide reference services and coordinate the facilities needs of other units delivering services within the Commons.

When the Information Commons was opened, an operations team was formed for the purpose of reviewing and resolving issues related to operations as well as making recommendations for and/or collaborating to implement service enhancements or new services. The team is sponsored by the Associate University Librarian for Client Services and the Associate University Librarian for Technology and Scholarly Communication and is chaired by the Head, Information Commons. Membership includes representatives from all of the units that contribute to the Information Commons' suite of services. The Information Commons Operations Team addresses all range of operations issues from finalizing software loads for public workstations, to dealing with user issues, to developing new services and identifying potential new collaborations. Issues beyond the scope of the operations team are referred, normally with recommendations, to the appropriate decision makers. The team is an effective vehicle for continued collaboration and service development.

One of four main user goals identified in planning for the Information Commons was "Acquire the skills I need to identify, locate, retrieve, and manipulate information."[6] A 50-seat classroom, with the option to partition into two 25-seat classrooms, is used regularly by library and Information Technologies staff to provide formal instruction. In addition to the information literacy instruction offered to numbered courses, a regularly scheduled suite of drop-in classes is offered to support learning about productivity software and research skills. Librarians and information technologists often collaborate to provide specialized instruction when the skills of both are required. For example, the sociology librarian, data librarian and a statistical analysis expert from Information Technologies work together to provide instruction to undergraduate sociology students preparing to write their first paper for which the use of data files is expected. Another example of combined instruction is the thesis production workshop that is very popular with graduate students. Information Technologies staff provide advanced instruction on Microsoft Word in combination with library staff, who instruct on the literature search process and the use of reference management software, and Writing Centre staff, who provide writing tips.

Focus on user needs and working in an environment where collaboration is the norm has fostered further grass-roots collaboration. During the first year of operation, 1999–2000, staff noticed that members of the teaching faculty were attending the various drop-in instruction sessions on the Microsoft suite of productivity software and electronic resources offered at the Information Commons. While faculty were welcome to attend these general drop-in sessions, librarians recommended that the Information Commons facilities and services could be showcased with the offering of a special multiday program for faculty during spring intersession. To ensure a well-rounded offering, staff from the university's Teaching and Learning Centre were invited to join Libraries and Cultural Resources and Information Technologies in the development and delivery of this program. Staff from the Teaching and Learning Centre work with faculty and graduate students in the development of teaching skills and the integration of technology into learning and their expertise was required to round out the program. Since then, Faculty Technology Days has been presented every year during spring intersession with staff from the three founding units continuing to collaborate in the planning, development and delivery. The most recent program offered sessions on such tools as concept mapping, blogging, formatting your dissertation, engaging students in large classes, bibliographic software, various new electronic resources in the library, and more.[7]

Working together to deliver successful programs in a collegial environment has fostered further collaborations with the instructional designers. The Teaching and Learning Centre included the Distance Education Librarian on the team charged with the review of the university's course management software. After that team selected Blackboard, the Distance Education Librarian continued as a key member of the implementation team and has been instrumental in assisting other Libraries and Cultural Resources staff, particularly liaison librarians, as they work with faculty to integrate links to library and information resources into Blackboard courses.

Late in 2004, a group of liaison librarians obtained a grant to develop an information literacy workshop consisting of both on-line and face-to-face instruction for insertion into blended learning courses being developed on campus. They worked with instructional designers and programmers from the Teaching and Learning Centre to create a tool that goes beyond simply training students on research tools. Based on the information search process research of Carol Kuhlthau,[8] the workshop has been developed with a holistic approach to the research process and is designed to guide students through all phases of the information search process. Librarians developed the content, the instructional designer provided guidance on sound instructional activities and ensured that a variety of learning modalities were considered. The instructional designer also recommended a number of simple technologies to increase interactivity. Technical experts developed the interface and navigation and created an online journaling mechanism. The project was completed with the creation of a tool called WISPR (Workshop on the Information Search Process for Research).[9] In its initial release, customization of content to meet the needs of specific courses could only be completed with the assistance of the technical experts. Further work was required to create a customization interface that could be used by librarians as they prepared instruction for integration into new courses. A second grant proposal was successful and librarians are currently collaborating with technical experts from Teaching and Learning to complete the interface.

While developing WISPR, librarians and staff from the Teaching and Learning Centre gained a greater understanding of the expertise each offered in support of the development of courses being designed to include opportunities for inquiry through blended learning (ITBL). As grants were awarded for the integration of ITBL opportunities into courses, Teaching and Learning Centre staff invited the appropriate liaison librarians to participate in the initial project planning meetings with faculty recipients. Information literacy skills are included in the curriculum at the will of the faculty instructors and this collaboration has helped increase faculty understanding of the benefits. The current blended approach extends our ability to provide relevant instruction within the context of the course without expanding upon the 50 minutes of in-class time normally afforded.

The enhanced visibility of the Maps Academic Data and Geographic Information Centre (MADGIC) and increased support for access technologies afforded by the inclusion of this service in the Information Commons ensured consideration of Libraries and Cultural Resources as a partner in the development of the Prairie Regional Data Centre. Staff from Libraries and Cultural Resources worked in collaboration with the Vice President (Research) office and faculty in the Faculty of Social Sciences to bring Statistics Canada's Prairie Regional Data Centre (RDC) to the University of Calgary in 2000. One of six regional facilities developed with funds from the Canada Foundation for Innovation (CFI), the RDC is staffed by a Statistics Canada employee. The Statistics Canada analyst is available to assist researchers in developing proposals to obtain access to confidential microdata sets for academic research. The RDC is a secure social sciences research laboratory with a closed local area network consisting of a powerful server supporting several high-end workstations and a wide range of statistical analysis software. Data librarians from MADGIC work closely with the Statistics Canada staff member to ensure appropriate referrals and to train researchers on the public-use microdata sets that are made available by MADGIC. The two units have collaborated to develop and equip a small electronic classroom for use by the RDC when hosting Data Training Schools for researchers from across the prairie region and by both MADGIC and RDC to support data training for university courses. This classroom is also available to staff from Libraries and Cultural Resources and Information Technologies for instruction of smaller classes when 15 or fewer attendees are expected.

In fall of 2007, the collaboration between Libraries and Cultural Resources and the university's Effective Writing Program was enhanced by a grant from the Students' Union Quality Funds[10] to produce a series of writing workshops supplemented by 12 hours per week of writing tutor office hours in the Information Commons.[11] The students have responded positively to the availability of these workshops and the availability of writing tutors for individual assistance. This project is an early harbinger of learning services that will be developed as the Information Commons evolves to become a Learning Commons.

PLANNING AND STRATEGIC TRANSFORMATION

The initial convergence of organizational entities to form Information Resources (now called Libraries and Cultural Resources) and the development of an environment conducive to collaboration in the delivery of information services can be traced to a campus-wide strategic transformation process during the late 1990s. In the fall of 1996, Terry White, President of the University of Calgary, established a Coordination Task Force to coordinate strategic transformation. That committee released a brief situation assessment document to the university community in December 1996 to set the context for the strategic planning process. In that document, the budgetary constraints facing the university were outlined,

Due to budgetary constraints, real government spending has been decreasing through the 1990's. Real government spending, as a percentage of the Gross Domestic Product (GDP), has declined from 23% in 1970 to 18% in 1996, and is projected to continue to decline. This will result in a reduction in transfer payments in the future.

Provincial funding will be targeted at government priority areas with the use of special funds. Accountability is required by the government. The resulting funding envelopes will form the basis of incremental funding for all post-secondary institutions in Alberta. Competition for these funds is inevitable.[12]

In February 1997, the Coordination Task Force announced five design teams and two situation assessment task forces and the nature of their assignments. Included among the design teams was the Information Resources team, chaired by Ken Hewitt from the Faculty of Fine Arts, with the following posted mandate:

The Technology Task Force (TTF) will work with resource people from across the campus with expertise in information technology, as well as student representatives to develop the skeletal action plan and associated key recommendations. It is intended that these recommendations will include better ways of managing the University's information technologies and of allocating appropriate resources.[13]

It is important to note that at this point in the strategic planning exercise, the term information resources was being used to refer to information technologies and the appropriate resources to manage those technologies. During the strategic transformation process, the term was assigned to the new organizational grouping of units responsible for the management of information resources including library, archives, media centre and, one year later, the museum. The TTF/Information Resources team was the first of the strategic transformation teams to deliver its report. The team recommended a fundamental shift in organizational planning and attitude, asserting that information technologies and resources should be regarded as institutional utilities (like heat and telephones) and not considered as supplemental to teaching and learning development. Among the recommendations in the final report:

- Establish a common, standards-based technology and support environment for academic and administrative information systems
- Enhance and expand broadband network capabilities (on and off-campus access)
- Create a consistent environment for information sharing and presentation
- Renew and integrate core business systems
- Establish a learning and professional development facility for information technologies
- Pilot and evaluate courses in technology-delivered asynchronous learning[14]

Another of the initial teams established by the Coordination Task Force was the Library Situation Assessment Task Force. Chaired by Keith Archer, then Associate Dean (Research), Department of Social Sciences, the posted mandate of the task force stated,

The library is one of the true community resources on campus. Serious concerns have been raised about the ability of the library to meet the research and instructional needs of the campus community in the years ahead. The process of scholarly communication is being transformed through the revolution in digital information. The Library Task Force is working to provide a comprehensive situation assessment of both the local and the national/global changes in scholarly communication in an effort to better inform the university about the strategies and choices available in the institutional redesign activities.[15]

The Library Situation Assessment Task Force consulted broadly with the university community and completed a detailed analysis of the library's budget and planning documents. The Task Force's final report, submitted in September 1997,[16] described the problems that had confronted the library for the preceding decade. Throughout the 1990s the University Library, like academic libraries everywhere, had been dealing with dramatic and unprecedented increases in the cost of academic journals and books coupled with continuous growth in the quantity of published scholarship. At the same time there was increased experimentation with electronic publications proliferating the modes of dissemination for scholarly communication. The University of Calgary had just completed a five-year cycle of budget cuts over which period the library's operating budget was cut by 19.4 percent and the collections budget had been frozen since fiscal year 1992–1993 (at approximately $3.32 million).[17] The situation was bleak. During the five-year period, the number of support staff in the library system had decreased from 240 to 180 and the number of librarians had declined from 44 to 30. Remaining library staff were dealing with ever-increasing job responsibilities, leading to high levels of stress.[18]

The effects of a static collections budget were equally devastating. In order to stay the effects of inflation, fewer and fewer monographs had been purchased and serial subscription costs had increased from $2.0 million in 1988–1989 to $3.2 million in 1995–1996, an increase of 60 percent over an eight-year period.[19] In fiscal year 1991–1992, the library initiated a systematic review of journal subscriptions and a significant cancellation exercise. That review was an annual event for the next four years and by 1995–1996 the number of journal subscriptions decreased by 17.9 percent from almost 14,000 to just less than 11,500. Even with these significant cancellations, the expenditures on serial subscriptions increased by 40.9 percent from $2.26 million to $3.19 million.

In their final report, the Situation Assessment Team clearly described the crisis in the University Library while complimenting staff and leadership within the library for their excellent work in weathering the crisis to date. The assessment team was also clear that many of their recommendations built upon directions identified in excellent planning documents produced within the library throughout the 1990s. The team made 19 recommendations in their final report, within the following groupings:

- Collections—4 recommendations
- Services and Staff—6 recommendations
- Budget and Funding—5 recommendations
- Partnerships—2 recommendations
- Leadership—5 recommendations
- Invisible Library—1 recommendation
- Conservation and Preservation—2 recommendations
- Library Space—3 recommendations
- Library Infrastructure—1 recommendation

Under the leadership heading, the Library Situation Assessment Task Force called for the creation of a Library Task Force Implementation Team to implement the transformational activities and other recommendations from their final report. It was recommended that this team "consist of the Team Leader, Library Task Force and one other academic member; the Chair GFCLC: the Library Director's Council; and the appropriate student representation."[20]

The university's budget committee responded immediately to the Situation Assessment Task Force's Final Report, canceling the next budget cut and infusing additional funds into the library's operating and collections budgets. In response to the call for an implementation team, the Vice President (Academic) established the Library of the Future Task Force (LFTF) in January 1998 with the mandate,

To envision the library of the future at the University of Calgary and to articulate ways of moving toward a new conception of the library suitable for the University we want to become.[21]

The task force was guided in its work by the situation assessment team's final report and the characteristics it heralded for a transformed library.

At the same time that the LFTF was beginning its work, a separate selection committee was in the midst of a search for two directors, a Director of Information Resources and a Director of Information Technologies to replace the position of Director of Information Services. The Director of Information Services had completed two terms and chose not to stand for a third. The two new directors were hired in a combined search with a common selection committee mandated to fill the positions with individuals who would work together to advance information services at the university.

The understanding that the position of Library Director was being replaced with a Director of Information Resources with responsibility for other information resource units freed the Library of the Future Task Force to think beyond the traditional library. In describing the transformed library, the task force stated that "In the future, the library will be defined more by its roles than by its building."[22] In defining those roles, the task force used inclusive terminology such as resourcing, archival, descriptive, mentor, place, creation, and publishing. Although the examples described within the report were from the library, the roles are common to all Libraries and Cultural Resources units and all staff could see themselves as part of the organization's future.

In describing the transformation of place, the final report heralded the creation of an Information Commons and maintained that the library building would continue to be a focal point at the university but with an increased emphasis on creating an environment for learning.[23] In describing the implications of this transformation, the task force identified that significant resources would be "required to renovate existing spaces, for such purposes as the creation of an Information Commons."[24] This identification of the need for renovated space to provide access to enabling technologies, both for access to information and to enhance learning, was echoed in recommendations made by the Technology Task Force ensuring that the concept was at top of mind among senior university administrators when the Government of Alberta announced the Knowledge Network funding envelope.

Early in the summer of 1998, the university received funding from the Knowledge Network envelope and assigned $2.2 million of that funding to the development of the Information Commons. The funding came with an aggressive timeline, the project had to be completed by spring 2000. From the beginning, the library recognized the need to collaborate with Information Technologies to ensure the success of the new facility. When the new Director of Information Resources arrived at the beginning of August 1998, one of his first actions was to invite the new Director of Information Technologies to work with him in steering the project and to name representation on the planning committee. The Director of Information Technologies responded positively to the invitation and assigned himself and two of his department heads to serve on the planning team. The nine-person team also included Information Resources' Assistant Director for Client Services as Chair and five other representatives from public and technical service areas in the library.

At the beginning of the planning process, the team recognized the need to focus on user needs in developing their concept. That perspective reduced political and territorial debates and led to a concept document that clearly described user goals and how they could be met within the renovated space. The user goals were articulated simply as:

- Acquire the skills I need to identify, locate, retrieve, and manipulate information
- Acquire the information I need

- Acquire the help I need
- I can use various spaces and workstations to complete my scholarly work[25]

The user goals were then translated to service goals and, from these, the various implementation elements were defined. The concept document was supplemented by documentation and photographs from best practice visits to three existing Information Commons and passed on to an implementation team to plan and implement the new services and provide input to the renovations process.

The user goals articulated in the concept document were confirmed by the findings of a joint research project conducted by Student Services and the Library Client Needs Group. With the support of a fellowship from the Learning Commons (later called the Teaching and Learning Centre), eight focus groups were conducted with students and faculty, and telephone interviews were conducted with 597 students and 155 faculty members to determine Learner Needs.[26] Help in the development of technology and information literacy skills and spaces that support learning were among the needs most frequently identified by students. These findings validated the work that was underway to construct the Information Commons and further informed planning to ensure the space was useful for other learning specialists as a place to deliver general instruction or tutoring.

The planning and implementation of the Information Commons were completed within a tighter than normal timeline. The Knowledge Network grant required project completion and expenditure of the funds to be in advance of April 1, 2000. This meant that the only window for completing the renovations was during spring and summer semesters 1999. As a result, planning, architect selection, and renovations all had to be completed within a one-year period. The newly appointed Director of Information Resources had experience leading projects to develop and construct new museums during his previous position as Director of Historic Sites Service, Alberta Community Development and understood the need to assign focused leadership to the project. A project manager was hired specifically to coordinate the project, becoming the single point of contact for university facilities planners, architects, and contractors. The project manager came on board just after the concept document was completed and worked closely with the implementation team until the facility opened. She also served as manager of the facility for the first term of operation. The assignment of a project manager was an essential component in the success of the project; her focus on the project ensured that the renovations were completed on time and within budget and, most important, were a complete match to the concept originally developed the previous fall. The facility was opened to the public two weeks before the beginning of fall term in August 1999. The project manager was an excellent communicator and had ensured ongoing community consultations and regular communication with staff and the university community throughout the project. As a result, the Information Commons was a heavily used, vibrant learning space from the date of opening.

In its first decade as a merged organization, convergence within Libraries and Cultural Resources occurred mostly with the development of new or reconfigured services. There have been only two examples to date of total unit mergers. The first was the merger of the University Archives with the University Library's special collections units to form Archives and Special Collections in 2003. The second was the merger, in fall 2007, of the Visual Resources Centre and the Fine Arts Library as described earlier in this chapter. Frits Pannekoek was Director of Information Resources from 1998 until 2005, when he was appointed President at Athabasca University. When he joined the University of Calgary, he came into an organization that was ready for change. He had the wisdom to use the final report of the Library of the Future Task Force as a guiding document as he led the organization in the development of a truly hybrid library. He nurtured innovation and collaboration within Information Resources and encouraged the leaders of the various units to consider collaboration with others in the university wherever possible.

Now, after a decade of working collaboratively, staff have learned to appreciate the strengths each unit brings to the organization. The new Vice Provost is another strong leader and is bringing his experience to bear on critical review and analysis that will lead to further convergence. The current focus of review is on collection management, the further development of discovery tools, and the integration of technical processing for archives and special collections and some museum holdings with the library's centralized technical services unit.

BUILDING FOR THE FUTURE, FROM INFORMATION COMMONS TO LEARNING COMMONS

Building upon the success of the Information Commons, Libraries and Cultural Resources led the development of a business case requesting funding from the provincial government for a new building. The new building will bring all of the Libraries and Cultural Resources units together. A key feature of the new building will be an expanded Learning Commons where staff from Libraries and Cultural Resources, Student Services, Information Technologies, and the Teaching and Learning Centre will collaborate to deliver services The facility will afford increased access to unique primary resources in addition to the enhanced provision of access to the technology and expert staff to support the use of information resources in all formats. In addition, new media experts and learning support staff would bring enhanced services into the facility to support the learning needs of our students. The years of preparation, collaborative planning, consulting with stakeholders and developing a comprehensive business plan paid off and, in March 2006, the government of Alberta committed $113 million to fund the new building. In December of that year the facility was named the Taylor Family Digital Library in honor of a donation of $25 million toward the project from Don and Ruth Taylor.

It is January 2008 and Libraries and Cultural Resources and its partners are ready to take another leap in the development of collaborative services for the Taylor Family Digital Library. Since assuming leadership in the summer of 2006, the Vice Provost (Libraries and Cultural Resources) and University Librarian, Thomas Hickerson, has worked with the new Provost, architects and others to bring the facility into existence. Early in the design phase, it was decided that the project would include two new buildings, the Taylor Family Digital Library and a High Density Library, and both are due to begin construction this coming spring. The programming for these new facilities builds upon existing collaborations and provides the impetus for the development of new collaborations. The most exciting of these new collaborations will be the integration of a suite of learner support services to be developed with the support and guidance of the new Vice Provost (Students) who joined the university in August 2007.

CONCLUSION

Convergence and collaboration in the delivery of information services at the University of Calgary have evolved in an almost organic manner. The converged Libraries and Cultural Resources unit has been able to leverage the expertise from its constituent units to become a national leader in digitization initiatives. The early success of the collaboration with Information Technologies in the creation and ongoing management of the Information Commons has led to an environment where staff from Libraries and Cultural Resources are comfortable initiating collaborations with other information services units on campus to meet the evolving needs of learners and researchers. Over the next few years, operational convergences will expand as all information services units work with student services and others on campus to complete the programming for the new Taylor Family Digital Library.

NOTES

1. University of Calgary. Office of the Provost and Vice-President (Academic), "Announcement: Changes in the Provost's Portfolio" (Calgary, Canada: University of Calgary, n.d.). Available at http://www.ucalgary.ca/provost/about/portfolio-changes (accessed January 2008).

2. Multicultural Canada, "Canada's Multicultural Historical Resources Online." Available at http://www.multiculturalcanada.ca/ (accessed January 2008).

3. Michael Eberle-Sinatra, "Synergies: The Canadian Information Network for Research in the Social Sciences and Humanities" (poster presented at Digital Humanities

INFORMATION SERVICES AT THE UNIVERSITY OF CALGARY 99

2007, Urbana-Champaign, IL) Abstract available at http://www.digital humanities.org/dh2007/abstracts/xhtml.xq?id=263 (accessed January 2008).

4. Note that during the initial planning, the committee called the facility an Information Hub. In response to feedback, the facility was renamed Information Commons soon after releasing the planning document.

5. University of Calgary. Information Hub Planning Committee, "Information Hub Planning Document" (Calgary, Canada: University of Calgary, 1998). Available at http://www.ucalgary.ca/IR/infocommons/ (accessed January 2008).

6. Ibid.

7. University of Calgary, "Faculty Technology Days 2007." Available at http://www.ucalgary.ca/ftd/courses (accessed January 2008).

8. Carol C. Kuhlthau, *Seeking Meaning: A Process Approach to Library and Information Services*, 2nd edition (Westport, CT: Libraries Unlimited, 2004).

9. Shauna Rutherford, K. Alix Hayden, and Paul R. Pival, "WISPR (Workshop on the Information Search Process for Research) in the Library," *Journal of Library Administration* 45, nos. 3–4 (2006): 427–43.

10. Over the past two budget cycles, the University Budget Committee has made funds available to be applied to projects, or the development of programs, that enhance the quality of the student experience. The Students' Unions is responsible for managing the funds and coordinate a competitive process for the awarding of grants that they have dubbed "Quality Money."

11. University of Calgary. Effective Writing Program, "Workshops." Available at http://www.efwr.ucalgary.ca/efwr/workshopsmain (accessed January 2008).

12. University of Calgary. Strategic Transformation Coordination Task Force, "Situation Assessment." Available at http://www.ucalgary.ca/Transformation/insert1/Page4.html (accessed January 2008).

13. University of Calgary. Strategic Transformation Coordination Task Force, "Design Teams Drafted." Available at http://www.ucalgary.ca/Transformation/Designteams.html (accessed January 2008).

14. University of Calgary, *Strategic Transformation Report Summaries: September 1998.* (unpublished report, Calgary: Strategic Transformation Coordination Task Force, University of Calgary, 1998), 8.1–8.2.

15. University of Calgary. Strategic Transformation Coordination Task Force, "Design Teams Drafted."

16. University of Calgary. Library Task Force. "Final Report—September 30 1997." Available at http://www.ucalgary.ca/lib-old/ltf/report/index.html (accessed January 2008).

17. University of Calgary. Library Task Force "Final Report—September 30 1997," collections numbers, p.15, operating budget, p. 23–24 (accessed January 2008).

18. University of Calgary, Library Task Force, "Final Report: Section 1—Executive Summary and Recommendations," 2 (of 8). Available at http://www.ucalgary.ca/lib-old/ltf/report/recommend.html (accessed January 2008).

19. University of Calgary. Library Task Force, "Final Report—September 30 1997," 17 (of 43) (accessed January 2008).

20. General Faculties Council Library Committee, a standing committee of the University's academic governing body in University of Calgary. Library Task Force, "Final Report: Section 1—Executive Summary and Recommendations," 6 (of 8).

21. University of Calgary. Library of the Future Task Force, Accelerating the Transformation of Information Resources, Section 2, The Transformation of the Library, 1 (of 6). Available at http://www.ucalgary.ca/lib-old/lftf/finalreport/transformation1.html (accessed January 2008).

22. University of Calgary. Library of the Future Task Force, "Accelerating the Transformation of Information Resources," Section 5. The Transformed Library, 1 (of 14). Available at http://www.ucalgary.ca/lib-old/lftf/finalreport/translibrary.html (accessed January 2008).

23. Ibid., 9 (of 14).

24. Ibid., 10.

25. University of Calgary. Information Hub Planning Committee, "Information Hub Planning Document."

26. Julie Kearns and Keith Scharnau, *Learning Support Needs: What U of C Students Need to be More Effective Learners*, Joint Research Project Final Report (Calgary, Canada: University of Calgary, 1999).

6

THE LIBRARY AS MODEL OF INTEGRATED STUDENT-CENTERED ACADEMIC SUPPORT ENTERPRISE

Jay Schafer and Anne C. Moore

It all started with a leaky roof. For years, the concrete decking around the 26-story W.E.B. Du Bois Library at the University of Massachusetts had been leaking into the building and the 58,000-square foot "garden level" floor below. This large and structurally open space is built like a double donut around a beautifully maintained courtyard and the elevator service core of the tower structure. For over 30 years, it housed both the major public service spaces (reference, card catalog/OPAC/electronic resources workstations, microforms, current periodicals, and large open study areas) and nonpublic, staff work areas (for reference services, technical services, and interlibrary loan) for UMass Amherst Libraries.

As work began to replace this exterior decking in 2004, planning for renovation of the interior spaces was initiated. A series of somewhat unrelated events serendipitously led to the creation of the Learning Commons and significantly changed not only the library and its services, but many other campus groups dealing with student and facilities support. Change of this magnitude on a university campus could only come about through new collaborations among services that had traditionally remained entirely separate fiefdoms, which are often referred to as silos. For organizational purposes, this chapter relates these collaborative efforts as grouped into four broad categories: campus support; faculty and pedagogy; academic support; and, internal library operations.

CREATING THE LEARNING COMMONS: COLLABORATION ACROSS THE CAMPUS ORGANIZATION

When it was clear that the Du Bois Deck Replacement Project was going forward in 2004, the UMass Amherst Libraries administration began planning for renovation of the Lower, or Garden Level. It was obvious this renovation would need to include more and updated technology in the public areas. Recent publications had promoted an "information commons"[1] and this concept was integrated into initial library discussions.

In unrelated conversations, an interdisciplinary group of faculty who had developed the program for an undergraduate minor in Information Technology was hoping to create a computing lab, similar to the Math Emporium at Virginia Tech. In a search for space, this group led by the Faculty Advisor to the Provost for Undergraduate Education, came to the library. Initial thoughts about a collaborative effort were reinforced by a NorthEast Regional Computing Network (NERCOMP) Program featuring Joan Lippincott from the Coalition for Networked Information (CNI) and Mike Edwards of the Virginia Tech Math Emporium held at the College of the Holy Cross, in Worcester, Massachusetts, on Tuesday, March 2, 2004. This program, "Learning Spaces: New Visions," was attended by individuals from the library, the Information Technology Minor, and Office of Information Technologies (OIT).

Lippincott's presentation was so timely to the UMass Amherst effort that she was asked to repeat her presentation on campus for a group of nearly 100 "interested parties" that included faculty, students, and administrators on April 6, 2004. This program and the brainstorming session afterwards formed the basis of a collaborative effort that is today the Learning Commons.

During the program, each attendee created a freehand drawing of his or her vision of the contents and arrangement of the UMass Amherst Learning Commons on an 11" by 17" blank placemat. These drawings formed the initial dataset that a grass roots planning group (Learning Commons Core Planning Group) representing the various interested constituents used to design the facility. Focus group interviews with undergraduates, graduate students, student assistants, faculty, and academic support service providers contributed additional data that the Learning Commons Core Planning Group analyzed during the planning process. The Learning Commons Core Planning Group worked through a careful process of conceptualizing desired services and the furnishings and configurations required to supply them.

The governing principle that determined which services would be included was a commitment from a campus agency that they were willing to provide their service in the Learning Commons. The principle was to include as many academic support services and creature comforts as feasible so students could remain in the library building until they had completed their academic tasks.

Previously, as soon as students got hungry, ran out of ink, needed a writing tutor, or reached a hardware or software technology problem, they left the building and most likely did not return that day.

The Learning Commons Core Planning Group worked for several months before composing the facility's mission statement:

As the heart of UMass Amherst, the Learning Commons (Learning Commons) provides a welcoming, flexible, and student-focused environment. Rich in services and technologies, the Learning Commons fosters community, innovation, and the creation of new knowledge. With long hours, peer support, and a relaxed and inclusive atmosphere, the Learning Commons encourages students to make the most of their educational experience. Campus service providers pool their expertise to provide convenient access to the core academic support services that enable students to succeed and excel at UMass Amherst. The Learning Commons strives to assist students to become self-directed learners and engaged adults to build a better future.

When the Provost announced she was funding the Learning Commons project in April 2005, she also indicated that it was highly desirable to have some part of it open by September 2005 when the students returned for the fall semester. To meet this schedule, it was obvious that collaboration among many groups across campus was necessary. Having direct support from the Provost, the Vice Chancellor for Student Affairs, the Vice Chancellor of Administration & Finance, and the Campus Chief Information Officer was essential in building this collaboration among groups not known for working effectively together.

To fast-track construction, the project was defined as a facilities renovation project rather than the development of a new facility. Renovation status allowed the project to be done internally using campus personnel rather than requiring an open bid process for outside contractors. A smaller subset of the Learning Commons Core Planning Group, the Provost's Learning Commons Committee (PLCC), was appointed by the Provost to enable faster decision making. The Faculty Advisor to the Provost for Undergraduate Education, a well-liked faculty member who had been working on special technology-related projects for the Provost, chaired the PLCC. Officially designating a smaller and Provost-sponsored committee improved communication with campus-level administrators and defused tension among major players, especially in the library and OIT.

Conceptual thinking about the initial project began as a relatively small 10,000 square-foot "test bed" for a variety of new furnishing and technology configurations for student study and collaboration. As discussions evolved, it was clear that Phase I or Learning Commons 1.0 would have a significantly larger impact if it encompassed approximately 25,000 square feet. Renovation work was limited to new paint, new flooring, and installation of new electrical and networking using a simple overhead wire cable tray arrangement. All furnishings were modular, off-the-shelf Herman Miller products that enabled wire management from the overhead metal tray. PLCC created the initial furniture layouts while interior design work (colors, carpeting, finishing, and final layouts/furniture specifications) was completed by the contract interiors firm representing Herman Miller. The minor architectural and engineering design work required for the project was done by the Facilities and Campus Planning personnel and actual renovation work was completed by the campus Alterations Department. The OIT designed and installed the networking and wireless technology required. This collaboration of campus trades groups greatly streamlined the design process and resulted in a remarkably successful final project.

OTHER CAMPUS AGENCIES HAVE BEEN INTEGRAL TO THE CREATION AND SUCCESS OF THE LEARNING COMMONS

The making of the Learning Commons facility in one summer seemed like an impossible task when first imagined. The decision to use campus-based services greatly facilitated the timely completion of this project. Ironically, this also had a major, unanticipated consequence. It was clear to all from the outset that this project, a space totally dedicated to student use, was the Provost's number one priority. As the project progressed, it became obvious that many organizations across campus bought into the philosophy behind the project and developed a real ownership of it. By the grand opening ceremony in October 2005, almost everyone on campus knew about the Learning Commons and many were openly proud that they contributed to the campus collaborations that created it.

Auxiliary Services

Food and drink in the library had been a long-standing issue. Over time, the policy had been liberalized to allow drinks in covered containers and the ban on food was rarely enforced. In conjunction with developing the Learning Commons on the Lower Level, library administration began discussions with the campus Auxiliary Services about creating a café on the entry floor of the Du Bois building. Auxiliary Services handles all food concessions on campus. At first reluctant because they did not think the facility would be profitable, the library obtained an agreement by underwriting all costs of creating the café. Space was extremely limited and no source of water was available, but a small, kiosk-like facility was created that sells coffee (from a local Amherst coffee roasting company), assorted bottled drinks, bagels, pastries, and packaged food such as sandwiches, salads, and snacks. A contest was held to name the café, and users selected "Procrastination Station," the winning entry submitted by a student. Today with gross sales of over $404,000, Procrastination Station is Auxiliary Services' busiest independent operation.

More coffee is sold in the library than anywhere on campus—in 2007 a total of 75,600 cups of coffee were sold in 184,000 transactions at an average cost of $2.20 per sale.

The Procrastination Station was open until midnight initially, but when students complained that they needed food services later into the evening, it opened until 3 A.M. As students continued to demand some type of food service during all building hours, the library worked with Retail Services of Auxiliary Services to add both a drink and a snack vending machine on the Lower Level. We overcame challenges to provide electricity to the only area that had sufficient wall and walkway space to accommodate the large machines. The downside was that the vending machines were next to the meeting space and both the normal operating and vending functions were annoying during presentations. The machines also require refilling at a much faster rate than those in other facilities on campus—nearly every day. By 2006, the Procrastination Station was open all building hours because business justified expanding the hours.

Custodial Services

Since the Lower Level was not originally carpeted, Custodial Services was involved in the initial renovation decisions which included applying a mixture

Photo 6.1: Procrastination Station Café, Entrance Level, W.E.B. Du Bois Library. Leslie Schaler, Communication Assistant, UMass Amherst Libraries.

of carpet and tile over the entire space. Special dry vacuum (dry vac) carpet cleaners were included in the original Learning Commons budget as indication of the importance and commitment to a well-maintained facility. While we anticipated the Learning Commons would be very popular with students, no one realistically anticipated the impact this renovation would have on Custodial Services. Upon opening, library gate count statistics almost doubled. The entire 26-story building is now open 24 hours per day, five days per week. We changed to a liberal food and drink policy in spring 2006, except in areas such as computer labs and Special Collections and University Archives, because it was impossible to stem the flow of students entering with food in backpacks and to accommodate all the café customers at its seven tables. Immediately, the need for bigger trash containers, more frequent trash pick-up and restroom maintenance, and many other maintenance issues became clear. High-level collaborations between the Provost and the Vice Chancellor for Administration and Finance demonstrated a campus-wide commitment to the importance of the Learning Commons and have provided a substantial increase to the custodial crew serving the library building.

Campus Police

Security in a 26-floor library building was a concern, even before the building opened on a 24/5 schedule. The Building Operations Desk, staffed by library Building Monitors and student assistants, was created to provide increased visibility and surveillance in 2005. It is staffed all times the building is open and is the central contact point for library staff and building occupants regarding safety, security, and building issues. A strong relationship has developed between the Campus Police and the Building Monitors. While not security personnel themselves, the Building Monitors have been trained on emergency and fire procedures and regularly patrol the building. If any problems arise, the Campus Police are radioed and appear within minutes from their office in the next building.

Follett University Bookstore

With increased hours and use of the Learning Commons, it became apparent that students needed various supplies during times when no other services were available on campus or that students just did not want to leave the building to purchase needed supplies. Library personnel worked with the Follett University Bookstore to develop and maintain an "office supply vending machine" in the Learning Commons from which students can purchase basic necessities—from pens and pencils, to thumb drives and CDs, to caffeine gum and aspirin—whenever the library building is open. This service has been tremendously successful because it enables students to remain in the building and continue to work productively. The collaboration with

Follett continues as requests from students for new items are forwarded to the Bookstore.

PEDAGOGY AND FACULTY

The convergences of teaching and learning may appear more subtle than other service provider relationships; however, they often lead to direct impact on student learning. Faculty are the key to reaching students. What faculty require students to use in their assignments are most often embraced and passed on from student to student. Library liaisons and other groups reach out to teach faculty to enhance student learning and faculty research success. Many learning convergences occurred at UMass Amherst over the last five years.

Center for Teaching

The Center for Teaching (http://www.umass.edu/cft/about.htm) was established in 1989 to provide support for teaching and learning on campus. It reports to the Provost and is advised by the Faculty Senate Undergraduate Education Council. The Center for Teaching was involved with the Learning Commons project from the very beginning and assumed an unusual role—one of support and input rather than direct service provision. It ran focus groups to gather input during the planning process and suggested service models such as peer tutors. A long-term collaboration grew out of the months spent together sharing ideas: both the library and the Center for Teaching think of one another as a matter of course. The two groups are collaborating with other campus representatives on efforts to rethink general education, develop an information literacy program, enhance the first year experience, and respect intellectual property. Once a close relationship is developed by two campus groups on a single, successful project, conversations naturally flow to other potential collaborations.

Office of Faculty Development

A Mellon-grant funded office established in 2006 became an immediate partner of the library and Learning Commons even before the grant was awarded. The three-person office is "developing an ambitious mentoring initiative for all new and underrepresented faculty" (http://www.umass.edu/cft/ofd.htm). The initial activity for the group was to coordinate information on new faculty and arrange a new faculty orientation each fall. Development of a longer term mentoring program was a follow-on activity. The library approached Mary Deane Sorcinelli, the grant coordinator, on behalf of its Academic Liaison Program to contact faculty as soon as they arrive on campus to orient them to available resources and identify future research materials to support their teaching and research activities and help them to succeed on campus. We hosted the first New Faculty Orientation in August 2006 in the midst of the Learning Commons itself with Jay Schafer, Director of Libraries, providing the welcome and the appropriate subject-specialist librarian sitting at the table with faculty new to the department. We also obtained a list of the new faculty and their departments for the first time ever. Liaisons eagerly contacted those who could not attend the New Faculty Orientation and took them to coffee. Long-term relationships between individual librarians and faculty developed out of these early conversations. Interestingly enough, new faculty and librarians bonded and are working together cohesively on information literacy, a multimedia center, streaming audio and video, curriculum development, and many other joint projects.

The Learning Commons brought undergraduate students into the library in droves increasing the gate counts by nearly 70 percent most months of the first two years of its existence. Typical building gate counts during the academic semester average 4,500–7,500 per day. Word travelled quickly through the student ranks of the Learning Commons' atmosphere as conducive to both socializing and collaborative study. Within weeks, graduate students requested quieter spaces specifically for them and faculty wanted to be in the building near students, but with facilities that met their unique needs—to be where the action was. Two quiet study areas were established on the second and third floors within the first year of operation, which appealed to both undergraduate and graduate students who wanted to study undisturbed by the noisier collaborations of the Lower Level.

Photo 6.2: Third Floor Quiet Study Area, W.E.B. Du Bois Library. Leslie Schaler, Communication Assistant, UMass Amherst Libraries.

The Center for Faculty Development, which was eager to support faculty in their research and writing, approached the library about the possibility of hosting a faculty writing facility in the W.E.B. Du Bois building. We identified a corner room on the sixteenth floor of the Tower that once held a Multimedia Lab for faculty and students. The room had been recarpeted and painted recently. With active network jacks, a PC with printer, office supplies, a dry erase board, tables, and comfortable chairs, the room with a lovely view of the campus became the Faculty Writing Place. Faculty come alone or in groups, check out the room key at the Circulation Desk, and escape from the activity in their offices and departments to focus on research and writing. Use has gradually increased and the second year (2007–2008) brought some programming opportunities that took advantage of the proximity of the adjacent library instruction room connected by a corridor. Friday programs with visiting editors and writing experts benefit from using both rooms. Small workshops are planned for the future. Faculty members are delighted to get away to such a contemplative environment that helps them maximize their writing productivity. The role of the library in supporting new uses of its spaces for unmet academic needs is part of the model of collaborative initiatives that followed the development of the Learning Commons.

Turnitin and Student Plagiarism

The library established a pilot of the Turnitin Plagiarism Detection Service in February 2004 because of frequent requests from faculty for a more sophisticated software solution to search for plagiarism in student papers than to type sections into Google. Turnitin indexed articles in the largest aggregator databases (EBSCO and ProQuest) subscribed to by the library on behalf of UMass students. Library staff in User Services tested the system and detected matches of quotations taken from articles in the two subscription databases through Turnitin. Incidences of suspected plagiarism were on the rise among both undergraduate and graduate students and faculty were reluctant to go through the official reporting procedure administered by the Ombuds Office because it strongly favored the student and placed the burden of proof squarely on the faculty member's shoulders. The Faculty Senate recognized the problems in teaching students the basics of respect for intellectual property and appointed the Ad Hoc Committee on Student Plagiarism in November 2005 to recommend how to:

- Conceptualize the issue of student plagiarism in the twenty-first century and communicate that concept to the academic community
- Teach to the issue of student plagiarism
- Support faculty in preventing student plagiarism
- Protect the student's right to due process in student plagiarism cases while ensuring a maximum of effectiveness and efficiency of the process with a minimum of bureaucratic "red tape"

- Improve any or all of its practices and procedures with respect to student plagiarism
- Revise and create documentation for students and faculty regarding plagiarism and academic honesty

The Committee formed two subcommittees that met steadily throughout the next two years. The Education Subcommittee designed a Web site (http://twiki.brianhoule.net/bin/view/Plagiarism/WebHome) of resources to inform both faculty and students about academic honesty. The Education Subcommittee approached the issue from a teaching and learning perspective. The Policy Subcommittee revised the policies and procedures for handling plagiarism cases and created an informal tracking mechanism that will help faculty discover if students have been suspected of plagiarism in the past: http://www.umass.edu/dean_students/code_conduct/acad_honest.htm. The Committee of the whole evaluated both MyDropBox and Turnitin as potential software packages to support plagiarism detection and prevention. Turnitin was eventually selected because it was more robust and indexed EBSCO (as well as ProQuest) databases. MyDropBox was purchased by Blackboard and has now been integrated into the Vista and Blackboard interfaces at no additional charge under the name SafeAssign. However, faculty who do not use the Course Management System for assignment submissions cannot benefit from the SafeAssign module, so we still license Turnitin both as a standalone product and integrated into SPARK through a Powerlink. UMass Amherst set up a segregated "node" to which all student papers are submitted rather than to the larger Turnitin database. Student intellectual property rights are protected because their papers are only available to UMass Amherst faculty during the grading process rather than to outsiders.

The student plagiarism project is an excellent example of the library assuming a leadership role and working collaboratively with individuals and groups all over campus to improve student learning and faculty success.

RefWorks

Most higher education institutions now offer a citation or bibliography management package such as RefWorks or Endnote to all students, faculty, and staff through a Web-based interface. At UMass Amherst the library conducted a trial of RefWorks in 2003 and licensed the service in 2004 for the entire campus population. RefWorks was one of the earliest Web-based academic support services licensed and completely supported by the libraries. Librarians teach specialized classes by reservation each semester, support and troubleshoot problems, and maintain instructions on how to extract citations from each of our subscription databases. The service has been heavily promoted to faculty, teaching assistants, and graduate students. Junior year writing, English 111, and the honors program Commonwealth College, all embrace the service with the support of the library. Over 5,600 users have accounts on the system as of January 2008. In 2007 the library added RefShare to enable researchers to share citations and bibliographies across the campus and with non-UMass colleagues across the world.

Electronic Reserves

The libraries have used Docutek ERES system to support electronic reserves since 2001. As UMass adopted WebCT as an integrated course management system for the Amherst campus and the UMass System adopted Vista for UMass Online, the myriad ways faculty provided Web access to courses gradually became centralized on the WebCT/Vista/Blackboard platform. It became clear that the library should try to provide access to electronic reserves through SPARK, UMass Amherst's name for the campus course management system regardless of the software platform. Finally in fall 2007, Reserves negotiated with the Office of Information Technologies to create a branded tool inside SPARK that can link directly into the Docutek course for a specific course without the student having to reauthenticate into Docutek. Since all reserve items in Docutek have been cleared through Copyright Clearance Center or directly with the copyright holder, this system adheres to copyright regulations. Through most course management systems, faculty can capture an item and store it permanently without receiving permission or paying appropriate fees. Now each online course that has electronic reserves uses them through SPARK and hence the library provides access to only cleared materials. Liaison librarians are called by electronic reserves staff to work with individual faculty members to identify replacement materials when one or more items they want to put on electronic reserves are not permissible.

Streaming Audio

During fall of 2007, the library initiated a pilot of streaming audio. Library Systems set up a streaming server and Web site to host the streams. Flash is used for the streaming audio. One faculty member requested streaming of several tracks and the experiment worked. Beginning in spring of 2008, the Music Reserve Lab Library Assistant III supervises studenst assistants to digitize heavily used items owned by the library and serve them through links to the streams through Docutek ERES to students enrolled in the course.

Streaming Video

Initial plans for streaming video began in fall 2007 with a pilot of two films distributed by California Newsreel that a faculty member in the Communication Department wanted to stream to the students enrolled in a course on advertising as social communication. Acquisitions will purchase the streaming rights to videos upon ordering for reserve and will negotiate streaming rights for films we own that are needed for reserve when possible. Film Media Group provides streaming via its own server. Many of their films we own are heavily used in current courses and might be candidates for the pilot. Academic Instructional Media Services (AIMS) collaborated with the library to experiment with formats for the streaming files at the beginning of the program.

Du Bois Initiative

UMass Amherst Libraries Special Collections and University Archives Department is the home of the papers of scholar and human rights activist W.E.B. Du Bois. Efforts to develop funding to digitize this globally important collection have created a collaboration of others who are interested in honoring the rich legacy of Dr. Du Bois. These include faculty from the Afro-American Studies Department (also named after Du Bois), the History Department, the Anthropology Department, and the community of Great Barrington, MA, where the UMass-owned Du Bois home site is located. The Du Bois Legacy Center is being established in the library to take current projects that are only loosely related, and put them under a single roof to realize benefits through integration. The Center will draw in other scholars working on related topics and, more generally, harmonize with and enrich campus-wide efforts to promote social justice.

Liaison Program

The libraries' Academic Liaison Program was established in 2002 to clarify the communication flow between the library and the academic departments. The only clear relationships before the formalization of the program were between bibliographers and some departments for the purposes of selecting library materials. The library moved to a model (similar to that of University of Colorado Aurora) of identifying a handful of selectors with fiduciary responsibility for expending portions of the collection development budget. These experts had additional training and the responsibility to fill in gaps, respond to faculty collection requests, conduct special projects such as serials cancellations, and spend their budgets by the annual deadline. The Academic Liaison Program (modeled after a successful program at the University of Connecticut) encouraged participation in relationships with academic departments and faculty by a broader number of librarians who had subject training or expertise in a particular discipline, but not necessarily the time or expertise to select materials. Liaisons could develop a customized relationship with the selector to recommend titles or actually order them through our approval plans with Yankee Book Peddler.

The Academic Liaison Program, however, ensured a single point of contact for every academic department to ask any question related to the library.

The libraries' liaison has to be an expert in all library services, systems, policies, and staff, to respond to most inquiries immediately and to forward other inquiries appropriately. The core responsibilities of the liaison beyond communication are reference, instruction, guide development, and database expertise. Increasingly, liaisons need to develop extensive knowledge on issues such as scholarly communication, academic honesty, information literacy, instructional techniques, and emerging technologies. Each academic department also has a library liaison and the libraries' liaison established a relationship with this faculty member as a conduit.

Image Collection Library

In 2006, the Dean of the College of Fine Arts and Humanities contacted the Director of Libraries about the library assuming control of the Art History Slide Collection. This was a very traditional slide library, used by the Studio Art, Art History and Architecture faculty and located close to faculty offices. UMass Amherst libraries do not have an Art/Art History/Architecture branch library. The Dean's major concern was the need to begin using digital images instead of slides and she knew she did not have the resources (human or fiscal) to deal with the transition.

Upon retirement of the classified staff employee who ran the slide library, UMass libraries took over administration of the facility and the collection. We hired a Visual Resources Librarian and half-time metadata cataloger from the salary savings of the retirement (plus additional funds from the library). We also began a collaborative relationship with our campus Office of Information Technology to implement the Luna Insight image presentation software.

Our goal, with the blessing of the Deans and the Provost, is to slowly turn the new Image Collection Library into a resource, primarily digital, for images from all campus disciplines (not just Art, Art History, and Architecture). We are also collaborating with the Smith College Visual Resource Library (and to a lesser extent the other five college digital image resources) to build a shared collection, as copyright and license agreements allow.

The major benefit of this arrangement is that the library is now in a position to lead the transition away from the traditional departmental slide collection into a campus-wide resource for the creation/acquisition, organization, use, and preservation of digital images for all disciplines including the sciences and social sciences. This is fundamental to our mission. The major con, as always, is that once interested in this concept, faculty are anxious to move forward, which puts a strain on limited resources, mostly staff.

First Year Experience

In 2006, the Provost and Vice Chancellor for Student Affairs appointed a Task Force of administrators, faculty, and academic support service representatives to analyze existing first-year experience programs and propose a new program that would be more effective in retaining students to complete college. The program has consisted of a variety of student residential options coupled with activities and information on academic decisions. The Learning Commons and Library were represented on the Task Force as we serve as the hub for integrating advising with the other academic support services in an environment that encourages student collaboration and socialization. Librarians are involved with helping students succeed academically through close interaction with faculty and linking students to any service they might need. As the campus experts in information literacy instruction, we were logical collaborators in the effort to increase student retention of first year students and to maximize student success.

After a year of discussions and planning, the Task Force settled on recommending a required first-year experience course for all freshmen and transfer students that could be satisfied through a number of courses: a standalone course taught by professionals (to include librarians) on campus or one offered by an academic department. The course would include student life (alcohol awareness, etc.), study skills, life skills, advising, research skills, information literacy, and career information. One key element of the course is contact with a professional staff member or advisor on campus who establishes and maintains an ongoing relationship with the student throughout the college adjustment period—an adult mentor who is a friendly and sympathetic resource for information and guidance about campus procedures and policies. Librarians are seen as key players in the development and administration of the course. And we would not have been considered without our recognized active role in coordinating the academic support effort on campus.

STUDENT AND ACADEMIC SUPPORT

Learning Resource Center

The Learning Resource Center (LRC; http://www.umass.edu/lrc/) has been offering tutoring and supplemental instruction services on the tenth floor of the W.E.B. Du Bois Library for nearly ten years. Managed by Susan Bronstein, the LRC was an initial collaborator in the Learning Commons effort. This extremely popular and successful academic support service offers walk-in, individualized tutoring by expert peer tutors whose schedule is posted on the Web. Another free service of the LRC is an extensive array of supplemental instructional sessions offered by a student paid to re-take a challenging course, to work closely with the faculty member, and to guide two 90-minute review sessions per week to answer questions, solve homework problems, and present test review sessions. Supplemental instruction is arranged for courses when students request it in sufficient numbers to make it worthwhile. None of the services of the LRC are remedial and student usage increases every year.

The LRC collaborates with the library completely in every endeavor from attendance at events to orienting others to the Learning Commons initiative to planning new services. A new academic support service provided out of the LRC, the Office of Undergraduate Research and Scholarship (OURS), assists undergraduate students in locating research opportunities (such as summer internships) both on and off campus. Most recently, the LRC agreed to offer individual test proctoring during certain hours each week. While the Faculty Advisor to the Provost for Undergraduate Education searched for a location to house a large scale testing lab, the campus did not offer any testing support at all. The library tried to satisfy individual student requests for proctoring through the Learning Commons and Technical Support Desk staff, but this proved to be complex and next to impossible to juggle from the busy service desk. The LRC stepped up to fill the need without hesitation.

Writing Center

The Writing Center was an underfunded and underutilized service that had been tucked away in the midst of the English Department and Writing Program offices. The huge building with long dark hallways was easy to get lost in. Hence, students would not go there after dark or on weekends. The Writing Center was open to the entire university population and featured highly trained undergraduate and graduate student tutors who provided 15 to 45-minute drop-in appointments. Yet, few students outside of English and the Humanities knew about this extremely well-hidden service. International students and those in the sciences (localized across the campus) rarely visited. The office provided approximately 400 drop-in sessions each long semester and was closed during intersessions and on weekends.

The library approached the Writing Center to set up tutoring hours Monday through Thursday evenings in four of our glass study rooms from 4 to 8 P.M., a time when students flocked to the Learning Commons after class. Use picked up very quickly and Sunday evening hours were added. By the end of the first semester, over 1,200 sessions had been offered between the original location (400) and the Learning Commons (800). When the Provost provided additional funds to expand the south end of the Learning Commons in summer 2006, the Writing Center asked for a dedicated space, so it could close its English Department location. Another motivator for the move was that the tutors were uncomfortable asking students to vacate the glass study rooms when Writing Center hours began each day. Once the new glass enclosure with four PC-equipped tutoring tables, a manager's office, a tutor break cubicle, and an intake desk opened, the Writing Center was constantly busy. International, ESL, doctoral, and science students streamed in for help. The Writing Center offered summer tutoring by appointment in 2006 and 2007. Scheduled appointments supplemented drop-in service beginning with fall 2007.

The addition of the Writing Center to the Learning Commons created instant visibility for the entire student population. Funding for tutors increased; shift managers and an overall manager were required; a student-staffed intake desk greeted students and scheduled appointments; and additional PCs were added.

An exciting synergy developed between the Reference and Research Assistance Desk and the Writing Center. The Writing Center tutors directed students who needed more or higher quality sources to the reference librarians while the librarians sent students who needed assistance with writing and editing to the Writing Center. The proximity of the two desks (within sight) was highly beneficial for collaboration. A reference librarian worked with one of the Writing Center managers to develop an online guide to writing. Learning Commons staff explained the full suite of services to tutors during their annual training session. Acquisitions ordered a list of Writing resource books selected by the managers of the Writing Center. These tomes were added to the Online Catalog and were available on a shelf outside the Writing Center enclosure for in building use by all. The area in and near the Writing Enclosure became a quieter, writing-friendly area of the Learning Commons. The Writing Center has been an exceptional success and both students and faculty say it has made a difference in student learning and success.

Photo 6.3: Writing Center, Lower Level, W.E.B. Du Bois Library. Leslie Schaler, Communication Assistant, UMass Amherst Libraries.

Office of Information Technologies

Two Office of Information Technologies units, Help Desk Services and Computer Classrooms, collaborated closely with library staff to design the services, equipment, and staffing of the Learning Commons and to establish and operate the primary service point in the Learning Commons: the Learning Commons and Technical Support Desk. Computer Classrooms operates the computer labs (called classrooms) on campus and licenses and key serves software for the campus population. Computer Classrooms has maintained computer classrooms on the seventh and sixteenth floors of the W.E.B. Du Bois building for many years and has always wanted to move its operations down to the Lower Level to increase the number of machines and facilitate staffing and support. The inconvenience of having only three elevators to service the first 16 floors of the building and two for the top 10 floors has also been an issue. Library staff had frequent contact with Computer Classrooms supervisors before the Learning Commons project because of proximity, building issues, and scheduling accommodations.

The Office of Information Technologies Help Desk has long operated as a telephone call-in service with limited walk-in periods at the beginning of semesters in another building on the science or north end of campus, far from the Du Bois building. Support was available only by phone between 8:30 A.M. and 5 P.M. Monday through Friday. The Help Desk provides nearly comprehensive technology support: networking, hardware and software configuration, accounts, Web hosting, virus and security protection, legal and policy issues, authentication, Vista, and so forth. This important group eagerly embraced the opportunity to extend hours and services with face-to-face help services from the shared desk in the Learning Commons. Regular Help Desk staff who had branched out to accept inquiries via Web form assumed hours on the Learning Commons and Technical Support Desk and supervised a group of students who extended the hours into the late evening and some holidays. Help Desk personnel take walk-up questions and configure personal devices at the desk. They work on trouble tickets submitted via the Web form as time permits, but do not handle phone calls, which go to the main Help Desk office across campus.

Students completely embraced the availability of comprehensive technology assistance in the Learning Commons. Library personnel at the LC & Technical Support Desk assist users with general questions, policies, and equipment troubleshooting, while Computer Classrooms personnel support the authenticated machines and staff the Calipari Instruction Classroom (used for library instruction, LC participant programs, and other events, but as a drop-in computer room when not scheduled).

The wild success of the Learning Commons & Technical Support Desk is unquestionably attributable to the long-term collaboration of extremely service oriented managers in the two OIT groups and the library. The team met weekly and communicated daily via email to design the services, policies, and procedures that would make the Learning Commons work smoothly. Every issue was discussed as many times as it took to figure out a mutually agreeable solution that would meet the needs of our users. Although our parent organizations might have differing viewpoints on an issue, we as a team worked out all the details together in a warm and supportive relationship because of our shared focus on the students, faculty, and staff.

Disability Services

For the convenience of students who need adaptive equipment, the Assistive Technologies Center (ATC) occupies a room on the Lower Level of the W.E.B. Du Bois Library. Most adaptive software is licensed by the Office of Information Technologies for the entire campus and is available on all authenticated classroom computers on campus. The ATC lab was one of the earliest multiservice-provider collaborations: the Library's Reference Department responded to user support questions from the Reference Desk; Office of Information Technologies maintained the hardware, software, and equipment in the room; and Disability Services trained new users to use the room and requested special access privileges on the student's email account through OIT. When the Learning Commons opened, staff and students from the library, OIT help desk, and OIT Computer Classrooms working at the Learning Commons and Technical Support Desk assumed responsibility for assisting users of the ATC. With the Learning Commons, the ATC collaboration grew and even more groups learned how to support users to succeed in the use of adaptive technologies. For the students, the availability of the equipment and software on a 24/5 schedule was extremely helpful.

Career Services

We discovered during the reconnaissance visits to University of Arizona and Indiana University Bloomington Information Commons in April 2005 during the planning of our Learning Commons, career services was the one academic support office the schools said should have been included, but was not. When we returned, the Library's Associate Director for User Services approached Career Services as a potential collaborator. They readily agreed to provide staff at one-half of the desk set aside for the Academic Advising Link. Career Services dispenses information on: potential employers; resume, interviewing, and cover letter preparation; career choice; and field internships. Career Services also presents job search workshops in the Calipari Instruction Room on the Learning Commons floor.

International Programs

International programs approached the library in 2006 with an interest in staffing a service point inside the Learning Commons to deliver education

Photo 6.4: Academic Advising Link and Career Services Desk, Lower Level, W.E.B. Du Bois Library. Leslie Schaler, Communication Assistant, UMass Amherst Libraries.

abroad and exchange information as well as to support international students. As all service points in the Learning Commons were occupied, we searched for a collaborator who would share space with International Programs Office (IPO). The Academic Advising Link readily agreed to train their student assistants about IPO services and keep a detailed notebook, handout materials, and Web links to assist students during their existing afternoon and evening hours. IPO staff present announced sessions on study abroad in the Calipari Instruction Room on the floor of the Learning Commons.

Campus Tours

While word of the Learning Commons spread rapidly among students, the early coordinators from the library and OIT thought it was essential to associate the facility as the hub of student life and academic support on campus beginning with the incoming student's first exposures to UMass Amherst. Library Learning Commons staff reached out to those coordinating the campus tours through the Robsham Memorial Visitors Center. We provided a script and orientation to the tour guides and provided updated information to the campus tour coordinator several times per year. Each campus tour brings prospective students, parents, and tourists through the Learning Commons and allows the folks to sit in our event space as the only break during the hour and 15-minute walking tour.

New Student Orientation

OIT Computer Classrooms had long scheduled the computer lab spaces that New Student Orientation (NSO) used for the advising portion of the summer and intersession (mainly transfer) program. The Learning Commons—with Herman Miller Resolve "pods" outfitted with a PC and plenty of space near the Academic Advising Link and the Calipari Room computer classroom adjoining—was an ideal space for academic advisors to meet with new students and assist them in signing up for classes in the PeopleSoft student system (SPIRE). Since the Learning Commons was not heavily used during the typical orientation weeks of summer and intersession, we began holding NSO in the Learning Commons in 2006. Students were brought on an initial tour to get the lay of the Learning Commons and Library and were shown where to report for the advising portion of their orientation. Learning Commons and Library staff also participated in an Activity Expo by setting up an information table in the hallway of the Campus Center during other portions of the orientation program when both students and parents would be milling outside the dining halls and could take a few minutes to learn about campus services. We also host an Academic Support Fair in the Learning Commons during the First Week of the fall semester in which all students are invited to enjoy food and music and visit tables staffed by all academic support services (including the Learning Commons service providers). The Fair targets freshmen who are brought over to the event by their dorm Resident Advisor (RA). Most RAs bring the students separately for a tour of the Learning Commons as well. By the time a freshman is in his or her second week at UMass Amherst, he or she has been taken to the Learning Commons at least four times and knows what services and facilities are available. Word travels quickly that the Learning Commons is the place to meet friends and get work done without the loud music and distractions of the dorm.

INTERNAL LIBRARY OPERATIONS

UMass Amherst libraries are certainly not alone when describing new collaborations with library operations. Technology has been driving change in libraries for several decades now. The traditional silos are being dismantled as the print-based world of libraries becomes electronic. As a result, new relationships are being developed within the departments of the library itself.

Reference and Acquisitions

Unlike the old paper indexes and abstracts, online electronic reference resources require a strong collaboration between the acquisitions department (vendor relations, licensing, online access, and fiduciary responsibilities) and reference desk staff. In large research libraries, these have traditionally been fairly independent tasks. However, reference questions no longer only

Photo 6.5: Glass Study Room and "Pods," Lower Level, W.E.B. Du Bois Library. Leslie Schaler, Communication Assistant, UMass Amherst Libraries.

Photo 6.6: Students with Laptops at a "Pod," Lower Level, W.E.B. Du Bois Library Leslie Schaler, Communication Assistant, UMass Amherst Libraries.

address "how do I use" a service, but now also very frequently include "how do I access" or "why can't I access" a service. The answers to these new questions require new relationships between "public" and "technical" services. At UMass Amherst libraries, building stronger collaborations among traditional departments includes taking vacant positions and creating new jobs such as a "Reference and Integrated Library System Support Librarian" and "Digital Interfaces Librarian."

Circulation and Course Reserves

Circulation and course reserves functions have also changed because of technology. Self-check machines for books are readily accepted by library users. At the same time, libraries are increasing the complexity of circulation duties by adding technology such as laptops, projectors, and digital cameras to the mix. This requires circulation staff to collaborate with the Library Systems Office in support of new services. Reserves staff are building new collaborations with liaison librarians as they work with faculty to integrate electronic reserves into the course management system, almost eliminating the need for paper course reserves, but increasing the job's complexity as additional skills like the ability to provide streaming audio and video become required.

24/5 Coverage

The Learning Commons has created new collaborations among staff. The Building Operations Desk was created when the facility became 24/5. This desk and its staff provide one central point for library users and library staff to focus facilities and security-related questions. During the midnight to 8 A.M. shift, the Build Operations Desk and the Learning Commons Desk are the only staffed operations in the building. A strong collaborative relationship has been built between staff at these two service points. They depend on each other for support and coverage although their individual tasks are quite different.

Cataloging and the Institutional Repository

The Cataloging and Processing Department has always provided bibliographic access to items added to the collection, regardless of format. This includes many electronic resources and digital objects including databases, Web pages, and individual objects such as images. Initial work on the UMass Amherst institutional repository, ScholarWorks, involves staff from cataloging in a new way. As ScholarWorks staff and library liaisons work with faculty, academic departments and research institutes across campus to deposit their material (either digitized or born-digital) into the repository, the skills of catalogers are being requested to help create metadata for these collections. Working with "end users" in faculty offices and in academic departments presents new challenges and new rewards for those in what might have been traditionally thought of as "back room operations."

As technology drives change in libraries, it is anticipated that even more collaboration will develop within. The silos of technical and public services diminish daily as our services become more electronic and our users located more remotely. Liaison librarians will be working with faculty on a variety of topics including copyright, intellectual property rights, and metadata and preservation of born-digital research. Library systems staff will be working with liaison librarians and instructional designers on interface design to assure user-friendly access to information resources. Interlibrary loan, document delivery, circulation, and reserves will work together so that resources, whether paper or electronic, can be delivered to the user—no matter where they are.

FUTURE INITIATIVES

The Learning Commons is a rich collaborative environment focused primarily on the needs and success of undergraduate students. The overwhelmingly positive response to the Learning Commons for all partners involved has been reinforced by requests for similar projects looking at graduate student and faculty populations.

Teaching Commons

Preliminary plans are in place for a Teaching Commons on the twenty-sixth floor of Du Bois Library. This space, a partnership between the Provost's Office, the library, Academic Computing, and the Center for Teaching, the Teaching Commons will provide a place where faculty can work on transitioning their course materials to include more instructional technologies, from basic, but effective, PowerPoint usage to fully online courses. With the help of an instructional designer and student IT helpers, along with reference librarians and information technology specialists, faculty members will have—at their fingertips—the help they need to find new and exciting ways to incorporate new technology into the learning experience of their students.

Research Commons

Interest is also growing in a Research Commons (RC). This is envisioned as a central location for support to faculty and graduate students in the complex research process. Like the Learning Commons, the RC will assemble groups and expertise now distributed across campus. It will provide the information resources, the technology and the place for scholars to pursue individual activities or to interrelate, both within and across the traditional boundaries of their disciplines.

CONCLUSION

The synergy and follow through for the Learning Commons project clearly came from the library. But this highly visible collaboration was just the beginning of what has morphed into a new role for the library on campus. The library is now viewed as a model for visualizing and guiding challenging projects that require the collaboration of multiple departments to succeed. Librarians and library staff participate actively in campus task forces, committees, councils, the Faculty Senate, and volunteer activities. We are involved in nearly everything that happens on campus. And we are invited to participate in these activities because of our eagerness and success at collaborating. We are seen as the glue that reaches out, pulls people in, and supports them to create something new together for the benefit of students. And yet, we have accomplished this revolution largely with existing personnel resources. An excellent example of our new role on campus is the amazing success of our development and communication librarian and her two support staff. They have engineered a staggering increase in donations ($170,000 in 2000 to $1.5 million in 2007) and publicity over the past five years. Academic departments, schools, and colleges want Emily Silverman to show them how to establish a successful fundraising program.

The transformation of higher education institutions to capture increasing numbers of students, coming in and out of educational opportunities, not geographically constrained, and able to select the institution that meets present needs is dependent on our ability to mobilize existing faculty, staff, and administrators to pool their knowledge to do more with the same or less. Harnessing technology, space, resources, and personnel in creative ways will help us transcend present obstacles.

NOTE

1. See Andrew Richard Albanese, "Campus Library 2.0," *Library Journal* 129, no. 7 (April 15, 2004): 30–33; Russell Bailey and Barbara Tierney, "Information Commons Redux: Concept, Evolution, and Transcending the Tragedy of the Commons," *The Journal of Academic Librarianship* 28, no. 5 (September 2002): 277–86; Donald Beagle, "Learning beyond the Classroom: Envisioning the Information Commons' Future: Conference Report," *Library Hi Tech News* 21, no. 10 (2004): 4–6; Donald Beagle, "Extending the Information Commons: From Instructional Testbed to Internet2," *The Journal of Academic Librarianship* 28, no. 5 (September 2002): 287–96; Jennifer Church, "The Evolving Information Commons," *Library Hi Tech* 23, no. 1 (2005): 75–81; Allison Cowgill, Joan Beam, and Lindsey Wess, "Implementing an Information Commons in a University Library," *The Journal of Academic Librarianship* 27, no. 6 (November 2001): 432–39; Charles Kratz, "Transforming the Delivery of Service," *College & Research Libraries News* 64, no. 2 (February 2003): 100–101; Joan K. Lippincott, "New Library Facilities: Opportunities for Collaboration," *Resource Sharing & Information Networks* 17, no. 1/2 (2004): 147–57; Laurie A. MacWhinnie, "The Information Commons: The Academic Library of the Future," *portal: Libraries and the Academy* 3, no. 2 (April, 2003): 241–57; Donald E. Riggs, "New Libraries Remain an Excellent Investment," *College & Research Libraries* 63, no. 2 (March 2002): 108–9.

7

THE UNIVERSITY OF GEORGIA STUDENT LEARNING CENTER

Florence E. King, Carla Wilson Buss,
Nadine Cohen, Deborah Stanley,
and Elizabeth White

The University of Georgia's Student Learning Center (SLC, http://www.slc.uga.edu) offers an interesting example of the convergence of campus information services.[1] It is unusual among research universities in that the building combines a large number of general classrooms with library and study space over four floors, totaling over 200,000 square feet. Since its opening in 2003, the SLC, as the students have come to call it, has become an integral, even dominant factor in the lives of undergraduates at the University of Georgia (UGA).

First conceived in 1996, it was recognized early in the planning stages that the Student Learning Center should be developed and operated in a collaborative manner. The three primary partners in this collaboration are:

1. The University Libraries (http://www.libs.uga.edu)
2. Enterprise Information Technology Services (EITS), the university's computing services (http://www.eits.uga.edu)
3. The Center for Teaching and Learning (CTL) Classroom Support Unit (http://www.ctl.uga.edu/)

The first two units report to the Provost and Senior Vice President for Academic Affairs. The third reports to the Vice President for Instruction who, in turn, reports to the Provost.

Over a year before opening, the three primary partners, working with additional support from other units of the Vice President for Instruction and units of the Vice President for Student Affairs, formed the Support Partnership to begin strategic planning of services and operations for the Student Learning Center. Thus began the convergence of talent and resources that sustains the SLC initiative. The Support Partnership's work began with agreement on specific areas of responsibility. This outline of responsibilities has allowed the collaborating partners the freedom to work in partnership with a fundamental understanding of accountability and authority (see Figure 7.1).

Issues such as identifying and selecting computer equipment, designing authentication protocols, defining building hours and use, finalizing the use of building spaces, developing the Web page and desktop image, and creating security policies were resolved. The formation of the partnership well in advance of the opening of the building provided ample time to form a cohesive and mutually respectful working relationship. It also developed ownership and knowledge of the building from all constituencies.

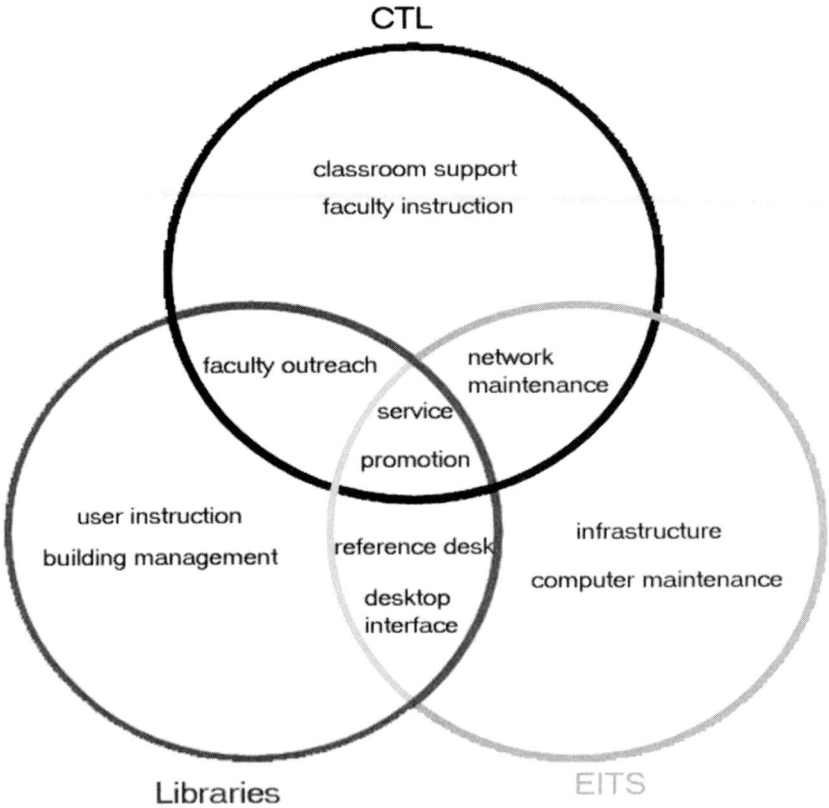

Figure 7.1: Collaboration in the SLC.

Administration of the building is shared with defined areas of responsibility. There is no single administrative leader for the building nor is there a single budget. The Partnership communicates frequently and assembles as needed to address new challenges that arise. Shared oversight and collaboration by the building partners have created a solid management and operations structure which ensures that the building continues to serve student and institutional needs.

HISTORY AND DEVELOPMENT OF THE SLC

Planning

The SLC was originally conceived in 1996 as a large general classroom building. The purpose was to address a documented shortage of classrooms. Early discussions quickly turned to the idea of combining classroom support functions as well as addressing other needs. The University Libraries had a shortfall in seating. Computer labs on campus were scattered. Students did not have space for group study. The senior administration of the University was supportive of expanding the plan for the SLC to include other functions as well as classrooms. The Office of the University Architect (http://www.maps.uga.edu) and the design firm of Cooper Carry of Atlanta (http://www.coopercarry.com) led the effort to develop a more comprehensive building program with assistance from a steering committee that included representation from all interested parties, including faculty and students.

Also early in the process, the libraries and EITS agreed that it would be in the best interest of students to merge functions wherever possible, to have a consistent set of workstations, and not to have physically separate computer labs. An understanding to this effect was reached and formalized by the University Librarian and the Chief Information Officer.

The SLC was designed with two underlying principles:

1. to be a collaborative academic environment for undergraduates, and
2. to emphasize direct support of instruction.

These underlying principles informed design decisions and services policies. Great care was taken to integrate online and on-site services, by merging classrooms, technology, and what was termed "The Electronic Library" into one experience. The initial vision was of a large space that integrated classrooms and study space to the extent that students coming out of a classroom would immediately be in an environment that supported learning and study activities. Thus, students would find immediately contiguous to their classroom space to study together, consult electronic resources, use computer workstations to develop projects, prepare a classroom presentation, meet with their instructor, have a cup of coffee, or simply sit and read a book.

The integration of classroom and study in the SLC resulted from a focus on the library as "process." The desire was to integrate in-class learning, gathering information, and consulting with research professionals under one roof along with the computing resources needed to complete assignments and group study rooms to work on a collaborative project or practice a presentation.

To an extent, however, the vision was toned down a bit by the reality of a multistory building. Because of the high ceilings needed for the larger rooms, the classrooms came to be clustered on the first and second floor and the study space on the upper floors. Indeed, the first floor was designated entirely for classrooms, the fourth or top floor entirely for study, while the second and third floors saw the realization of the contiguous access that was desired. While this was somewhat disappointing, the students have not complained and, indeed, the variety of spaces is a positive development.

The SLC was planned to allow students to make use of electronic resources to the fullest extent possible. In addition to 500 workstations, an extensive Ethernet network with over 2,000 drops was integral to the concept of the building. Students would be able to plug in, and thus have access to library and other network resources throughout the building. Over the course of planning the building, wireless networks matured and an extensive wireless system was included. Following the usual delays and cost adjustments (euphemistically termed "value engineering"), planning for the SLC was completed in 1999 and ground was broken in fall 2000. The building was completed and opened three years later, in time for the start of the fall semester on August 18, 2003.

Description of the Building

As constructed, the SLC encompasses over 200,000 square feet and is comprised of four floors of approximately 50,000 square feet each. The building is designed to integrate the two components (Classrooms and the Electronic Library) so that students can quickly shift from classroom activity to research or study. Located in the center of campus, the SLC is both a place to move "through" and a place to move "to" on campus.[2]

The Classrooms are managed by the Center for Teaching and Learning Classroom Support Unit and include the following:

- Offices for staff who support the classrooms
- Twenty-six classrooms in a variety of configurations ranging in size from 24 to 300 seats with a total of 2,200 seats
- Advanced classroom technology controlled with instructor podium and equipped with state-of-the-art presentation technology
- Three Faculty Preparation Rooms for use by instructors for class preparation

- An interactive computer lab dedicated to faculty technology development
- Classroom support offices for on-site classroom trouble shooting and a lab for technology training for faculty

The Electronic Library is managed by the Libraries and EITS and includes the following:

- A total of 2,300 seats in a variety of configurations, including carrels, study tables, and soft seating
- Five hundred PC-based workstations
- Ubiquitous wireless plus extensive Ethernet wired access
- Six help desks located throughout the building, five of which provide technical help from student computing staff and one of which provides support from both a librarian and student computing staff
- IM-chat, phone and email support
- Ninety-six group study rooms seating 6–10 people each
- Four instruction labs (seating 16–38 students) dedicated to teaching electronic research, information literacy skills, and technology
- Digital Media Lab for audio/video editing
- Event spaces for academic activities and functions, such as freshman orientation or alumni events
- Traditional cherry library furniture by Thos. Moser, using a design that was created for this building
- Comfortable study areas furnished with soft seating
- A traditional reading room
- Twenty-four-hour access to about 25 percent of the building for study
- A coffee house

Expectations and Assessment

When the building opened in 2003, the University Librarian posed several expectations and suggested that testing those expectations would assist in measuring the success of the building and also in helping to change course if the assumptions proved wrong. The assumptions posited were:

- Use of the building will be heavy
- Students want to study in groups
- There will be greater informal interaction between students and faculty
- Use of the Main and Science Libraries will not decrease

Experience gained over the past few years allow those assumptions to be addressed.

Use of the Building Will Be Heavy

This assumption proved to be correct. Using hourly counts and infrared people counters, we found that the SLC has an average of over 8,000 visits per day when the university is in session, totaling more than 2.25 million visits over the 2007 academic year. Moreover, traffic has been increasing each year.

It should be pointed out that this figure does not count traffic to the classrooms on the first floor because no reliable method has been found to measure this activity due to the many entrances to this floor. There are a relatively small number of access points to the upper floors and people counters were installed at those points.

Students Want to Study in Groups

The 96 group study rooms in the building are in high demand and frequently all of them are in use, so this assumption has proven to be correct. The original program called for 150 group study rooms, but 54 rooms were cut to keep the building within the allocated budget. However, there is no doubt that this larger number would have been used.

There Will Be Greater Interaction between Students and Faculty

This assumption has also proven to be correct. Through surveys, faculty and students report that the coffee house, the group study rooms, the open table environment, and the soft seating areas promote both informal discussions and formal study sessions.

Use of the Main and Science Libraries Will Not Decrease

This was, perhaps, more a hope than an assumption. In fact, there has not been a significant decrease in the gate count at the main or science libraries. It is apparent that the SLC is used by students who had been studying somewhere other than those two libraries. Surveys of the Main and Science Libraries indicate that some students prefer those libraries to the SLC because they are quieter and have fewer people, and, of course, they also feature significant print collections. Clearly, use and acceptance of the SLC has surpassed expectations.

Challenges and Lessons Learned

Over the initial years of operating the building, it became evident that even the best planning cannot anticipate the actual behavior and needs of students. There were many challenges and many lessons learned. Perhaps the greatest lesson was the need to remain flexible. As situations have arisen, the staff and administration have attempted to respond in a timely fashion.

Most decisions are made at weekly staff meetings where everyone has the opportunity to voice an opinion. For example, as color printing was instituted, we had to decide on a pricing structure and ways to advertise the additional service. Another example is the creation of a digital media lab, which would allow students the opportunity to create and edit digital materials. The original plans for the building included a room for photocopiers. Actual experience with students found that the need for copying was very small. This room was converted to the digital media lab using funds from the student technology fee. Again, this was a joint effort between the Libraries and EITS.

An immediate and continuing challenge has been finding the services offered in the building. Signage, especially directional signage, was not provided beyond room numbers and very basic signs designating areas. These signs did not have the visual impact needed to guide users in such a large space. This problem has not been entirely resolved, although increased signage has helped. Fortunately, while the building is large, it is very symmetrical and can be easily navigated.

Least surprisingly, policies to handle day-to-day activities common to libraries everywhere had to be developed, but developed within the partnership. For example, "Lost and Found" procedures were needed quickly because students and faculty frequently left valuable items. Again, most of the policies were hammered out at staff meetings. This style of decision making had the benefit of including our partners in the SLC, especially the staff of EITS. This had the dual effects of improving communication and minimizing conflict.

It became apparent that not having a public administrative function such as provided by the circulation services in a traditional library setting hampered our ability to manage certain activities. "Lost and Found" procedures as mentioned above, giving or taking money (e.g., for pay-for-print or vending refunds), providing a place for student workers to sign in and out for work, and designing a check out system for laptop computer loans were remarkably difficult without a check-out system to fall back on.

One notable challenge that the library staff faced was getting the patrons, mostly students, to understand that they were actually in a library, even if there were only a few books. Students could be overheard whispering into their cell phones, "I can't talk now, I'm in the Library," but they tended to see the SLC as a space and not necessarily a resource. They were and are especially slow to realize that professional reference assistance is readily available. They frequently spend hours working on their own or with their peers, without any attempt to seek assistance from the professional staff. Faculty can also be slow to seek assistance.

It also became apparent that the original "reference" desk in the SLC was not well located. During the planning, it was seen as a destination in the east wing of the third floor. While the original desk was located near the largest collection of public workstations, not all traffic passed this desk. It was soon discovered from actual experience that assistance was most needed in an area where the classroom function and the Electronic Library function converged, in the middle of the third floor. A temporary desk was placed at this site and it quickly received more activity than the original desk. Around the beginning of 2006, plans were made to build a permanent desk and to relocate library staff to the new desk. The new location is at the top of the stairs between the third and fourth floors. Now students using the stairs have a clear view of a desk and most patrons associate a desk with a place to seek assistance.

The staffing model at the six service desks uses student computing staff at all locations; at one central location both a librarian and a student computing staff member work together. Research referrals are made as needed to the "reference desk." Working with the student workers at the desk has, by and large, been a positive experience for the library staff. Student workers tend to stay in their positions in the SLC and staff and students forge strong bonds. Several of "our" students have migrated to full-time positions in the libraries and elsewhere on campus. Library staff have been invited to wedding showers, weddings, graduations, baby showers, and birthday parties. The generational divide has been easily bridged and working more closely with the students has been a positive experience for all of the staff. In addition to the friendships, both librarians and students traded skill sets, which only served to improve service at all levels.

The classroom support model for faculty in the building has been highly successful. The assumption was that most faculty do not want to teach very far from their office, or to teach at any times other than between 10 A.M. and 2 P.M. Because of the training that the faculty get with the technology, the design and comfort of the classrooms, and the support for any problems, faculty prefer to teach in the SLC. Classrooms are almost completely booked during all class periods of the day and the technology model has set the bar at a higher standard for the rest of campus.

We also stressed that no partner could simply overlay existing policies onto the SLC. Everyone soon recognized that it was a new entity and that policies needed to be adjusted. For example, at first, staff resisted food and drink in the building. However, the physical layout of the building with its many entrances was not conducive to a single checkpoint to control food and drink. More importantly, it is the students' building and they should be allowed to eat and drink there if they want. Attention turned from restrictions to how to deal with clean-up, spills, and trash.

Building and service hours also had to be rethought. Designed to be a 24-hour space, we were unable to offer that service until 2007. Even so, we had extended hours during finals and for some of the partners, it meant offering help at night and weekends, with no additional staffing. In 2007, in large part due to lobbying by the Student Government Association, 24-hour access was instituted throughout the semester.

Focus Group Interviews

Starting in 2005, students and faculty have been surveyed and focus groups have been formed to gather information on how the SLC might be improved or changed. Some comments from the focus group interviews and changes made as a result follow:

- Several students remarked on the need for better advertising and signage. Most participants were unaware of the full range of services available in the SLC.
- Students report that they do not conduct research at the SLC. Instead, they do most of their research at home, where printing is "free," or in the Main or Science libraries where it is quieter and print resources are available.
- In 2005, complaints were received about the quality of help received from student workers at the service desks. Efforts were made to train the students more effectively and comments were more positive in 2007.
- Problems with the computer workstations were identified in a focus group interview before they were widely recognized as a problem. This has led to improved monitoring of the workstations.
- In 2004, a focus group noted that noise was a problem and asked that "quiet areas" be designated. This was done but this concern also led to the purchase of ear plugs that are given to students free upon request. This has proven to be a popular service.
- As with most campus facilities, concerns have been raised about parking.
- Perhaps reflecting the maturation of the building, the focus group interviews in 2007 found the building to be "an attractive, comfortable environment. Each floor has a specific purpose (especially the 4th floor as a quiet space)." This group also stated that they liked the availability of earplugs.

Impact of the SLC on Roles and Responsibilities of Partners

Staffing patterns ensure that research assistance from professional librarians is available, but students do not seem to be aware of it. This has continued to be a frustrating and sometimes ego-deflating issue.

Working in an all-electronic environment required some retooling by the librarians. The librarians who originally staffed the service desk all came from a busy reference desk environment. The transition at first was a bit shocking. Possibly due to the lack of visible print resources, students tended not to see the staff behind the desk as information providers or research assistants and research questions have been uniformly low in number. This phenomenon was very frustrating for the Reference staff and resulted in librarians having less opportunity to make use of their skills. In preparation for opening the building, Reference Department staff compiled a list of ready reference materials and those materials were shelved at the desk on a book truck. They were rarely used, as students relied heavily on e-sources or the Internet. In order to maintain their reference skills, most librarians continued to have a reference desk shift at the Main or Science Libraries at least once a week.

While librarians' reference skills may have been adversely affected, their technical skills were enhanced. Students were more likely to ask for assistance in formatting a Word document or an Excel file and librarians quickly became adept at assisting with this type of question. Always seeking a teachable moment, librarians sought ways to incorporate library instruction into their responses. For example, when students were adding data to an Excel file, the librarian might ask if the patron had found enough information and suggest other data sources.

Librarians also learned many new skills from working with the EITS student workers. Before the opening of the SLC, student workers were cross trained in library skills, with the intent of empowering them to answer basic reference questions. This cross pollination had the added benefit of librarians developing and enhancing their own computer skills. Again, this reflects the meaningful benefits of the partnership.

Due to their limited activity at the SLC reference desk, librarians working there have assumed responsibility for the UGA libraries' remote reference IM/chat service. Librarians monitor IM/chat while staffing the reference desk at the SLC.

Another response to the lack of reference questions was to teach significantly more library instruction sessions in the SLC. This served two purposes. First and foremost, the sessions offered a forum in which to drive home the fact that the SLC is a library and that the librarians were able to answer questions in depth. Second, these sessions provided an opportunity to guide students to quality electronic resources. Increasing information literacy is a goal of the libraries and these sessions are the perfect opportunity to work toward that goal.

Overall, librarians have found that they are providing more technical assistance and less traditional reference service. The EITS staff, who are primarily student workers, find the level of support that they are providing to be more complicated than in traditional computer labs.

Over time, student perceptions do seem to be adjusting as they see the library and research component of the SLC emerging. This is evidenced in the following findings from focus group interviews:

- 2004: Aware of library affiliation, but not research assistance availability. Presence of librarians not recognized.
- 2005: Many students unaware of the range of services and confused by who is offering them. They do not distinguish between computer help, research help, and Writing Center help.
- 2006: Signs that use the word *help* or *research* do not tell students that librarians are present. A suggestion is made that signs should say "librarians available." Participants were not aware of chat reference service. They were interested in using it when told about it and suggested it needed to be better publicized.

- 2007: Participants remarked that they appreciated the availability of help and tutoring services for their research.
- 2007: A growing number of participants were aware that there were librarians available at the SLC.

Impact of the SLC on Academic Life of Students

Students are regularly surveyed regarding their use and perceptions of the SLC. Table 7.1 offers a summary of responses to the question "What do you do in the SLC?"

The SLC is a multidisciplinary academic space offering general classroom space to all disciplines, thus, students and faculty alike have the opportunity to interact with colleagues whom they might not normally see. Students use the SLC during small breaks in their schedule. They can use a spare hour at the SLC, which previously they might have wasted. Centrality comes into play here again, as they can stop by on their way from one class to another.

Again, comments from the focus group interviews emphasize how this building has affected their academic careers:

- 2005: "Love it. It's where I hang out because I'm always on North Campus. Can just drop in to do email, write papers. Much less distracting than home."
- 2006: "You can do everything in one building; computers always available and have great graphics software; great for group work."

According to Michael F. Adams, president of the university,

The Student Learning Center continues to function as the academic hub of the campus. Nothing pleases me more than to walk through the SLC late in the evening and see the activity there. Students have taken to that facility with an enthusiasm that has exceeded our expectations, and the faculty who have the opportunity to teach there love it as well.[3]

Table 7.1
What Do You Do in the SLC?

Activity	Year		
	2005	2006	2007
Study alone	32%	22%	22%
Attend class	18%	18%	20%
Do research	17%	17%	11%
Write a paper	14%	14%	14%
Study with a group	10%	20%	20%
Go to coffee shop	10%	10%	11%
Tutoring	n/a	1%	2%

New Programs and Collaborations

Building upon the success of the SLC, programs have been added and new collaborations founded since the building opened in 2003. Some of these programs were initiated by the Partnership of the Libraries, EITS, and CTL while others include new partners.

Following are some of these new programs and activities:

- Instruction and Information Literacy: Because of the integrated nature of the classroom and library environment, librarians at the SLC have an increased opportunity to promote information literacy to classes in a variety of subjects. EITS also offers courses in various software packages to the general student population.
- Laptop Computer Loan: In 2005, the SLC began loaning laptops. This allowed even greater freedom of movement for students. The libraries purchased 10 laptop computers and EITS worked with the libraries to maintain them. We purchased a docking station and developed a routine for check out/check in. As with other policy decisions, the libraries and EITS worked closely to develop a practical policy and to train all staff in the procedures.
- Digital Media Lab: Opened in 2007, this specialized lab provides students with workstations, media, and Web development software as well as onsite support and training to help them create their own digital multimedia projects for courses.
- Writing Center: The UGA Writing Center offers walk-up services on-site which have proven to be very popular (http://www.slc.uga.edu/students/writing_center.html). The Writing Center staff saw the importance of being in the SLC because of the high concentration of students. Staffed in partnership with Academic Enhancement and the English Department, the Writing Center works closely with the reference librarians in the building to advertise the service and schedule sessions for students. Students use the Writing Center throughout the entire semester and use has increased to the point at which the Center has been experimenting with double staffing. The extended hours of the SLC also allows the Writing Center to be more flexible in its scheduling and thus more appealing to students. This has become a very popular service and students begin to ask for it the very first week of classes.
- Academic Tutoring: As with the Writing Center, Academic tutoring staff wanted this service to be at the SLC because that is where the students are. Parents and students are specifically told to come to the SLC for tutoring during freshman orientation. The Tutoring program offers free tutoring in core level math, science, language, and business courses by appointment and drop-in sessions.
- Art: Not surprisingly, there are many empty walls in the SLC. Images from the Libraries' Special Collections are used to enliven the walls, give users a glimpse into the past, and highlight the Libraries' collections. The SLC has also been home to many student fueled artistic events and is expanding its support of student artists by offering exhibit space in SLC called "Art SLC" (http://www.slc.uga.edu/artslc/cfp2007.html).
- Undergraduate Research Awards: Librarians in the SLC spearheaded an Undergraduate Research Award funded by the UGA Libraries. These awards are given out to students conducting research within their coursework. The students are required

to meet with a Librarian to discuss appropriate resources for their research, and they must write a reflective essay about their research process. These essays are judged by librarians, and prizes are offered to the students who utilized library resources the best and had gained a thorough understanding of the research process.

- Center for Undergraduate Research Opportunities (CURO): This campus unit is part of the Honors Program and promotes research by undergraduates. Librarians in the SLC work closely with the staff and The CURO Research Symposium Awards are held in the SLC.
- Student Life: After 5:00 P.M., the SLC classrooms are heavily booked as meeting spaces for registered student groups and campus departments for student meetings, tutoring, or other activities reinforcing that the building has become the location of choice for a variety of student pursuits.
- Freshmen Orientation: The SLC has become a host site for freshmen and transfer orientation sessions that are held throughout the summer, featuring parent receptions, testing, and course registration. The SLC houses many of the orientation sessions, including registration for the largest group of students: those in the Franklin College of Arts and Sciences. We also offer diversions for the parents of students by providing a video viewing area complete with popcorn which screens humorous films from our media collections.
- Events: Several areas in the SLC are conducive to hosting events that encourage collaboration between faculty and students, or provide a space for departments to host small conferences, presentations, or speakers (http://www.slc.uga.edu/policy/eventspace.html).
- Departmental Tables: University departments, such as Study Abroad, and many student groups set up tables, usually near the coffee house, to take advantage of the heavy traffic of students and distribute information.
- Film Series: The SLC screens foreign films for the University and local community. Each semester several films from a particular foreign country are selected based on artistic merit and cultural importance.
- Blue Card Events: The College of Arts and Sciences sanctions certain cultural and academic events as Blue Card Events. Students who attend complete and submit a card. Certain perquisites are earned depending upon the number of events attended, such as being allowed to register early for the next semester. The SLC hosts many of these events, as well as offering Blue Card Event opportunities to students, including the Film Series, the Bulldog Book Club, and information sessions on the Libraries.

THE FUTURE

The programs and services of the SLC continue to evolve. Ideas from the students are sought through ongoing surveys and focus groups. We expect to implement some of the following enhanced partnerships in the near future:

- Continued collaboration with Writing Center: Extended hours and staffing are planned as is the incorporation of writing assistance specifically geared toward students for whom English is a second language. We also plan increased collaboration with Librarians to provide research assistance alongside writing assistance.

- Tutoring Center: With the Division of Academic Enhancement, we are planning the development of an SLC Tutoring Center where students can come for specialized tutoring in a wide range of academic disciplines spanning first year coursework to graduate level needs.
- Campus Career Center: Discussions are underway to provide research workshops for career planning (e.g., Hunting for Company Information, Resume & Cover Letter Preparation, and Interview Workshops).
- Increased instruction in the Information Literacy Labs: We are fortunate to have three well equipped classrooms for Information Literacy sessions. The use of these classrooms or labs for open workshops and training sessions for students and faculty will be expanded. Topics that will be covered include using the Libraries' online research databases; RefWorks and EndNote; super-searching in Google; RSS feeds for research and scholarship; Web 2.0 tools for the active researcher; savvy Web-searching, avoiding plagiarism, and so on. The objective is to promote information literacy/fluency across the University community.
- Digital Media Lab: This facility is still relatively new and will be promoted heavily in the future. The Libraries and EITS will work closely together to provide open workshops and training sessions for students and faculty on using software and equipment in the Digital Media Lab and throughout the building.
- Faculty outreach to promote "library literacy": The integration of classrooms and libraries in the SLC offers a unique opportunity to market library resources and services. There is a sense of camaraderie in the building that should be conducive to these efforts.
- Develop and target the print collection: As mentioned above, there is a traditional reading room that can seat 100 and can house a noncirculating collection of about 7,000 volumes. The collection is less than half that size and while it includes some excellent titles, including the complete Penguin classics, we need to focus future growth to make the collection more of a draw to students. Based on a 2007 survey of students who use the reading room, we hope to add a small collection of magazines, acquire more graphic novels and popular culture titles, and develop a collection of faculty and alumni publications.

CONCLUSION

By any quantitative measure, the SLC has proven to be a highly successful convergence of functions and collaboration of programs in one building. Surveys of students indicate a remarkable level of satisfaction that is borne out by the fact that use has risen since the building opened and passed 2.25 million visits in the 2007 academic year.

Despite the success, librarians face one almost existential question: What is the SLC? Is it a library, a student union, a classroom building, a vast computer lab? Many students express surprise when they hear the building referred to as a library or when they learn that librarians are available to help them. Given the time and effort that they devote to the SLC, it would be understandable if the librarians felt slighted. It is to the credit of the librarians who work there that they do not. Rather, they focus on how to improve upon and promote their services and do not worry about user perceptions of who or what is behind those services.

In the final analysis, the important thing, the only thing really, is whether students are learning. No matter what students think it is, all evidence points to the fact that as an academic facility, focused on integrating classroom instruction and independent learning, the SLC is a resounding success. Again, quoting from University of Georgia President Michael Adams:

The opening of the Student Learning Center may have had the greatest impact on the intellectual climate of this institution since Old College was constructed (in 1806)...Every time I am there the place is alive with academic activity....I do not know of another facility on this or any other campus where design so fully meshes with function....For decades to come, the Student Learning Center, with its combination of Electronic Library and classroom spaces, will be a defining experience for almost all UGA students.[4]

NOTES

1. Photos and a QuickTime video are available at http://slc.uga.edu/press/educause.html (accessed June 1, 2008).

2. Floor plans are available at http://slc.uga.edu/facility/floorplans.html (accessed June 1, 2008).

3. Michael Adams, "State of the University Address," University of Georgia, Athens, 2008. Available at http://www.uga.edu/news/artman/publish/080117 SOTU2008_text.shtml (accessed March 5, 2008).

4. Michael Adams, "State of the University Address," University of Georgia, Athens, 2004. Available at http://www.uga.edu/news-bin/artman/exec/view.cgi?archive=7&num=977 (accessed March 5, 2008).

8

FROM FACTION TO FUSION: THE COLUMBIA UNIVERSITY LIBRARIES AS INFORMATION SERVICES ENTERPRISE

James Neal

The Columbia Libraries are an exemplar of collaboration and convergence, attracting and integrating independent and disparate programs and projects from across the University to advance an enhanced and innovative merging of information service ventures. By bringing together academic computing and research library and entrepreneurial vision, Columbia has created a unique and powerful organizational strategy.

ORGANIZATIONAL CONTEXT

The basis of any organization is individuals and groups carrying out roles and working together to achieve shared objectives within a formal structure and with established processes. Organizations define the systems through which goals and priorities are established, decisions are made, resources are allocated, power is wielded, and plans are accomplished. They determine the degree to which administrative responsibility and authority are distributed and shared, operations and procedures are integrated and flexible, and policies and standards are designed and enforced.

Organizational models focus on a set of parameters defined by: centralization and decentralization, hierarchy and adhocracy, bureaucracy and distribution, simplicity and complexity, formality and informality, administration and entrepreneurship, authority and collaboration. They can be viewed, among many characteristics, in terms of layers and rigidity of structure, direction and effectiveness of information flow, sources and impact of leadership, participation in decision making, freedom of action, and levels of ambiguity. Particularly important are the health of the industry, the level of competition, the speed of technological change, the extent of globalization, the degree of professionalization in the field, and the rapidity of new knowledge creation. These have been critical considerations as the libraries' organization has expanded.

Libraries have struggled to distribute authority, integrate key operations, break down bureaucratic processes, achieve less rigidity in structure, promote more cooperation across units, and build more matrix-type approaches to the work. As a result, centralized planning and resource allocation systems coexist with broadly distributed and loosely coupled structures and an expanding array of maverick units like research centers and entrepreneurial enterprises.

Columbia University was an early integrator of information technology and information services functions under a single administrator. By the early 1970s, all computing and telecommunications areas were administered by a Chief Information Officer (CIO), reporting to the executive vice president for academic affairs. By the mid 1980s, this structure was expanded to include the University Libraries, but now under the direction of a vice president and university librarian. By 1989, the pendulum had swing back in the other direction, with administrative computing and telephone services moving to an administrative vice president. Academic computing, network services, electronic mail, electronic classroom support, computer labs, videoconferencing, security authorization and authentication, the data center, technology training, helpdesk and the libraries continued to report to the librarian, and the unit was expanded over time to include electronic publishing, digital library, instructional technology, and research computing units. In 2004, another reorganization pushed all administrative, network and telecommunications technologies under a new CIO position. Academic computing and the libraries were assigned to the university librarian.

The Columbia Libraries and Information Services recently implemented a rationalized organizational structure, creating four administrative groups under the direction of the Vice President for Information Services and University Librarian. One group is responsible for administrative services, including budget and finance, facilities and building projects, and human resources. A second group, Bibliographic Services and Collection Development, includes units responsible for serials acquisitions, electronic resources, monograph acquisitions, copy and original cataloging, database maintenance, metadata services, collection development, and the offsite shelving facility. A third group, Collections and Services, includes three multidisciplinary library divisions for history and humanities, social sciences, and sciences and engineering; the global and distinctive collections in the Starr East Asian Library, the Avery Architecture and Fine Arts Library, the Rare Book and Manuscript Library, the Global Resources Program, and the Burke Theology Library; and Access Services including circulation, interlibrary loan/document delivery, collection management, reserves, and building security. The fourth group, Digital Programs and Technology Services, includes the Libraries Digital Program, the Library Information Technology Office, the Preservation and Digital Conversion Division, the Center for New Media Teaching and Learning, the Center for Digital Research and Scholarship, and the Copyright Advisory Office.

CONVERGING UNITS

The Electronic Publishing Initiative at Columbia (EPIC) was an early partnership between the Libraries and Columbia University Press. It has advanced innovative scholarly communication projects in close collaboration with the faculty and the wider research community. Two examples are Columbia International Affairs Online (CIAO) and Earthscape, knowledge centers bringing together Web resources and original work in these multidisciplinary areas. These databases have been licensed to libraries and government organizations around the world, producing a modest income stream to sustain the publishing projects and seed other initiatives. EPIC also launched a series of research and development projects with major grants from foundations and federal agencies. Examples include: the Gutenberg e-project which supported new college faculty in the preparation of their first scholarly monograph as an electronic book and monitored the impact on scholarly reviews and career advancement; an assessment of the growth of electronic resources on the work of libraries, publishers, and researchers; and the National Science Digital Library initiative to develop a robust repository of curricular materials and tools to support teaching and learning in the sciences in the nation's schools. EPIC as a unit focused on electronic scholarly publishing has been phased out to allow a new concentration on support for faculty research and scholarly communication.

The new Center for Digital Research and Scholarship (CDRS) seeks to facilitate cyberscholarship through the development of Web-based customized and personalized research and discovery tools; collaboration and communication virtual spaces; mechanisms for data-driven scholarship, especially data access, review, mining manipulation, and reuse; platforms for dynamic content creation, preservation, organization and distribution; systems for intellectual property management and author management of their work; new and innovative approaches to scholarly communication and repository development; and means for sustaining academic conversations through distributed network communities, conferences, and structured user contributions. CDRS is building strong campus partnerships with a wide variety of Columbia academic and research groups. These include: the Center for International Earth Science Information Network, the Global Health Research Center of Central Asia, the new Harm Reduction Journal, the Women in Silent Film project, a faculty/researcher intellectual inventory project with the Office of Research and Grants, the HIV Center for Clinical and Behavioral Studies, the Earth Institute, and the Columbia University Press, for example.

The new Copyright Advisory Office will support the Columbia community by providing educational and consultative support in copyright issues arising in the creation of original works and in the use of copyrighted works for teaching, research and service. The Office operates in close coordination with the administration, particularly the university counsel, and with many academic units. Based in the Libraries, and providing internship opportunities for students in the Law School, the Office educates through Web-based information, publications, training programs, and conferences. It will monitor legislative and legal developments affecting copyright and their application at the University. It will advise the University on copyright policy development affecting academic programs and faculty publishing activities.

The creation of the Copyright Advisory Office solidifies the libraries' expanding role in this area. The libraries must be knowledgeable resources for the campus, sources of current and accurate information about copyright. The libraries must advocate through political action for the public and academic interest. The libraries must educate students, faculty, and staff to respect copyright and to practice responsible and appropriate uses of copyrighted works. The libraries must document the impact of changes in copyright laws on the ability to serve users. The libraries must effectively negotiate licenses to achieve terms that advance and do not erode fair use. The libraries must promote author rights and promote open models of information access.

The Columbia Center for New Media Teaching and Learning (CCNMTL) is based in the libraries with the mission to enhance education through the purposeful use of technology and new media. CCNMTL forges partnerships with faculty and with academic departments and schools to provide support in everything from the construction of course Web sites to the effective use of Courseworks, the course management system, to the development of advanced projects. CCNMTL is committed to leadership in instructional technology, to research and development, to the assessment of the impact of technology on learning, and to the engagement of faculty collaborators in the reinvention of education in the digital age.

CCNMTL employs an iterative cycle of research, development, and evaluation which looks at the curricular context, identifies the challenges, articulates, and clarifies a set of hypotheses, advances the design, delivers the educational experience, interprets and evaluates the results, and folds this research into a new cycle of analysis, improvement, and innovation.

CCNMTL encourages instructors to go beyond the basic use of the course Web site and to develop rich learning environments through simulations, multimedia treatments of seminal texts, communication and collaboration tools, case studies, training environments, and digital archives. The service philosophy is to provide a supportive environment for faculty in utilizing new media technologies. Technologists, with extensive pedagogical training and discipline expertise, provide advice and direction. CCNMTL has advanced the development of flexible tools in support of engaging study environments adaptable to classroom and online learning environments. These include visualization and modeling tools, real-time data collection tools, data sharing programs, annotation and study tools, simulations, and multimedia capabilities. Projects emphasize collaboration, interaction, and student activity.

The Triangle Initiative creates digital tools and capacities to serve the intersecting interests of education, research, and community service. For example, CCNMTL is teaming with researchers from the School of Social Work and the School of Public Health to build effective HIV prevention and management programs, for teaching students, for generating research data, and for assisting social workers and health professionals in New York and around the world.

The Digital Bridges project works in partnership with Columbia faculty and librarians to bring students into deeper contact with digital collections by promoting active and hands-on use of digitized materials from the library collections. New learning environments enable students to interrogate curated source material with interactive technologies.

COMPELLING TRENDS

The libraries are building the digital library, recognizing that quality increasingly equals content plus functionality, not just the ability to locate the information but what can be done with it. The digital library includes published and licensed content, primary content digitized from special and unique resources, open Web content, sites and documents of quality and relevance to collection development priorities, and institutional content, the uncontrolled and often grey literature produced across the institution. Digital content is increasingly multimedia, integrated with services, and dependent on sophisticated software tools. At Columbia, digital library development has required partnerships with the information technology organization to support the processing and preservation activities and with academic departments to develop the intellectual rationale and framework for digital collections. Partnerships with Google and Microsoft are supporting mass digitization of historical book collections. Large-scale and in-house projects are drawing upon unique special collections. Multi-institutional projects like the Advanced Papyrological Information System, Digital Scriptorium for medieval manuscripts, and the John Jay database, for example, are transforming scholarship on a global scale and building rigorous collaborations for content and functionality.

The libraries are preserving and archiving the scholarly record. Archiving means repository (hold), persistence (access), curation (secure), and stewardship (care). It focuses on the legacy and continuing growth of analog resources, materials digitized, and information born digital. It requires an institutional commitment to architecture, policies, tools and standards. It recognizes the dynamism, fragility, and vulnerability of digital content. It encourages a new copyright policy framework that supports routine capture and preservation of works through technology without permission.

The libraries are advancing the repository movement, the diverse places where scholarly work is deposited and accessed. We are moving beyond licensed publisher repositories to discipline, institutional, departmental, individual, government and national repositories. We face the challenges of navigation and discovery, version control, and sustainability. The work of the library is being reshaped by the scope, rigor, and diversity of the scholarly infrastructure.

The libraries are leading the campus conversation and the transformation of scholarly communication, that is the creation, transmission, evaluation, and preservation of new knowledge. Focus on the crisis in scholarly publishing, the dysfunctional market, the concentration in the industry, the transfer of ownership from author to publisher, the inflationary pressures, and control of access and use are all important themes. The library community wants a competitive market, easy distribution and reuse of scholarly work advancing to more open access, innovative applications of technology, new approaches to quality assessment, and permanent archiving.

The libraries are pushing an information policy agenda focused in the challenging arenas of intellectual freedom, privacy, civil liberties, federal and state education and research programs, telecommunications, government information, and copyright. Leadership is increasingly based in the library for monitoring, educating, advocating, and implementing legislative change.

The libraries are participating in the entrepreneurial academy, leveraging assets, and seeking new markets for educational and research products and services. This has expanded under the impact of financial, competitive, and prestige mandates. It requires significant development and risk capital, business planning and market analysis, and a cultural and legal firewall between the library and its commercial initiatives.

The libraries are expanding a research and development (R&D) agenda committed to the creation of new knowledge and to the solving of real problems in real situations. R&D activities create a laboratory for experimentation, serve as a magnet for new skills, present the potential for capitalization and technology transfer, support decision making, open faculty collaboration opportunities, foster a culture of risk taking, and attract federal foundation and corporate investment.

The libraries are preparing for heightened accountability and assessment. This is a product of institutional expectations and government and funder mandates. It means effective and broadly embraced measures of user satisfaction, market penetration, success, impact, cost effectiveness, and usability.

Ultimately, the future prospects for successful convergence in the Columbia Libraries will be constructed on a redefinition of the physical, expertise and intellectual infrastructure and a new understanding of the geography (where), psychology (why), and economics (how) of innovation.

Collections of significant depth and breadth have supported the development of academic partnerships based in library space. Over the last several years, the libraries have acquired the archives of the world's leading human rights organizations and papers of important advocates for human rights. This enabled the creation of the Center for Human Rights Documentation and Research, a multidisciplinary initiative focused on educational, research, and programming activities in human rights. The Center for American History based in the Herbert Lehman Suite in the libraries, similarly launched because of remarkable archival collections, is administered by a senior scholar in history and supports classes, speakers, conferences, and social events for faculty and students. A distinguished archival collection on Chinese, Korean, and Japanese film will promote a new Center on East Asian Film. The prospective donation of one of the world's largest collections of sound recordings and related realia and papers will lead to the founding of the Center for Popular and World Music. The Avery architecture collections, among the most distinguished in the world, are linked to the Wallach study center, a major repository for architectural drawings, personal papers, and archives, and to the unit that creates the *Avery Index to Architectural Periodicals,* a major publishing enterprise in partnership with the Getty Foundation.

An important example of convergence is expressed as well in the design and development of new and innovative physical spaces in the library. Digital centers will be implemented in succession over the next three summers in the social sciences, humanities, and science libraries on campus. All build on existing partnerships among the Libraries, Information Technology, CCNMTL, and CDRS in the areas of electronic text, GIS, and electronic data centers. These "research commons" will also combine with existing reference service desks to advance critical service objectives. The digital centers will provide flexible user workspaces, furnishings, diverse software, and high-end technology to support collaborative group work. They will enable sophisticated professional assistance to users with research and technical assistance needs. They will provide space, equipment, and software to support presentation practice and design.

An important partnership was forged in 2005 between the Libraries and Research Administration to implement GENIUS (Global Expertise Network for Industry, Universities, and Scholars) as part of a new grants management system. GENIUS stores curriculum vitae information including employment, education, publications, patents, committee work, grants, and research interests. It seeks to foster collaboration among researchers at the University and worldwide, and the profiles are searchable. The role of the libraries was to supply publication and patent data drawing from a variety of published and Web sources for nearly 6,000 faculty and researchers at Columbia. This intellectual inventory produced initially over 135,000 publications. A secondary goal is to repurpose the data to create an expanded component of the institutional repository to reflect the full text of published works.

A recent initiative to define a Web 2.0 strategy for the libraries forges a new working relationship with both student services and information technology organizations. Social networking Web sites and related technologies offer new ways for the libraries to have a new presence in the lives of students and other users. Sites such as YouTube, Flickr, Wikipedia, and My Space, for example, are increasingly used not only to express and explore personal interests, but also as important components in learning and research. Tools such as blogs, wikis, RSS feeds, widgets, and microformats offer ways of sharing ideas, experiences, and information, and connecting content with services.

A critical partnership forged with the medical and science research community at Columbia is being advanced through the library-based task force on e-science. New research methodologies and approaches are enabled by network capabilities and vast amounts of data, and driven by the increasing dispersion of research teams across geography and disciplines. E-science alters the ways investigators carry out their work, the tools they use, the types of problems they address, the research communities that are forged, and the nature of research inputs and outputs. E-science is large scale, computationally intense, dependent on new tools for extraction and visualization, and linked to simulations in support of teaching and learning. Can the University build the cyberinfrastructure, the technologies, the standards, the expertise to support big science? The task force will develop a plan of action for the management and sustenance of support for scientific research, including appropriate policies, resource requirements, and organizational strategies.

The Columbia Libraries remain focused on core roles, that is information acquisition (get), information synthesis (organize), information navigation (find), information dissemination (deliver), information interpretation (answer), information understanding (learn), and information archiving (preserve). But new roles and responsibilities are advancing as the Libraries expand as information intermediaries and aggregators, as publishers, as educators, as a research and development organization, as entrepreneurs, and as policy advocates. The shifting vision of the library is defined as a combination of: legacy, responsible for centuries of societal records in all formats; infrastructure, the essential combination of space, technology, systems, and expertise; repository, guaranteeing the long-term availability and usability of the intellectual and cultural output; portal, serving as a sophisticated and intelligent gateway to expanding multimedia, interactive content and tools; enterprise, expanding concern with innovation, business planning, competition, and risk; and public interest, advocating for supportive national and global information policy.

The libraries in their work with University partners are very much focused on enhancing the faculty experience and supporting faculty desires: enabling personal advancement and recognition, contributing to the scholarly literature of their field, having high quality instructional experiences, working with successful students, collaborating with colleagues on innovative projects, and having access to excellent laboratory and library support and opportunities to experiment with technology.

Similarly, the libraries need to enhance the student experience and respond to student expectations: enabling technology ubiquity and network access anywhere and anytime, providing self-service Web capabilities, creating technology sandboxes as places for experimentation and fun, maintaining places to work with protection and privacy, delivering support services when needed at appropriate level of expertise, supporting information fluency and understanding as lifelong skill, and sustaining post-graduate access to the advantages and capabilities enjoyed as a student.

This translates into an essential partnership among the libraries, Information Technology, and the academic divisions in the development and support of the course management system. The libraries should be focused on such areas as content creation, storage and management of learning materials, distribution and access to course materials, rights management, and collaborative tools. The libraries need to integrate electronic resources and professional services into the learning environment. Online learning demands interactivity, flexibility, administrative functionality, support for diverse learning styles, assessment and innovation; and the libraries can advance these values.

Ultimately, the success of the libraries is determined by responding to user expectations: more and better content, access, convenience, new capabilities, cost management, individual control, and individual and organizational productivity. How do collaboration and organization convergence support these objectives?

CONCLUSION

As an academic research library, the Columbia Libraries have defined their strategic focus to enable and advance essential convergence with academic and technology partners. Key elements include distributed electronic access to content, tools and services, high-quality physical spaces, high-quality electronic spaces, special and distinctive collections, global collections, and the archiving of analog and digital content. Also critical are: innovative applications of technology in support of learning and research, high-quality technology infrastructure, staff development and professional engagement, new knowledge driven by investigation, and expanding integration into the academic fabric of the University. These goals create the opportunities for collaboration and convergence across the University and with partners on a global scale.

9

LIBRARIES AND CONVERGENCE AT YALE

Alice Prochaska

My own background as a museum curator, briefly, then an archivist, academic historian and university administrator, and eventually a library administrator, gives me a certain perspective on convergence in the academic context. I sometimes feel as though I have perched on the borderlines of each of these professions. Fully committed to each job and each organization during my tenure there, and yet gifted or cursed with the quizzical perspective of an outsider, I am not sure whether I have spent more time in my working life explaining people in different disciplines to each other, or having them explained to me. At all events, a lifetime of outsider experiences lends zest to the idea that the different constituent parts of a university campus offer untapped riches to the common good.

Yale University, like every other case, offers some very specific variations on the theme of converging academic resources. It is first of all, an ancient and wealthy university founded on thousands of highly specific endowments. The University Library system (consisting in itself of libraries in some 22 separate buildings) and the galleries and museums, work with a myriad separate funds that are limited to particular activities in different ways. The University's academic departments and many interdepartmental programs are criss-crossed with similarly complex funding arrangements. The search for new donors and sources of support is part of the university's way of life. Add to this the usual array of competitive factors and well-guarded territories, and the environment does not necessarily conduce to sharing resources.

In recent years, however, collaboration and convergence have become more common at Yale. The present campus is relatively compact. Although it is laid out on an elongated grid that makes different areas appear more distant from each other than they really are, nevertheless geographic proximity favors collaboration. Against this background, some long-standing traditions have grown up that counterbalance the divisions.

In 2008, the university is poised to embark on some remarkable transformations. The acquisition in September 2007 of a new campus, the 136-acre site of the former Bayer Pharmaceutical Company campus in West Haven, about 10 minutes' drive from the center of New Haven, will be a catalyst for changes that are still in their planning stages. Meanwhile, Yale plans to build two new residential colleges in New Haven, bringing in approximately an additional 600 undergraduates. The new topography on the campus will transform the use of buildings and spaces adjacent to the new colleges, including library spaces. Planning is already advanced for the compression of library provision for government documents and the social sciences into one of two buildings.

It is difficult therefore to predict the future of convergent collaborations at Yale. A competitive environment with many separate funding streams and semiautonomous institutional governance built into the structure, has fostered nevertheless some promising partnerships. The extraordinary opportunities offered by new space and resources will develop against a background of some discernible, not necessarily compatible trends.

CURRICULUM REFORM AND THE GROWTH OF INTERDISCIPLINARY STUDIES

In 2004, a Committee on Yale College Education (CYCE) recommended wide-ranging reform in the subject content of the Yale undergraduate curriculum. It asserted the importance of the arts in the undergraduate experience, but also insisted on the need for a sound training in quantitative reasoning and enhanced competence in language, which meant both English writing skills and knowledge of foreign languages. The university set up a new Writing Center and greatly strengthened its Center for Language Studies. It also announced that within a matter of a few years, every undergraduate student at Yale should have some extended experience of study abroad. Interdisciplinary programs such as African American Studies, American Studies, Gender Studies, Judaic Studies, and History of Science and Medicine, have flourished at Yale for some time. New majors now being introduced add to this trend, with the two most recent being Middle Eastern Studies and a major in Computing and the Arts.

The CYCE report built on preceding polices that included a strong international thrust. The MacMillan Center for International and Area Studies supports area studies councils, each composed of faculty members from a number of subject-based departments; and the councils in turn support the international programs of the University Library system. In 2007 the East Asia Studies Library completed an elegant renovation of its reading and seminar rooms and office spaces within the central library building, Sterling Memorial Library, funded by the East Asia Studies Council from its Sumitomo Mitsui endowment. In another example of collaboration, the Middle East Studies Council includes support for the library's Near East collections in its grant applications, and the library in turn derives support and advice when it applies for grants for important electronic programs such as AMEEL (An Arabic and Middle Eastern Electronic Library).[1]

Among other international programs at Yale that included the library as an integral part was the PIER program (Programs in International Educational Resources) set up by the MacMillan Center to help colleges and businesses in the regional community. PIER fellows from Connecticut community colleges came to Yale as interns and used library resources, with help from the area studies librarians, to build up a bank of information and expertise. A different type of fellowship, the Yale World Fellows Program which brings world leaders in mid career for a few months of intensive study and intellectual interchange at Yale, also relies on library support to help the fellows navigate the system's resources and get the most from them in their limited time at the university. Regular library symposia give the fellows the opportunity to speak to a broader audience about their work.

The CYCE report on the curriculum was less explicit about *how* students learn than *what* they learn. Although its electronic version includes an appendix on training in the use of information, which the Library provided, this was not a major focus (see http://www.yale.edu/cyce). The fundamental role of librarians and library resources in educating students to find information in all formats, to order and use it, might be described as a zone of developing awareness for many universities. At Yale, the library has worked in fruitful collaborations with a number of other campus organizations to develop services that members of the faculty may not have known they needed, but which they increasingly appreciate. Adventurous members of the faculty have played a key role in these collaborations. One program in particular has led, through grant-supported initiatives and with at times a fragile momentum, to the establishment of a permanent innovative facility in the intensive-use, newly renovated, and renamed Bass Library.

The Yale library's Electronic Library Initiatives (ELI/Davis program) is "a focused effort to facilitate and study the use of digital images and other materials in teaching, learning, and scholarship" (see http://www.library.yale.edu/eli). It grew out of a program supported originally by the Gladys Krieble Delmas Foundation and then the Getty Foundation to encourage use of digital images relating to American history ("Imaging America"). With a major grant from the Davis Educational Foundation, this continuing program has turned into a source of custom-designed course support for professors teaching in numerous disciplines. The work involves close collaboration with members of Yale's Information Technology staff, the Graduate School's McDougal Graduate Teaching Center, the Center for Language

Study, and others. It figures prominently at the annual Innovative Teaching Technologies fair on campus. More than 30 separate courses have now been designed with library support, drawing on collections that are then digitized selectively, to provide students with enhanced access. Growing out of this program is the new Collaborative Learning Center based in the Bass Library, a rebuilt and reconceived library on two floors underground. Designed for intensive use, it is the place where students and faculty find the core materials for each discipline in the curriculum. The new Bass Library provides different sorts of spaces to fit different modes of study: group study rooms, individual study carrels, and open spaces with soft seating. We describe the Collaborative Learning Center, located on the lower floor, as "a resource for the Yale community designed to foster dynamic interactions among Yale students, faculty and staff from across the campus in the support of teaching and learning." It brings together the services of the Library, ITS Instructional Technology Group and Media Services, and the Center for Language Study in a space which functions as a kind of extended learning commons, with two adjacent classrooms. These spaces are designed as flexibly as possible to facilitate consultation and teaching. A Librarian for Undergraduate Library Research has her office in this area, and a technology trouble-shooting office next door is staffed by students on rotation. Special sessions known as "Teaching with Technology Tuesdays" introduce different facets of library technology each week, with presentations from staff and faculty in many different parts of the University. A session on using the tools of social bookmarking, for instance, was run by a professor of the History of Art and a librarian from the Yale Center for British Art, drawing on the facilities provided in the library.

The library's work at the center of teaching and learning relies at every step on collaboration with the providers of our electronic infrastructure, the Information Technology Services (ITS). It has acquired an important, heightened profile through the Collaborative Learning Center; and it also functions in virtual space. One important point of convergence between the two organizations is the Teaching and Learning Portal, based on Sakai software, which provides electronic course support for the entire campus, gives access to student financial and administrative information, and also includes a library role, for customized access to library resources. Generally it is true to say that ITS supplies the infrastructure and mechanisms while the library supplies content, but there are closer intersections and overlaps as well. ITS runs a Center for Media Initiatives, and in several instances it has handed over projects that began in response to ad hoc faculty requirements, for the library to develop and run at a sustainable scale. This has happened, for instance, with an exciting multimedia course on Dante that is now supported by the library's ELI program. A project run by the library to digitize some 200,000 slides in the Visual Resources Collection for teaching purposes, grew out of faculty needs and a collaborative approach between ITS and the Library, funded by a significant donation and by the office of the Provost.

RESEARCH SUPPORT AND THE EXPOSURE OF COLLECTIONS

Research support relates closely to the Library's work in support of teaching, but with an emphasis on exposure of collections, and in particular to the challenges of surfacing "hidden" collections, and bringing together materials with disparate forms of description. The goal of the Collections Collaborative, funded by a grant from the Andrew W. Mellon Foundation, is "to enhance access to and use of the museums, galleries, and library special collections across the university. These collections comprise an extraordinary wealth of resources for teaching, learning, and research" (see http://www.library.yale.edu/collections_collaborative/). This program of convergence at Yale starts from the proposition that an alliance between different collection-based units will add a new dimension to the service that all can bring to the University. Generated in discussions between the Mellon Foundation and librarians at Yale, it taps into nationwide trends bringing libraries, archives, and museums closer together. Its program in turn has supported a movement within the University to provide a much higher level of electronic infrastructure than previously existed, to support the needs of faculty and staff in all disciplines.

The Yale Collections Collaborative works by sending out calls for proposals, which must involve more than one Yale repository, and then giving re-grants to those selected by its steering committee. The program as funded by the original grant ended in the spring of 2008, but there will be ways of sustaining at least some of the momentum for convergence that it has set up. It supported the following projects:

- A finding aid authoring tool, developing a shared and centrally supported tool for the creation of finding aids in Encoded Archival Description (EAD)
- Two projects on "The World War I Experience." The first selected and digitized a range of materials in many formats and media to provide primary source documentation of the impact of the Great War in Britain and America, as a prototype for improving description of and access to nonstandard published materials. The second developed a cross-collection search interface to provide access to digital collections in various Yale repositories.
- Digitization of the papers of two of the major figures involved in establishing the Peabody Museum of Natural History at Yale, O. C. Marsh and G. R. Wieland. Both scientists left their papers to the library's Manuscripts and Archives, and their specimen collections to the Peabody Museum.
- Unlocking digital data collections across the sciences. This initiative formulates a common workflow and generates a cost model for metadata production for digital data collection. It involves the Kline Science Library, the Peabody Museum, Library Metadata Services and the Academic Media and Technology Unit of Yale ITS.
- The Archivists' Toolkit, an open source database application that provides a tool for many of the most common activities undertaken by archivists. The aim is to

develop a model implementation across four Yale repositories with a view to investigating the Toolkit's value university-wide.
- Subject-based guides to collections at Yale, providing an overview of particular strengths across the range of the University's special collections and museums. The project is beginning with African American Studies, British Studies, Modernism, and Photography.
- A project to coordinate and reach agreement on common or compatible practices for descriptive and imaging metadata, and to develop a metadata registry and a metadata application profile for Yale.

These projects, grouped together into a systematic program, exemplify some of the opportunities for convergence that a research university such as Yale provides, with its long traditions of innovative and interdisciplinary scholarship. The convergence between Peabody Museum and Library collections, for instance, taps into a continuing habit of splitting archival paper and artifact collections between the two separate units. Hiram Bingham, the anthropologist and explorer who made the Inca civilization known and celebrated by a worldwide audience through his work on Machu Picchu, left a rich collection of personal papers and notes, and some thousands of artifactual remains (brought to the United States following careful negotiations with the Peruvian government of the day). Today, his papers reside in the Library's Manuscripts and Archives and the artifacts in the Peabody Museum. In the present day this pattern is replicated by another distinguished anthropologist, the Philippines expert Harold Conklin, who is dividing his archive of papers, photographs, maps, and so forth between the library and the museum.

Similar examples come from the School of Medicine, some of whose illustrious history is now preserved in the papers of scientists held by Manuscripts and Archives. There are crossovers, too, with the Lewis Walpole Library, with its extensive collections of eighteenth-century prints, and the Medical Historical Library's Clements Fry collection which includes prints illustrating and satirizing medical practices of the same period. As these collections are digitized, scholars can create their own convergences in ways that might not have happened earlier. The same is true for the history of medical missionaries, illustrated in some important collections both at the Historical Medical Library and in the Day Missions collection of the Divinity Library.

Yale's well-established professional schools, some of which are rated among the best in the country, sometimes also introduce innovative shared programs that draw on resources from across the campus. Thus for instance, students from the Yale School of Medicine may take a course on the skills of observation, based on portraits and other works of art in the Yale Center for British Art. Yale Law School students recently initiated a project to support the preservation in situ of the records of truth commissions in different trouble spots of the world. Manuscripts and Archives then sponsored work financed by the U.S. Institute of Peace, to investigate the need and opportunities for this work on the ground, taking Peru and Sierra Leone as their examples. The Dean of the School of Architecture has worked closely with Manuscripts and Archives to collect the archives of leading architects with Yale connections; and this work in turn closely relates to collections and exhibits at the Yale University Art Gallery. A full-time position of Architectural Archivist is one of the fruits of this collaboration. From the Yale School of Management come further examples. The Beinecke Rare Book and Manuscripts Library provides abundant primary sources for teaching the history of finance; and a recent project to make part of the Economic Growth Center collection held in the Social Sciences Library digitally accessible drew on sponsorship from the director of the Center for the Study of Globalization as well as the School of Management and the Economics Department at Yale. Connections between the Yale School of Music and the Gilmore Music Library as well as the Beinecke Library include support for concerts and performances in the Beinecke, and joint support to establish the Oral Histories of American Music (supported by donations and grants for nearly 40 years) as a permanent part of the Music Library.

CHANGING CONFIGURATIONS OF SPACE

Often when collaborative programs develop successfully, they involve repurposed space. A suite of rooms at the front of Sterling Memorial Library was vacated when the new Arts Library opened in the summer of 2008. Plans are now in hand to turn the ornate Arts of the Book room and a smaller room above it into a reference center for international studies. Staffed by reference librarians with specialist expertise in area studies, it will promote use of our extensive international collections and provide a way into their more intensive use in teaching and research. The center will also offer practical help with preparing students and faculty for their overseas visits: everything from information about research libraries and collections at their destination, to help in planning for the student programs such as "Bulldogs in Beijing" and "Bulldogs in London" that offer international experiences as part of the undergraduate curriculum. This is another way in which the well-established habit of collaboration between the Library and the MacMillan Center for International and Area Studies can promote effective use of shared assets: the programs of the center and the Library's collections and curatorial expertise come together to form a new service.

The success of the new Bass Library presents the University with a timely model for further development. Residential colleges are one of the hallmarks of Yale, starting with the 10 originally built in the 1920s and 1930s, and extended with two new colleges designed by Eero Saarinen in the 1960s. Planning for two additional colleges to be built in an area of the campus close to "Science Hill," much of which will be vacated by social science departments when the School of Management moves to a new site a few blocks to the east, has an impact on library space among much else.

Planning for the new colleges requires that one library building will be vacated completely, and the Social Science and Government Documents collections, with some others, compressed into the renovated Seeley Mudd Library. This building sits at the northwest corner of the site for the new colleges, where it will become less isolated and potentially far more important in student life. Currently the Mudd Library and the Social Sciences Library between them house something like three million volumes of the Yale Library's collections. An ambitious project to re-house little-used collections appropriately among central campus and off-site shelving will reduce the collection in the Mudd Library drastically, but at the same time it presents an opportunity for new services. Not only does the Bass Library present an appealing model for combining the social amenity of a café with the adjacent study spaces and collections, but its Collaborative Learning Center also suggests ways in which similar but distinctive services could be offered elsewhere. In the case of the Mudd Library, the Statistics Laboratory run by Yale ITS, and a satellite of the School of Art's Digital Media Center for the Arts are candidates for housing in the reconceived building. Bringing these facilities together with Library services focused on the social sciences presents an intriguing set of possible new convergences. Student learning increasingly depends on the skills needed to expose, manipulate, and present electronic materials. Here, in a multidisciplinary environment facilitated by librarians and information technologists, new generations of Yale students will experience those skills in new ways.

Yale's plans extend beyond the addition of hundreds more undergraduates on the New Haven campus to a major expansion of laboratories, collection housing and processing, and more, on the newly acquired West Campus. It is inevitable and desirable that new partnerships will spring up. A shared preservation facility has long been planned, but only now is there adequate space to make it a reality. Here in shared space, the Art Gallery, the Library, and the British Art Center will apply the best expertise, equipment, and resources available to the University, to preservation and conservation treatments for collections that range from sculpture to furniture to papyri, and from photographs to watercolors, to personal archives in typescript and manuscript. Alongside the shared preservation facility, a shared in-house digitization facility, which would be based on a partnership between the University Library and the University Press, probably also involving advance capabilities for three-dimensional digitization shared with the museums and galleries. Science departments and the Yale School of Medicine will draw on library services on the new campus in various ways. It is possible to imagine convergence between preservation experts and the Chemistry Department in studying the science of paper, and a range of other possibilities will become apparent as the new facilities develop.

Convergence between units at Yale works in an environment of expansion, but also one where there is an awareness that the University needs to catch up in some ways with its own aspirations. Much of Yale's New Haven campus resembles a building site. New spaces in the many new and renovated buildings reflect the attack in recent years on a decades-long problem of "deferred maintenance." Both the University Library and the Art Gallery are beneficiaries of these developments, with truly innovative programs taking root within the new spaces. Now the University is turning its attention to the equally pressing problem of deferred maintenance in the electronic environment. It is doing so at the right time to take advantage of the movement towards shared resources and open access. A new digital repository service, building on a pilot "rescue repository" that the Library set up in 2004 for shared use with the Art Gallery and others, will provide the virtual space in which the library, galleries, and museums, and also faculty in all disciplines, can preserve their databases and digitized materials, and also design new purposes for them, use them for teaching, and share them in new interdisciplinary projects.

CONCLUSION: THE UNIVERSITY AND ITS COMMUNITIES

When an organization expands, the opportunities for collaborative work can seem almost infinite; just as times of constraint will sometimes engender conservatism, protection of territory, and competition for scarce resources. But it does not have to be a stark contrast between those two conditions. Recent experience at Yale, where space and funding have often been constrained in relation to the work expected, suggests that necessity can be the incubator of partnership. Much of the on-campus convergence described above has grown out of years when separate units of the University have looked for ways to do their work more effectively within serious limitations. Now that the University has entered on an expansionist phase, much of the previous struggle to stretch resources, and to turn grant-funded projects into longer-term sustainable programs now appears as useful groundwork.

Yale's relatively fortunate position engenders or at least brings sharply into focus a new kind of necessity. That is the imperative to share resources beyond the confines of the University itself. There is a political drive to hold private universities with generous endowments accountable for sharing their wealth. In addition to that, Yale from its early days has cultivated a sense of civic and social obligation, which the University has developed in recent years in numerous directions. For example, some 80 percent of undergraduates undertake some form of social service while they are at Yale; the University has a long-established policy of need-blind admission, now extended to international as well as U.S. students, which provides financial aid to all students who are admitted and need it; and its current president, Richard Levin, has proclaimed this fourth century of Yale's history the one when the University will realize to the full its potential as an international and global organization.

One effect of Yale's outreach is to create further convergence within the organization. This can take the form of the Library working with the MacMillan Center to support international research and learning, as described above. Another instance is the collaboration between different parts of the University Library system and local school teachers. The Medical Library and the School of Medicine support the local Career High School with programs for their teachers and students. The Medical Library also supports a Public Health Information network based on the New Haven Free Public Library. A recent grant from the Teagle Foundation supported collaborative work with liberal arts and community colleges in Connecticut to encourage teaching with special collections. The Library's Manuscripts and Archives work in close partnership with the New Haven Colony Historical Society, and encourage undergraduate seniors to use the Society's resources for the original research that is mandated for Senior Essays at Yale. Meanwhile the library's Human Resources department sponsors courses for local school teachers, and an annual book drive to give books to elementary school children. The Library is also a partner in a program to bring interns from Historically Black Colleges and Universities to study librarianship and medical informatics at Yale alongside the Library's staff.

Further afield, two current projects draw together the library's resources with those of the Medical School and the School of Forestry and Environmental Studies respectively, in partnership with United Nations agencies to provide free access to networked information on health and the environment to professionals working in the poorest nations in the world (the HINARI and OARE programs).[2] Just one more example draws on Divinity Library funding and expertise to partner with the Uganda Christian University (UCU) to archive and microfilm Christian records in Uganda and the Great Lakes region of East Africa. The records cover the history of the Anglican Church of Uganda and are kept at the UCU archives located in Mukono, about 15 miles northeast of Kampala.

The communities that the University serves form a complicated network of intersecting interests, from the local to the global. Many parts of the network involve the Library and the other collection-based units at Yale working together in convergent activities. Informing the whole agenda of outreach is a shared sense within the University that there are benefits to be shared with other communities. Convergence at Yale thus is partly a function of the University's own mission, and of its complicated interaction with the world at large.

NOTES

1. To quote from its Web site, http://www.library.yale.edu/ameeel, AMEEL will be a Web-based portal for the study of the Middle East, including its history, culture, development, and contemporary face, and within this portal, will integrate existing

scholarly digital content to make such material easier to find and use efficiently and freely. AMEEL will then become an electronic library about the Middle East, that is, a digital collection of information, hopefully as rich and intricate as its subject.

2. HINARI, the Health InterNetwork Access to Research Initiative, of which the Yale Library is one of the institutional partners, is a World Health Organization (WHO)-sponsored program providing free or very low cost online access to the major journals in biomedical and related social sciences to local, nonprofit institutions in developing countries. The initiative was developed in the framework of the Health InterNetwork, introduced by UN Secretary General Kofi Annan at the Millennium Summit in 2000, and officially launched in 2002. There are currently 1,300 institutions in 103 countries registered for HINARI. During 2003, users at these institutions downloaded over one million articles (see http://www.who.org/int/hinari/en). OARE, Online Access to Research on the Environment, works on similar principles in partnership with the United Nations Environmental Program, UNEP (see http://www.oaresciences.org/en).

10

THE POETRY CENTER AT SUFFOLK UNIVERSITY

Fred Marchant and Robert E. Dugan

On May 15, 2006, the Mildred F. Sawyer Library at Suffolk University in Boston opened its new library. Within the library were the Poetry Center and the Zieman Poetry Collection. The opening of the Poetry Center and the Zieman collection illustrates 50 years of stewardship, accountability, and a renewed relationship between the library and the College of Arts and Sciences' English Department. The beneficiaries of this collaboration are students, the wider university community, and the evolving literary cultural partnerships with our Beacon Hill neighbors, including the Boston Athenaeum.

THE GIFT

Irving Pergament Zieman (1891–1970), a local Brookline building contractor, gave a collection of his personal books to Suffolk University in 1956. An article published in the university's student newspaper, *The Suffolk Journal*, at the time of the donation and rediscovered in 2005–2006, noted the university's acceptance of an "unusual gift" of an "extensive poetry collection consisting of approximately two thousand books and pamphlets" that would be organized in book cases in a comfortably furnished room "off the College Library," intended to stimulate an interest in poetry among the students. The 2,000 items, which included 600 leather-bound volumes, several first editions, and 1,200 books of modern poetry, would be known as the Irving Zieman Poetry Library. The gift also included book cases with locking wired mesh fronts.[1]

Early Years

Zieman chose Suffolk University to receive this collection because "he enthusiastically supports Suffolk's philosophy of education—the opportunity for an ambitious student of limited means to acquire a good education." Fifty years earlier, Suffolk School of Law opened as a night school to serve men working during the day with an opportunity to study law. The poetry collection, close to the library, would "be available to young people who he [Zieman] feels are deserving of this privilege."[2]

Although in the same room, the 600 leather-bound and first-edition classics were shelved in the book cases with the locking wire mesh front donated by Zieman, while the more numerous and general volumes comprising the balance of the gift were arranged in open shelving. Because of space and other constraints, the comfortable reading area housing the collection and open to students was soon converted into a Faculty Lounge. The Zieman Poetry Library became a background for the scholarly atmosphere of the room.

Technically, the collection was under the shared custody of the library and the English Department. The 1956 student newspaper article also noted that Zieman "pledged himself to accelerate the growth and expansion of the collection by additional financial contributions." It is unknown whether or not this happened. It is nonetheless certain that the presence of the collection inspired English Department faculty member and Chairman Stanley M. Vogel to acquire additional books to add to the collection in the 1960s.

Soon after the student-accessible space became faculty space, and as demand for shelving other resources in the faculty lounge increased, the open-shelved general books from the Zieman poetry collection began to be relocated to the undergraduate library. The earliest accession record for adding a Zieman collection book to the library was 1966; the last accession record was 1972. This accession effort clearly indicates that the intent was to make the collection part of the research and instructional resources of the library overall.

When the undergraduate library was relocated to a renovated university building in 1982, the classics in the Zieman Poetry Library and their wire mesh-front bookcases were also moved and situated in what was designated as the library's Faculty Reading Room of some 160 square feet on the second floor of the library. The balance of the Zieman Poetry Library was shelved in the general collection on another of the library's floors. The classics collection sat dormant for years, occasionally perused by those interested in what was shelved behind the wire mesh. The library was rededicated and renamed the Mildred F. Sawyer Library in 1995. While the general collection of the Zieman Poetry Library was cataloged in the 1970s, 1980s, and 1990s, the classics collection was cataloged and added to the online catalog during the late 1990s and early 2000s. The library's Faculty Reading Room, infrequently used, was converted into a student video viewing room in 1999. The shelved and locked classics collection remained in the room.

The English Department

The Creative Writing Program was begun in 1996. An early intent for the program was to serve as the basis of a graduate MFA writing program. However, as Fred Marchant, Director of the Creative Writing Program, carefully considered the missions of the university and the College of Liberal Arts and Sciences, it became clear that the core constituency, and thereby the need, was undergraduate based. Therefore, he decided to focus on providing a first-rate undergraduate writing experience rather than on graduate writing programs.

Another idea generated by the Program's director was to start a literary journal that would have national prominence. In June 2000, Marchant investigated the costs for establishing and maintaining such a journal, and discovered that the costs were at the time prohibitive. If a creative writing MFA and starting a literary journal seemed at that time beyond the institution's financial capabilities, the question for him became, What else could or should be undertaken to support the Creative Writing Program?

Marchant met with the long-time Dean of the Colleges of Arts and Sciences, Michael Ronayne. A chemist by education, Dean Ronayne took the long view of higher education, and his leadership style was one in which entrepreneurship and thinking/doing outside of the traditional bounds of the academy was always welcomed and considered if not always approved and implemented. Marchant proposed the concept of a Poetry Center as the next reasonable and practical step in the growth of the Creative Writing program, and as at least a temporary alternative to the creation of an MFA program and/or the creation of a nationally prominent literary journal. As initially imagined, the Poetry Center would plan and host literary events with an emphasis on poetry. It would provide a venue for poets and writers to read their works and discuss their creative processes. The primary audience would be our undergraduate students, but we would make every effort to connect with the broader community of the city. Dean Ronayne supported the concept and allocated exploratory funds for the project. The first poet to read in a Poetry Center event was Naomi Shihab Nye, herself a nationally prominent educator and poet from San Antonio, Texas, and author of over 10 books and winner of multiple honors and awards.

The Mildred F. Sawyer Library

The university's regional accrediting agency, NEASC, was scheduled for its 10-year, peer-reviewed site visit in October 2002. The university convened a committee and working group structure in 2000 to undertake the required self-study, including library and information services. Because the Sawyer Library's physical facility was a concern to many in the university community, Library Director Robert E. Dugan had begun outlining space needs and objectives early in the self-study effort. The library's section of the self-study found that the Sawyer Library as a physical facility was inadequate to meet the study and information services needs of the twenty-first-century college student.

In May 2003, Dugan met with university President David Sargent because of concerns arising from the accreditor's formal report. The concerns were based upon the visiting site team's submitted document and related to space and usage constraints in the Sawyer Library, then housed in the Frank Sawyer Building. Dugan's written report to the president provided a summary of the information from the self-study and the statistical documents compiled and provided to the visiting team's documents/work room. Soon thereafter the president concurred with the assessment of needs, and thus began a process designed to find space that would meet the library's and other academic needs.

Neither an early library facilities and space planning document outline dated October 5, 2000, nor the fall 2002 university self-study submitted to NEASC mentions either the Zieman poetry collection or the concept of a poetry center.

Shall We Cooperate?

In 2002, Marchant had heard longtime rumors that the Zieman poetry collection, its size and location murky, had been sold by the undergraduate library. Marchant wanted to learn if there was any basis to the rumor and if so, were any funds remaining from its sale to apply towards the evolving concept of a poetry center and its hosted speaker series. Upon his arrival at the undergraduate library and inquiry about the Zieman collection, he was directed to the University Archivist and history professor, Robert Allison, who had been relocated to the library's video viewing room (the former Faculty Reading Room) as a result of flooding in the basement area occupied by the Archives collection in September 2001. Dr. Marchant asked about the Zieman collection. Dr. Allison gestured to the locked, mesh-front cabinets behind him. "It's right here."

Members of the Sawyer Library staff were aware of the Zieman collection, and the newly appointed Assistant Director of Technical Services had begun creating online catalog records for those books in the locked cabinets in late 2000. The balance of the collection remained shelved with the general collection; the Zieman poetry collection was simply viewed as a long-forgotten gift, and the age and condition of the classics collection was appropriate for nonpublic, locked shelving. However, faculty and others could gain access to the locked collection by making a request at the library's Reference Desk.

Soon after rediscovering the Zieman poetry collection, Marchant scheduled a meeting with Dugan. The Zieman collection was discussed, as well as Marchant's vision for a Poetry Center. The Sawyer Library immediately joined in a cooperative effort with the English Department's Creative Writing Program to host/sponsor Poetry Center events on campus, with a hope to do so in new library space in the future. Such a cooperative venture at Suffolk University was somewhat unusual because the rarest and most valued campus asset was physical space, closely guarded by those possessing it. However, at this time, the cooperative project was to co-sponsor Poetry Center–related events—a dedicated space was not envisioned.

CONVERGENCE

The English Department and the Creative Writing Program were developing the concept of the Poetry Center while the Sawyer Library was separately cataloging the Zieman classics collection and making those bibliographic records available through the online catalog in order to make it more accessible since few knew of its existence. The concept of the Poetry Center as a place to host literary events was adopted by the library in a cooperative undertaking with the Creative Writing Center, using the Zieman classics collection as a backdrop. Convergence between the Creative Writing Program and the Sawyer Library occurred when the initial concept of the Poetry Center as a place anywhere on campus hosting literary readings transitioned into the planning and designing of a literary center. Both Dugan and Marchant quickly agreed that the collection's academic objectives and future development goals of such a center would best be served by a dedicated physical space within the Sawyer Library.

Although the books in the Zieman classics collection had not been sold as rumored, their monetary value was unknown. If this collection of bound leather volumes and first editions was as valuable as hoped, it had to be properly insured and protected or, if possible, sold as a means to endow the speaker series and, hopefully, provide seed funding for space for a physical Poetry Center on campus.

To gauge its value, Marchant asked Boston's Brattle Book Store owner, the internationally regarded antiquarian book dealer Ken Gloss, to review the caged Zieman classics collection and provide his valued opinion. Gloss deemed the collection as being essentially worthless if we were judging on the basis of rare books. These were, he said, old books in good condition, but none of them qualified as "rare" or unique, as they were likely to be found in other public and academic libraries. Gloss indicated that if he were buying the collection, he would be willing to pay $15,000 for it, which is a very modest sum in the world of antiquarian book dealing. In short, the truth was this was Zieman's personal collection rather than a carefully developed rare book collection.

As Marchant and Dugan later considered this unexpected finding, the point for Zieman collecting these books was revisited. To both, the reason became clear: here was a vivid example of the love of books and a love of literary art.

It was also a primary example of the love of learning for its own sake. Thus it became clear to Dugan and Marchant that the collection's primary usefulness was for teaching and learning—for exploring and wondering why these books were specifically acquired and read by an individual. They also could be used as evidence of publishing trends and tastes ranging from the seventeenth century to the twentieth century. One could indeed do historical research on the history of poetry and the history of the book using this collection. And because these books were not technically rare, students could, within the confines of the Poetry Center have some hands-on experience with studying these old, but well-kept books.

At that moment, the custodial importance of maintaining the Zieman classics collection became clear. As a result, a dedicated physical space within the library to properly shelve the Zieman collection and host Poetry Center literary events was outlined and refined.

As stated earlier, Dugan presented Suffolk University President Sargent with the need to replace the inadequate library in May 2003, and a search commenced to locate physical space in the surrounding campus area. In September 2003, Dugan submitted a supplemental FY2004 budget request which was approved to contract for a space planner to assist in developing a library building program.

To incorporate the concept of the Poetry Center into the library's physical space, library staff and Marchant envisioned space which could serve several programming purposes including:

- As a more public and visible home for the classics in the Zieman Poetry Library
- For the development and housing of newly acquired poetry resources
- As a room for authors to read their works and accommodate 40 listeners, adjacent and visible to the Zieman collection.

In December 2003, the staff prepared the first draft of the library's objectives for its space/building program, which included the now articulated poetry center. This planned space need was then carried forward to the first draft of the space/building plan created with the program consultant on January 14, 2004. During the next several months the Poetry Center as physical space survived numerous challenges to become part of the final draft of the building program completed in June 2004. Space was planned for 357 linear feet of wall-mounted shelving for the Zieman classics collection, 800 square feet for the programming area to support the Poetry Center's activities, and 150 square feet to store the Center's tables and chairs when different room arrangements were desired.

Also at this time, Dean Kenneth Greenberg, replacing the recently retired Dean Ronayne, envisioned re-engineering the curriculum to increase the academic rigor for undergraduate students in the College of Arts and Sciences.

One of the objectives focused on bringing scholars to campus to work with faculty and students. Two examples of such scholastic involvement included writers Jim Carroll and Maxine Hong Kingston, both National Book Award winners. Carroll is presently a Distinguished Scholar in Residence, and Kingston makes an annual weeklong visit to Suffolk as a Distinguished Visiting Scholar. In 2005, during her second campus visit, Marchant brought Maxine Hong Kingston to the Sawyer Library to see the Zieman classics collection and to talk about the planning for the physical space of the evolving concept of the Poetry Center.

While Kingston was reviewing the titles in Zieman's classics collection, she saw a studio photograph of Zieman hanging on the wall. Based upon the clothing he is wearing, his posed stance, and the papers he is holding, Maxine quietly observed, "Oh, he is about to read one of his poems." Maxine's statement was an epiphany. The Zieman collection was not just a personal collection—Zieman acquired and used this collection to teach himself about, and to later write, poetry. Indeed, Maxine was right. A slightly different studio photograph of Zieman from what appears to be the same photography session appears in a book of Zieman's poetry published in 1961.[3] Collecting, learning about, and composing poetry was Irving Zieman's lifelong passion. In fact, included in the collection of books donated by Zieman in 1956 were three manuscripts of his poetry written in the 1940s (from the 1956 article rediscovered in 2005–2006). The three manuscripts identified in the article, along with a fourth, were published after the donation of the collection.

As far as we can learn, Irving Zieman had no formal education after high school. In addition to the collection being used as a teaching tool for creative writing, it also becomes a personal learning opportunity for students—"if Zieman can do it, you, with all of the advantages provided by a college education, can do it." To help make that point, the Zieman classics collection needed to be visible, and freed from its locked wired cabinets.

As a result, the concept of the Poetry Center further evolved. It would not only serve as a physical place for hosting speakers, it would provide space with tables and chairs for faculty and other scholars to work with students in a creative writing environment, and incorporate Zieman's personal collection as a physical and important motivational backdrop.

The initial cooperative project of hosting literary events had converged into a determined effort of the Creative Writing Program and the Sawyer Library to plan and provide a dedicated physical library space:

- to provide an inspirational space for study and reflection as well as self-improvement as part of Zieman's vision.
- to shelve properly and make more accessible Zieman's personal classics collection not only to honor Zieman's passion to lifelong learning, but as an example of the university's serious commitment to stewardship of a gift given a half century earlier.

- as a functional and visible yet esthetically pleasing environment to foster creative writing.
- as a well-designed, flexible, and technically enhanced space to demonstrate the university's ongoing commitment to scholarship and especially to writers wanting to communicate directly with their readers and audience.
- as a selective repository of the written, visual and audio contributions of those writers presenting in the Center and elsewhere within the College, carrying forth the recorded audio learning concepts deployed by the English department in the 1950s.[4]
- as a space for members of the university community to gather and deliberate.

STRATEGIES

On June 10, 2004, staff learned that the library would relocate to a commercial office building known as "73 Tremont Street" at the historic corner of Boston's Tremont and Beacon streets. Three partial floors with about 55,000 gross square feet would be renovated to accommodate the library based upon its building program. The library's share of the 13-floor building included more than 170 windows, many of them facing historic Boston sites such as King's Chapel and the Granary Burial Ground.

During early architectural design, the university wanted to convert the physical space planned and programmed for the Poetry Center into a multifunctional room, and assigned it space with small windows and an outside view of a modern office tower on the Beacon Street side of the third floor. Administration and "shared staff" (e.g., locker room and kitchen) space was located on the same floor overlooking the treed historic Granary Burial Ground. Dugan and Marchant viewed the Poetry Center as a priority, and wanted to elevate the Poetry Center to a first class design/finish status (e.g., high quality wood trim, paint, and furnishings)—to make the center a signature space within the new library facility. Furthermore, we wanted to relocate the Poetry Center from the Beacon Street office building side to the bay window areas overlooking the Granary Burial Ground, essentially swapping space with library administration and staff.

At this time, Marchant and Dugan undertook a joint and planned effort to place the Poetry Center into their desired space location and design changes. This would require changing senior administrators' minds through information and influencing change through persuasion and persistence. Marchant articulated the vision of the Poetry Center, talking with university officials to increase their understanding of the concept. Dugan managed the physical space details by revising the architectural drawings as they were drafted and progressed, moving the Poetry Center from its initial planned location to its desired location on the Granary side of the building, and by continually renaming the physical area assigned to the space on the drawings as the Poetry Center rather than the Multi-Function Room.

The joint effort worked and a compromise was reached. The Poetry Center was designated as a signature space resulting in application of first-class building materials and furnishings and located on the Granary side of the building. It would be equipped with video projection, videoconferencing, ceiling-mounted speakers, audio- and video-recording devices, and other requested audiovisual necessities such as a wireless microphone system. Tables would be on wheels so as to be easily placed within the Poetry Center as well as moved to and from storage as needed. Stackable wooden chairs which could also be moved in and out of the room as the function/event required were also approved. In exchange, the Poetry Center would include a built-in movable partition which could be unfolded from its in-room closet and, once unfurled, would create three temporary group study rooms for use during the last two weeks of the fall and spring academic semesters.

Construction of the new library began on September 15, 2005. During the nine months of construction, Dugan and Marchant enthusiastically conducted dozens of hard hat tours of the Poetry Center space as it progressed into a signature space within the library.

THE RESULTS

The Mildred F. Sawyer Library opened on May 15, 2006. Since opening, the Poetry Center has met its objective of becoming an inspiration and signature space, hosting more than 250 events including lectures and film viewings, presentations, conferences, student and faculty group meetings, institutional and departmental receptions, and writing classes. The room has served as a backdrop for photographs and for conducting interviews, and several Suffolk University centennial events were held there. As a literary meeting space it has hosted writers and translators including:

- Nguyen Duy and Nguyen Quang Thieu, of Vietnam
- Robert Hass, Poet Laureate of the United States (1995–1997)
- Larry Heinemann, National Book Award winner
- Maxine Hong Kingston, National Book Award winner
- Martha Collins, of Oberlin College
- Grace Paley, renowned poet and prose writer
- Rosanna Warren, of Boston University
- Helen Vendler, renowned critic, Harvard University
- David Rivard, James Laughlin Award winner
- James Carroll, National Book Award Winner

It has also been used, as promised, to provide three additional group study rooms during the final two weeks of both the fall and spring academic

Photo 10.1: The Poetry Center Arranged as Lecture Space.

Photo 10.2: The Poetry Center Arranged into Three Group Study Rooms.

Photo 10.3: The Poetry Center Arranged as Creative Writing Space with the Zieman Poetry Collection in the Background.

semesters. The partition is unfolded and the stackable chairs and the tables on wheels are placed inside each of the three partitioned spaces. The main door to the Poetry Center, locked when not in use for an event, is open when the Poetry Center is in "group study room mode."

In addition, the existence of the Poetry Center has enabled the Creative Writing Program to expand its offerings in a variety of unexpected ways, most notably by inviting an already well-established, Boston-area literary journal, *Salamander*, edited by Jennifer Barber, to join the Suffolk community and be published with the support of the university. In addition, the library holdings too have benefited by the Poetry Center's existence. Not only does the library acquire signed editions by writers who visit the campus, but in May 2007, the noted novelist John Updike made a donation of his complete "run" of *Transatlantic Review*, an internationally important journal from the mid-twentieth century.

INTENTIO DILATO (CONVERGENCE EXPANDED)

The Poetry Center's pleasant environment with its seasonal beauty provided by the Granary Burial Ground and its south-facing direction, the availability of movable and flexibly arranged furniture, and its installed audiovisual and other technology capabilities, has resulted in a frequently used and requested space that has exceeded all expectations. The Creative Writing Program and the Sawyer Library are jointly creating a Poetry Center collection development plan. The goal is to expand carefully and not lose sight of Zieman's original intentions, while at the same time meeting the expected needs of the twenty-first-century student and scholar. Furthermore, the convergence of the English Department and the Sawyer Library's interdepartmental relationship, along with the success of the Poetry Center space, has enabled us to envision several new academic objectives which would support the missions of Suffolk University, the College of Arts and Sciences, and the Sawyer Library:

- to become a cultural space for the university
- to create a triangle of partnerships of cultural institutions encompassing Park, Tremont, and Beacon streets
- to become a recognized cultural space for Boston's poetry community
- to become a print, audio and visual repository of twenty-first-century poetry and other Poetry Center–presented works
- to become an intellectual space as we develop the vision Zieman may have had when building his own collection—seeking and reading the world's best poets to teach others and to appreciate the artistry of poetry.
- to sponsor conferences and other public service events on issues of current interest and import, especially as they are reflected in the literature of our times.

CONCLUSION

Convergence occurred when the Sawyer Library and the Creative Writing Program took their cooperative undertaking to the next level, planning a physical space within a new Sawyer Library to convert the concept of the Poetry Center into a dedicated reality. The convergence was facilitated by the shared vision of the directors of the Creative Writing Program and the library, as well as the professional opinions and expertise provided by Ken Gloss and Maxine Hong Kingston. As planned, programmed, designed, and constructed, the Poetry Center reaffirms the educational mission of the university as well as the role of gift stewardship of "doing the right thing" as donors intend. It also celebrates the Centennial vision of the university's founder as well as Zieman's vision in providing the collection to the library 50 years later.

While we still do not know the answers to some of our questions concerning the original gift in 1956 and Irving Zieman in particular, we are certain that Zieman would be pleased and that the Poetry Center fulfills his 1956 vision and intent. It took us 50 years to arrive at this point; it may take another 50 years to fully realize these new objectives. That is fine; Suffolk University and its departments are good stewards.

Photo 10.4: The Zieman Poetry Collection.

NOTES

1. "Library Granted New Collection," *The Suffolk Journal* (Fall 1956).
2. Ibid.
3. Irving Pergament Zieman, *Founders to Bounders: Boston in Rhyme* (Cambridge, MA: Starr Books, 1961).
4. "Library Granted New Collection."

11

COLLABORATIVE INITIATIVES TO DELIVER AGRICULTURAL INFORMATION

Barbara S. Hutchinson, Jeanne L. Pfander, and George B. Ruyle

Collaboration is a term much in vogue these days and often used very loosely to describe almost any project or initiative that involves more than one individual or entity. As defined in the 2000 *American Heritage Dictionary,* to collaborate is "to work together...to cooperate."[1] The thesaurus in *Microsoft Word 2008* lists as synonyms for collaboration, terms such as teamwork, partnership, alliance, and relationship. However, as scholars have studied the dynamics of collaboration, they have identified more of a multidimensional process than might be initially assumed based on the dictionary definition. This is not surprising, given that anytime people work together and are "in relationship," complexities can be expected. In fact, the literature on collaboration describes a variety of types of collaborative models that can be categorized and analyzed to understand better not only how partnerships work but how operational strategies can be implemented that will serve to strengthen them.

A work by the Drucker Foundation describes collaboration as existing on a continuum, ranging from "philanthropic" to "transactional" to "integrative" with varying characteristics of "collaboration mind-set," strategic alignment, collaboration value, and relationship management.[2] Each stage provides markers for understanding the collaboration and for determining actions to guide its development. For instance, at the philanthropic level, grants may be given with little interaction and with the mind-set as one of gratefulness, but also separateness. At this level, alignment is minimal, there is an unequal exchange of resources, and there are minimum performance expectations for the collaborators. At the transactional level, increased understanding and trust characterizes the collaborative mind-set, shared visioning begins to create greater alignment, there is more value given to the exchange of resources, and an emerging infrastructure increases communication and personal connections. Finally, at the integrative level "we" has taken the place of "I," the relationship is itself a strategic tool among the partners, projects are developed at all levels of the collaboration, and deep personal relationships exist across the organization that facilitate sharing of resources and ideas.[3] As can be seen, integrative collaboration represents the more fully developed level of collaborative effort and requires more time and commitment to achieve and maintain. At the same time, the benefits of this type of collaboration can reach far beyond what might be achieved by an individual or one organization alone.

Similarly, Bess de Farber, creator of the CoLAB Planning® Series and collaboration development consultant, drawing on the work of the Wilder Foundation, describes three modes of working together: Cooperation, Coordination, and Collaboration.[4] Each entails increasing levels of risk and formality and depth or pervasiveness of relationships. At the first level of "cooperation," there are few risks, relationships are informal, and resources and rewards are maintained separately. As a group progresses to the level of "coordination," it will become more formalized with some planning and defining of roles, increased communication channels, and more mutually acknowledged rewards. At a true level of "collaboration," however, there is a full commitment to a common mission, an organizational structure is in place, and comprehensive planning defines roles and procedures. In the collaboration stage, participating organizations essentially change the way they do business to adopt the collaborative relationship(s) as part of their normal business practice, with this attribute being the strongest distinguishing characteristic.[5] In the move from cooperation to coordination to collaboration then, both resources and rewards become more integrated and tangible to each partner. This emphasis on "joint effort and joint ownership" that leads to "leaving a legacy" also is noted in other works on collaborations.[6]

Thus, the steps toward and characteristics of successful collaborations include a grounding in shared purpose and a joint understanding of the end the collaboration is hoping to achieve. James E. Austin emphasizes the importance of ensuring strategic fit and suggests that potential partners develop a partnership purpose and fit statement based on six questions:

1. What are you trying to accomplish through the collaboration?
2. Where does your mission overlap with potential partner's mission?

3. Do you and your potential partner share an interest in a common group of people?
4. Do your needs match up with your partner's capabilities, and vice versa?
5. Would the collaboration contribute significantly to your overall strategy?
6. Are your values compatible with those of your prospective partner?[7]

Reflection on the answers that each partner gives to these questions can serve as the basis for development in the early stages of a collaborative relationship and also guide assessment or evaluation at later stages.

At the same time, the literature points out numerous pitfalls that may cause the best-intentioned collaborations to fail. Both Austin and de Farber describe issues of turf concerns, differing resource bases or lack of resources in general, changes in leadership, lack of sufficient, consistent, and/or quality communication, and lack of accountability as well as other difficulties that must be overcome if a collaborative effort is to become a sustainable entity.[8]

Given the level of effort, commitment, and potential hurdles to be overcome, why would academic libraries and their campuses want to try to initiate and sustain such collaborations? There are several forces or drivers in the present (and likely future) higher education environment that compel the movement toward collaboration. Collaborations may be first driven by budget constraints but, on a more positive note, can also be motivated by a "service first" interest or philosophy.[9] Other forces include the complexity of the challenges facing our institutions, the blurring of boundaries, a demand from our constituencies for accountability, agility, and responsiveness, and (as noted in this book's introductory chapter on convergence), advances in information technologies. As such, collaboration is recognized as a constructive and productive response to these forces and can result in:

- Better use of scarce resources (cost savings)
- Potential for organizational and individual learning and growth
- Ability to create or achieve something you wouldn't be able to do on your own
- Higher quality, more integrated product or service for the end user[10]

These outcomes have been the primary motivators for the authors of this chapter and the many individual and institutional partners that have worked toward collaboration in the Agriculture Network Information Center (AgNIC) initiative and the Western Rangelands Partnership. This chapter describes the history and evolution of these two related initiatives which both seek to use collaboration and collaborative relationships to deliver quality agricultural information through the Web. It will also provide insights into how the Western Rangelands Partnership is perceived by its collaborators and summarize lessons learned from both the AgNIC and Western Rangelands collaborations.

THE AGRICULTURE NETWORK INFORMATION CENTER: A MODEL ALLIANCE

The Agriculture Network Information Center (AgNIC, http://agnic.org) is conceptualized as a distributed discipline-oriented source of agricultural information in electronic form over an international network of networks. Agricultural information is defined in its broadest sense to include basic, applied, and developmental research, extension, and teaching activities in the food, agricultural, renewable natural resources, forestry, and physical and social sciences... AgNIC's mission is to facilitate and advance [seamless] electronic access to people, agricultural information, and other resources for use by public and private components of agriculture.[11]

For 13 years, much has been written, presented, and discussed about the Agriculture Network Information Center.[12] Developed as a model alliance of equal partners, the strength of AgNIC in working to achieve its goals has been a commitment to collaboration at all levels. From the outset, AgNIC was conceived as an initiative that would build on the long-term relationship among land-grant universities and U.S. Department of Agriculture (USDA) agencies that would draw on technical guidance from the National Science Foundation (NSF).[13] To achieve this end, the National Agricultural Library (NAL) and the Cooperative State Research and Extension Service (CSREES) hosted a Planning Workshop of key stakeholders in December 1994[14]:

to provide an opportunity for direct interaction among the participants to consider the issues of most concern related to the establishment of the AgNIC pilot, the services to be provided by AgNIC, how they will be provided, and to set up Task Forces to take the lead on the next steps required for pilot implementation.[15]

As part of this process, the AgNIC Organization Work Group headed by Dr. George Strawn, then Director of the Computation Center at Iowa State University, recommended an alliance structure over the more traditional hierarchy of a consortium—a move, as has been noted, very much in conformity with academic theory for achieving a successful collaborative venture.[16] He noted that

The Alliance would be based on the importance of member selection (shared vision, compatible culture and service orientation, technological responsiveness) and cooperation among equal partners (independent organizations bound by a common interest, each participant retains its own identify and autonomy, and all areas of cooperation are voluntary).[17]

The characteristics of the alliance as envisioned included:

- consensus decision making where possible
- cooperation rather than competition among members

- little overhead or central bureaucracy
- a dynamic structure with most work accomplished by committees[18]

Following completion of the AgNIC pilot phase that resulted in a set of distributed services including an online reference project, an AgDB directory of links to evaluated Web resources, a calendar of events, and a directory of experts in agriculture, the first official institutional members of the AgNIC alliance turned to formalizing operating guidelines.[19] In 1998 a Task Force on Governance was convened to develop bylaws and procedures for the organization and administration of the alliance. The final document outlined the initiative's aims, membership requirements and responsibilities, and governance through an Executive Board, Coordinating Committee, and an AgNIC Secretariat.[20]

Specifically, the *aims and objectives* section specified that partners were to provide access to small, vertical segments to a broad range of authoritative agricultural information and resources which would benefit all agricultural communities. Information products included linked Web sites on targeted subjects and the provision of online reference services in each subject area. Further,

the alliance is based upon the collaboration and cooperation of independent participants bound together by common interests and goals, namely providing electronic access to reliable, evaluated agricultural information enhanced by the application of shared technology and standards.[21]

To date, after more than a decade of largely voluntary effort, the AgNIC membership numbers 59 self-selected partners and Web sites, primarily from land-grant libraries, but including international organizations such as SIDALC (Agricultural Information and Documentation System for America), the Canadian Agriculture Library, and the International Rice Research Institute (IRRI). Besides maintaining distinct Web sites, full partners are to provide metadata records for resources to be made available through a global search interface. In addition, partners may contribute to an international "Calendar" of agriculture-related events and "News" items from around the world. However, in actuality, most of the core services for the alliance are managed by the central AgNIC Secretariat housed at NAL and described below. Following in this pattern, a new feature called AgOAI has been developed by the Secretariat. This service pulls in metadata from full-text, open access repositories, such as *African Journals Online, Organic Eprints,* and university-based institutional repositories (Auburn University, Purdue University, and Texas A&M University). It also contributes nearly 15,000 additional metadata resources to the AgNIC database and is an example of OAI harvesting of selected full-text repositories.[22]

Membership requirements include the expectation that partners will contribute freely accessible, quality electronic information and resources of benefit to the extended agriculture community around the world, and that they will actively participate in decision making, policy making, and governance. In addition, partners adhere to agreed upon technical standards, keeping current Web site content and links, and the inclusion of legal disclaimers to ensure appropriate use of provided information. Categories of membership have undergone revision over the years to accommodate different levels of involvement and support. *Sustaining partners* are full members who contribute content, provide online reference services, attend annual meetings, vote on issues, serve on task forces and committees, and submit annual reports and usage statistics. *Strategic Partners* participate with AgNIC through Memorandums of Understanding, collaborative projects, and may serve on committees and task forces although not as voting members. *Sponsoring Partners* provide funding support of AgNIC's mission and may serve on committees and attend annual meetings. In addition, working relationships with other entities are pursued as appropriate to specific projects and goals.[23]

The AgNIC alliance *governance structure* provides a model for more dynamically and less hierarchically organized partnerships. The original Governance Task Force reviewed the bylaws and alliance agreements of the Big 12 Plus Library Consortium, the Library of Congress's cooperative cataloging program, OCLC User Council, and the U.S. Agricultural Information Network (USAIN) prior to drafting tentative operational guidelines. The resulting guidelines were formalized as the alliance's bylaws and, although they are revised periodically, the basic structure remains the same as first defined in 1998. An AgNIC Coordinating Committee consists of two designates, primary and secondary, from each sustaining partner organization. The Committee meets annually to set policies, operating procedures, content and standards for the AgNIC Web sites, and to create agendas for outreach and dissemination. Each sustaining partner organization has one vote that includes approving changes to bylaws and electing an Executive Board from the membership of the Coordinating Committee. The Executive Board, comprised of a Chair, Chair-Elect/Vicechair, Past Chair, and three Members-at-Large, elected in alternate years, is primarily responsible for reviewing applications for membership, conducting needs assessments, organizing Coordinating Committee meetings, creating task forces and committees, and drafting guidelines and changes to alliance documents. To manage day-to-day operations, NAL houses the AgNIC Secretariat. This includes the AgNIC Coordinator, NAL Liaison to AgNIC, and technical and content staff as needed.[24] The Secretariat also operates a number of listservs and wikis to facilitate communication and sharing of ideas among the partners. Under this flexible structure and collaborative environment, AgNIC has created a strong foundation to realize its early vision for a distributed and broad-based information system for agriculture; and in fact, much has been achieved toward that end. However, at the turn of the Millennium, expected gains and advancements had been limited in spite of the great promise that such a collaboration held.

Steps Taken to Strengthen Support for the AgNIC Alliance

As has been pointed out, one of the primary pitfalls that may contribute to maintaining a formal collaboration is the lack of or uneven distribution of resources. Related to this, members of the AgNIC Executive Board and general membership increasingly recognized the importance of high level support if AgNIC was to gain critical funding needed to maintain an engaged and diverse membership as well as the ability to evolve and adapt new technologies to meet new user demands. At the same time, and largely in parallel to AgNIC member concerns, a USDA Blue Ribbon panel was convened in 2000 to review and assess NAL's programs and services. Included in the final report was the recommendation to build on such initiatives as AgNIC as the foundation for a national digital library for agriculture.[25] To that end, a series of meetings were held between 2004 and 2006 to gain input and seek support from a variety of stakeholders.[26] First, Library Deans and Directors, as well as Extension Directors, were contacted and discussions were held in conjunction with the American Library Association (ALA), the Association for Research Libraries (ARL), and a meeting of the National Extension Directors.[27] Included in these sessions were members of comparable initiatives such as CyFERnet, the Plant Management Network, and the newly formed eXtension. In addition, similar to the originating meetings held in the mid-1990s, a Planning Group for a Leadership Council for Agricultural Information and Outreach was convened three times by NAL and AgNIC members. This Group brought together representatives from NASULGC, USDA, CSREES, land-grant library directors, Extension and Experiment Station Directors, and members of AgNIC who underwent a visioning process for defining a digital agricultural information system. In the summary of the 2006 meeting, the Group substantiated the need for a system that would provide "seamless access and discovery to a broad scope of authoritative collections and services across a flexible, networked, and collaborative system."[28] In addition, a request was made by many of the participants in these meetings to conduct a benchmark survey to inventory and document current library, Cooperative Extension, and Agricultural Experiment Station collaborations and cooperation.

To accomplish this end, the University of Arizona's Dean of Libraries and Director of Cooperative Extension co-sponsored a preliminary survey of ARL Library Directors and Cooperative Extension Directors in 2004 with the results made available at the 2005 Planning Group meeting. This led to an expanded survey to target all land-grant libraries and to also include Agricultural Experiment Stations. The resulting report, published in 2006, held particular insights for AgNIC and for land-grant libraries in general who were looking for opportunities to develop collaborations across their campuses. Of the 49 land-grant libraries, 22 extension units, and 23 agricultural experiment stations responding to the survey, eight institutions identified AgNIC as an initiative involving significant formal library-extension-experiment station collaboration. Other findings noted eight land-grant libraries collaborating with Colleges of Agriculture in projects to preserve and archive agricultural materials, and nine libraries stated they were actively pursuing plans to develop institutional repositories that would include digital archives of extension materials. Additionally seven libraries already hosted extension materials online.[29] The results of the survey suggested a growing trend in library-extension-experiment station collaborations, but also pointed out that the impetus for such cooperation appears to emanate principally from the library communities. Specifically, as in the case of AgNIC, resources often were primarily provided by institutional libraries, although with a few notable exceptions where a more equitable sharing of costs had been achieved.

Characteristics of AgNIC Collaborations

Examples of AgNIC collaborations involving campus partners as well as external organizations and agencies are numerous and include many not documented in the 2003–2004 survey[30]:

- *Cornell University:* Mann Library works with the Tropical Soil Cover and Organic Resource Exchange (TropSCORE), Cornell's Soil Health Program Work Team, and the Northeast Organic Network, Corporacion Artemesia, and other international institutions and programs on development of a *Worldwide Portal on Soil Health*.
- *Kansas State University:* K-State Libraries partner with the K-State Grain Science and Industry Department on a *grain milling and processing* Web site.
- *Michigan State University:* AgNIC sites on asparagus, maple syrup, bedding plants, blueberries, elderberries, viticulture, cherries, and the USDA Home and Garden Bulletin Publications are hosted by MSU Extension while the MSU Library provides e-mail reference services in each subject areas. Both units contribute to the update and maintenance of the sites.
- *National Agricultural Library:* NAL hosts an *invasive species* AgNIC Web site for the National Invasive Species Information Center (NISIC) for the National Invasive Species Council.
- *Pennsylvania State University:* The Life Sciences Library and the College of Agricultural Sciences collaborate on a *youth development* Web site.
- *Purdue University: AquaNIC* was created through grants from USDA-Extension Service, the Illinois-Indiana Sea Grant College Program, and Purdue University Libraries.
- *University of Illinois at Urbana–Champaign:* maintains Web sites on *agricultural communications, corn,* and *soybeans* as collaboration between the College of Agricultural, Consumer, and Environmental Sciences and the University Library.

- *University of Nebraska–Lincoln:* The University of Nebraska's libraries cooperate with the University's Institute of Agriculture and Natural Resources on a *water quality* site.
- *University of Wisconsin–Madison:* The *American cranberry* Web site content and organization are determined by librarians at Steenbock Library in collaboration with faculty from the departments of Horticulture and Plant Pathology at UW-Madison, including UW-Extension specialists.[31]

In spite of these clear examples of successful collaborations, the obvious agreement on a shared vision for AgNIC, and the extensive nature of voluntary contributions to the effort (i.e., traditional library "service orientation"), AgNIC has not yet achieved the level of external support necessary to fully sustain the effort and, as such, may not yet completely fulfill the requirements for an integrative collaboration. The reasons for this are discussed in the conclusions at the end of the chapter in relation to insights gained from the literature on collaborations as are steps that are being taken now to overcome these obstacles.

THE UNIVERSITY OF ARIZONA AGNIC EXPERIENCE: A COLLABORATIVE WEB SITE FOR RANGELAND MANAGEMENT

One of the more intensive and extensive collaborative initiatives under the AgNIC umbrella is the University of Arizona's (UA) project on rangeland management. Although the UA was not part of the original 1994 discussions for developing AgNIC, nor the subsequent preliminary negotiations between NAL and the General Services Administration for initial funding, a move taken by outgoing Arizona Senator Dennis Deconcini caused a sequence of events that tied the UA to its initiation. The Senator became interested in AgNIC as part of an opportunity to involve Arizona in a number of initiatives related to the use of new technologies before his departure.[32] Thus, through the influence of the Senator, NAL's original October 1994 proposal to GSA to develop AgNIC as an Iowa Communications Network (ICN) Pilot Project turned into a March 2005 Memorandum of Understanding between GSA and Arizona State University (ASU) in Tempe, Arizona.[33] This MOU provided a $3 million grant for five technology-related projects, only one of which was for AgNIC:

ASU will sponsor a proposal from the US Department of Agriculture/ National Agricultural Library to establish a prototype Agricultural Network Information Center to serve the global community of people who share an interest in agriculture. The Center will provide electronic access to people, information, and resources on a global basis via the Internet.[34]

Subsequently, a month later, an Interagency Agreement between GSA and NAL outlined an AgNIC pilot project in partnership with "Arizona State" for a sum of $225,000. By that time the University of Arizona, Iowa State University and other land-grant universities, including Cornell University's Mann Library as a provider of digitized historically significant agricultural literature, were named as cooperators along with CSREES and Cooperative Extension.[35] The final piece in this paper trail was a September 1995 Cooperative Agreement between NAL and the University of Arizona Libraries (UAL) for nearly $52,000 to "Develop More Advanced Approaches to Disseminating Electronic Information."[36] At this point, AgNIC had turned into a four-pronged initiative: an online "Reference Assistance Pilot project," a directory of agriculture-related resources in electronic form, a set of frequently asked questions (FAQs), and leadership in finding ways to "involve the entire land grant library community in this process."[37] A 1996 project progress report documents that by April of that year, four AgNIC Web sites were operational and ready to implement the distributed reference pilot (Agricultural Economics at Cornell; Animal Science at ISU; Food and Nutrition at NAL, and Range Management at the UA). At the same time, a central database of events had been implemented, there were plans for a directory of experts, and the Society for Range Management (SRM) had approved a digitization project with the UAL to provide electronic access to the back issues of their two journals.[38]

What had happened behind the scenes demonstrates the vagaries of the governmental funding process. Senator Dennis Deconcini brought $3 million to Arizona and, specifically, Arizona State University, but in doing so rerouted funds that had been requested for the development of AgNIC and the leadership of ISU. However, the UAL, as representative of Arizona's land-grant university, garnered the AgNIC portion of the GSA agreement largely due to its already working relationship with NAL. Although the GSA funding eventually provided to NAL for AgNIC was much reduced from the original request, it was now designated with the stipulation that the UAL would be the cooperating entity. This, in turn, led to the Cooperative Agreement between NAL and UAL which finalized the deal, although for some reason the AgNIC brand was not mentioned in that agreement.[39]

During the early months of 1995, a pivotal step was taken by the University of Arizona (UA) Libraries' agriculture librarian to ensure UA involvement in AgNIC would be a collaborative venture from the start. The UAL librarian contacted the librarian who ran the Arid Lands Information Center (ALIC) in the College of Agriculture and Life Sciences (CALS) for assistance in the project and the head of the College's Network Support Group. Brainstorming ideas for how to implement what they understood of the vision for AgNIC and the components of the likely GSA-funded project, one of their first discussions focused on the selection of a topic for the UA's contribution to a vertical segment of AgNIC. The idea of a topic with substantial relevance to Arizona and to the Western United States in general was agreed upon and the management of Arizona's extensive rangelands almost immediately became the area of interest. It was soon after this that a meeting was held with a School of Natural Resources professor of rangeland science and the UA's rangeland management Extension Specialist to engage them in the project. To their credit, they recognized the importance of information dissemination through the Internet and agreed to participate in the development of a rangeland management Web site. Thus, from the outset, the UA's contribution to AgNIC was based on an interdisciplinary approach, with librarians as the primary organizers, rangeland scientists and extension personnel contributing authoritative content and a user focus, and Internet technicians providing the technical foundation for the system.[40]

As the UA AgNIC team took on the development of the original Managing Rangelands AgNIC Web site, the members determined a set of informal operating guidelines that continue to influence the direction of the site's development today.[41] There was an early recognition that authoritative Web sites are not likely to be developed by a single individual. If the site was to be more than a set of links to other resources, rangeland specialists and other knowledgeable stakeholders were needed to help develop customized content specifically to meet the information needs of private landowners, agency land managers, range researchers, students, and policy makers. In addition, a user-friendly Web interface required the skills of Web and graphics designers, and later Web database specialists. At the same time, as the complexity of the site developed, knowledge of metadata standards and Web indexing became increasingly important and these were areas where librarians could particularly contribute. The understanding that partnering would create a better product and help generate opportunities for external funding also led to an active marketing effort by members of the UA AgNIC team involving presentations at a variety of meetings on-campus and around the state.[42]

These efforts resulted in gaining direct user input to guide improvements and enhancements to the Web site and led to the development of a number of external collaborations. For instance, the Arizona Common Ground Roundtable, made up of ranchers, environmentalists, academics, and agency land managers, approached a member of the Team about creating a module of practical information about conservation ranching and together the two groups created the "Toolkit for Profitable Conservation Ranching" (http://rangelandswest.arid.arizona.edu/az/toolkit/toolkit.html). In addition, collaboration with the Arizona Office of the Natural Resources Conservation Service (NRCS) provided geospatial access to NRCS Ecological Site Guides, land management, and planning tools used by multiple agencies to identify and characterize land resources including soils, vegetation, hydrology, and climate features, as well as interpretations of wildlife, recreation, and grazing (http://seth.arid.arizona.edu/arizona/). Leveraging funding from a NASA-funded Raytheon project in which ALIC was involved, led to the design of a special section on "Geospatial Applications for Rangeland Management" in collaboration with the Arizona Remote Sensing Center (ARSC).

This interim page provides explanations of remote sensing technology and its potential as a tool for rangeland management as well as links to specific range-related geographic information system (GIS) applications (http://rangelandswest.org/jsp/module/az/geospatial/index.jsp).[43]

Turning AgNIC's Managing Rangelands Web Site into Western Rangelands: A Collaborative Portal

By 2000, the UA AgNIC Rangelands Team had worked together for nearly five years. For some time, there had been recognition that even the UA's interdisciplinary team could not cover all the issues related to the understanding and management of Western rangelands. Similarly, it was clear that these same issues do not stop at political boundaries. This led to a decision to present the idea of inviting other Western land-grant universities to join in the effort and move from an Arizona focus to a Western regional emphasis. To this end, in the winter of 2001, Team members gave a presentation to the administrations of the UAL and CALS.

This presentation and the subsequent discussion resulted in an invitation [from the UA Director of the Agricultural Experiment Station] to demonstrate this concept to the administrators attending the Land Grant College of Agriculture Western Regional Joint Summer Meeting in July 2001 at Keystone, Colorado. The positive feedback from various land-grant representatives at the meeting, including the Western Council for Agricultural Research, Extension, and Teaching (WCARET)...led the UA AgNIC team to make plans to host a workshop in March of 2002, with the goal of bringing key library and rangeland specialists together to discuss establishing a Western Regional AgNIC Rangelands group. Letters were sent to both Library and College of Agriculture Directors, and where appropriate, to Colleges of Natural Resources, requesting their participating in the effort by selecting representatives to attend the workshop. At the same time, letters were sent to designated library and rangelands contacts at many of the Western land-grant universities.[44]

The result then as now has far exceeded original expectations. At the first meeting in 2002, 12 states sent representatives including both librarians and range specialists in keeping with the collaborative, multidisciplinary model begun at the UA. Also attending were representatives from SRM, AgNIC, and NRCS. The primary purpose was to explore the possibility of forming a loosely structured consortium, similar to the AgNIC model, to provide access to evaluated rangelands information, resources, and learning and decision-making tools. The delivery mechanism would be through state-specific Web sites (e.g., Montana Rangelands, Kansas Rangelands, and California Rangelands) and an umbrella Western rangelands gateway to link all together (first called Rangelands of the Western U.S. and now called Western Rangelands). The meeting resulted in a unanimous decision to pursue this common agenda.[45]

Western Rangelands Operating Structure

For the first five years, the UA continued to lead the effort—organizing the annual meetings and facilitating action planning. However, by the fifth year, the collaboration was strong enough and expansive enough (now including members from all 19 Western states) to begin planning for sustainability.[46] One step in this process had been to apply for Western Coordinating Committee (WCC) status within the agricultural experiment station (AES) system at the suggestion of the UA Director of the Agricultural Experiment Station. With the assistance of the Director, this process was successfully navigated in 2004 and has resulted in legitimizing Western Rangelands work and travel as officially sanctioned AES activities.

In addition, in 2005, with help from a UAL facilitator, a governance structure was drafted and voted on by the members of the Western Rangelands partnership. Similar to the AgNIC alliance model, there are levels of membership; although in this case Core members are identified as those from land-grant universities and other qualified institutions whereas Affiliate members include other institutions, agencies, and groups such as nongovernmental organizations (NGOs). Leadership is provided by elected officers that involves a three-year commitment coming in as Secretary, then moving into the Vice Chair, and Chair positions respectively and, if possible, alternates between librarians and range specialists to maintain the cross-disciplinary collaborative model. The majority of the work of the Western Rangelands Partnership, as now called by its members, is conducted through Committees and Task Forces—both self-selected and assigned by the Executive Committee. These include Outreach, Technical, Annual Meeting Planning, Policies and Standards, Grant Writing (as needed), and, currently in discussion, a committee on Evaluation and Assessment. In addition, Content Working Groups have formed around the six broad categories that constitute the browse function on the Western Rangelands home page with each Group selecting a leader who is responsible for organizing necessary updates, reviews, and discussions on new content ideas.[47] Although the Partnership has had some success in gaining extramural funding, specifically a Western Sustainable Agriculture Research and Education CSREES grant from 2005–2007, the work of the Partnership is still largely voluntary and progress is necessarily limited by the time and resources members can commit to the effort.

Results of a Survey of Western Rangelands Partners

An e-mail survey with the five following questions was sent to 34 individuals from the 19 Western Rangelands partner institutions:

1. Please identify your affiliation: __ Academic department __Cooperative Extension __ Library __ Other

2. If applicable, please characterize the extent of any internal/local campus collaboration in the development and operation of your state's Rangeland West Web site: __ None __ Some __ Moderate __ Considerable
3. What do you see as the primary benefits and challenges of working collaboratively with your campus Western Rangelands partners?
4. What do you see as the primary benefits and challenges of working collaboratively with other states in the Western Rangelands partnership?
5. Do you have any other comments or observations about the Western Rangelands collaboration?

Twelve completed surveys were received for a 32 percent response rate. It was a fairly balanced response, with seven academic departments, four Cooperative Extension units, and five library/librarian affiliations.[48]

Most respondents indicated only "some" (or fairly low) level of collaboration in development of their state site. Only one institution showed "considerable" (high) level of collaboration from all partners (both Extension/Academic and librarian). In other cases where both the Extension/Academic partner and librarian responded, the librarian indicated "considerable" collaboration in development of the state site, while the Extension/Academic indicated "some." Comments on involvement showed that collaboration on Web site design, functionality, and content plus shared support from both library and college administrations.

In responding to the question of the primary benefits of collaboration with the campus/local partner, the most common benefit identified was the different but complementary skills, knowledge, expertise, and points of view that the extension, academic, and librarian partners bring to the initiative. One respondent wrote "Working with colleagues from other departments and fields provides opportunities to learn and to create more useful products and services." A librarian wrote "Since I don't have extensive subject area expertise, I have relied on our range specialist a lot." An academic department partner wrote "Their skill at the internet and at information archiving has made easy work of my part." Networking, relationship building, and a sense of community were also described as positive outcomes of collaboration.

The challenges of working collaboratively at the local/state level are seen as primarily related to issues of scarce time and heavy workload, in addition to constrained funding resources. Communication and decision-making challenges are usually related to the issues of time and workload. Physical/geographic distance between partners in some states can be an impediment to face-to-face communication. Another challenge mentioned several times is that of technical programming/IT support. One person wrote "Dealing with programming issues is currently the major difficulty," and another "Very little cooperation from university IT department (usually difficult or impossible to get Web statistics)."

At the regional level, respondents described similar benefits and challenges to working collaboratively with other states in the Western Rangelands partnership. Many respondents commented on the networking benefit. For example, "Having the opportunity to meet and develop collegial relationships with people from different locations and disciplines is a uniquely rewarding experience." Another wrote, "The benefits are the opportunities to meet and discuss mutual problems with those from other campuses." Yet another commented on "shared resources for rangelands info; fun; sense of community and shared purpose."

Several commented on the benefit of regional collaboration as the "sum is greater than the parts":

- "We made something substantial happen that would not have happened if each individual state had to do this on its own."
- "The energy exchange between states strengthens and amplifies inputs into the organization from our team. The free exchange of ideas between states allows your imagination to develop and investigate new ideas that you may not have realized by yourself."

Regarding communication issues, one respondent stated that communication is "both the major benefit and the challenge." The challenge of communication on a consistent basis was reiterated by others who wrote "We don't communicate with others on a regular basis"; "Uneven participation—not much communication throughout the year"; and "Time for communicating effectively also can be a challenge." Again, heavy workloads and competing priorities are probably a root cause of communication problems. As one respondent wrote, "All of us get busy and the Western Rangelands Partnership sometimes has to take a lower priority than other work."

Several people commented on the challenge of financial support. One writes "The primary challenge is to achieve financial sustainability to maintain ongoing involvement." Another asserts "Funding is a sticking point. If we had more grant money and funding, we might be able to hire more people or offer money to libraries or academic departments to hire grad students to help or students to work on Web page projects."

Technical issues at the regional level, just as at the state level, are a concern. A respondent observed, "I think the organization is at a critical juncture and believe, in hindsight, that the reorganization of the regional site structure should have been approached in a different fashion. The need to re-do previous work seems to have negatively impacted the group and sapped, or diverted its energy. I have seen this to be the fatal blow to other volunteer organizations and hope we can rebound in a positive way."

In the end, however, respondents have positive opinions about the Western Rangelands collaboration. Comments include "It is a unique effort of portal development and a role model to other areas"; "It has been very rewarding to work on a project with both local and regional implications"; "This is important work. Information about rangelands is critical for research, decision-making and public awareness"; and "It has been a great experience and a great group to work with. I have learned a tremendous amount and look forward to continuing in the partnership for a long time."

CONCLUSION: LESSONS LEARNED FROM THE AGNIC AND WESTERN RANGELANDS COLLABORATIONS

In reviewing the history of both the AgNIC and Western Rangelands collaborations and the responses of some of the Western Rangelands partners to the survey described above, we can see how the continuum of development from philanthropic to transactional to integrative and the variations of cooperation, coordination and collaboration have played out. There are a number of lessons to be learned.

For AgNIC, even with extensive voluntary commitment and buy-in that might be considered features of integrative collaborations, there is still a need for ongoing high-level support and considerable institutional resources to sustain the collaboration over time. Longevity, commitment by individuals, and singleness of purpose has not been enough. Resources are needed to evolve and enhance the technical infrastructure and to support content development, perhaps by buying-out people's time. The AgNIC collaboration could benefit from considering a new business model for future financial sustainability and, in the interim, an active program to attract external funding. To this end, two new initiatives are currently being discussed by AgNIC members that could expand the initiative and potentially lead to gaining new resources for the development of a national collaborative repository of "born digital"[49] and "reborn digital"[50] agricultural resources and materials.[51] Already, the committees for these efforts involve both land-grant librarians and extension personnel as well as others. Thus, AgNIC is continuing to build on the collaborative mode it has practiced from the start to further strengthen the alliance and to build broader support for its products and services.

In the Western Rangelands Partnership, it is clear that interdisciplinary collaboration is a strong point and that growing deep personal and complementary relationships among the partners are key to its successful operation. The interdisciplinary approach is on the whole seen as critical to developing authoritative Web content focused on direct user needs. To this end, the collaboration benefits from the contribution of:

- Content experts (extension agents and faculty) who have "front-line" exposure to clients who need and use the information resources
- Information experts (librarians) who understand how to organize, categorize, and present information
- Technical infrastructure and Web design experts who give functionality on the Internet

It should be noted that the lines between these areas of expertise are not hard and fast and that there are cases where one individual possesses a combination of these capabilities.

The Western Rangelands Partnership can be viewed from different levels of collaboration or involvement, particularly at the local or state level. This can be influenced by the culture at each institution but mainly it is a matter of time and opportunity for building relationships. For example, the University of Arizona team has had ten years to develop local collaborations. Other states involved in the development of Western Rangelands have only been working in extension/faculty/librarian teams for five or fewer years. Nevertheless, as indicated in the survey responses, the relationships and sense of shared purpose and accomplishment that have developed over time are seen as a unique strength. Similarly, "Joint ownership" of Western Rangelands has been understood and appreciated by the partners from the beginning. This was represented by the two-part goal that included both the main/regional portal site and the independently created state sites allowing for resources and rewards to be shared at both levels. However, in spite of this, engaged and consistent communication, most particularly between annual meetings, is still viewed as a challenge. Thus, while some levels of integrative collaboration have been attained, these are still components of the Western Rangelands Partnership that denote earlier stages of collaborative development.

In hindsight, it can also be seen that Western Rangelands partners initiated the effort largely without a full understanding of the complexity of collaborations and, in fact, with some resistance to spending the time necessary to establishing formal governance and collaborative understandings. People were understandably eager to build their state sites and to develop quality content actions still central to the partnership's credibility and usefulness. However, the authors perceive an opportunity to begin partnership strengthening—perhaps using some of the questions and other tools found in the works referenced earlier in this chapter.[52] In reality, it might be better timing for such work at this stage rather than earlier, given the need to gain initial interest in a collaborative venture in which most people did not know each other and, also, to build a necessary foundation of trust.

Overall, the lessons learned from the convergence and collaboration both within individual institutions and between institutions in the AgNIC and Western Rangelands initiatives can be summarized in the following statements:

- Librarians and extension personnel have missions and professional cultures that focus on outreach and collaborations, therefore both AgNIC and Western Rangelands have a solid foundation for the future as long as time, energy and resources can be sustained.
- It is critical to keep partners engaged through effective and consistent communication, and to maintain a shared sense of purpose.

Progress is not always linear or one-directional. Collaborative organizations and partnerships naturally move back and forth between stages and modes of working together, although hopefully finding a gradual tendency toward the "higher" end of the continuum and true integrative collaboration. By keeping AgNIC and Western Rangelands moving forward on this track, the goal of delivering agricultural information to our campuses, states, nation and society can be achieved.

NOTES

1. *American Heritage Dictionary of the English Language*, "Collaborate." 4th ed. (Boston: Houghton Mifflin, 2000). Available at http://www.bartleby.com/61/ (accessed February 25, 2008).
2. James E. Austin, *The Collaboration Challenge: How Non-Profits and Businesses Succeed through Strategic Alliances* (San Francisco: Jossey-Bass, 2000).
3. Ibid.
4. Bess de Farber, *Collaboration Basics*. Unpublished presentation delivered at the University of Arizona, September 1, 2006.
5. Ibid.
6. Russell M. Linden, *Working across Boundaries: Making Collaboration Work in Government and Nonprofit Organizations* (San Francisco: Jossey-Bass, 2002).
7. Austin, *The Collaboration Challenge*.
8. Ibid.; de Farber, *Collaboration Basics*.
9. Linden, *Working across Boundaries*.
10. Ibid.
11. Agriculture Network Information Center, *Draft Concept and Prototype Pilot Project* (1994), 1–2. Available at http://www.agnic.org/about/leadership/background/DraftVision (accessed February 17, 2008).
12. Agriculture Network Information Center, *About Section* (2008). Available at http://www.agnic.org/about (accessed February 17, 2008); Melanie Gardner, Jean Gilbertson, Barbara Hutchinson, Tim Lynch, Janet McCue, and Amy Paster, *Partnering for Improved Access to Agricultural Information: The Agriculture Network Information Center (AgNIC) Initiative. ARL Bimonthly Report* 223 (2002), available at http://www.arl.org/bm~doc/agnic1.pdf (accessed February 27, 2008); Barbara Hutchinson, *Major Agricultural Information Initiatives: With Emphasis on Developing Country Services.*, prepared for Cornell University and the Gates Foundation for the WorldAgInfo Symposium, October 2007, available at http://worldaginfo.org/files/Agricultural%20Information%20Initiatives.pdf (accessed February 17, 2008); Barbara Hutchinson et al., *Making the Case for a Next-Generation Digital Information System to Ensure America's Leadership in Agricultural Sciences in the 21st Century*. A Background Document. Commissioned by the United States Agricultural Information Network (USAIN). October 2006 (updated December 2007) (in review); Douglas E. Jones, George Ruyle, and Barbara Hutchinson, "Building a Collaborative AgNIC Site as an Outreach Model: Rangelands of the Western U.S.," *The Reference Librarian* 39, no. 82 (2003): 125–40; M. Lonsdale, *Global Gateways: A Guide to Online Knowledge Networks* (Australian Council for Educational Research, 2003), available at http://www.educationau.edu.au/jahia/webdav/site/myjahiasite/shared/papers/

global_gateways_v3.pdf (accessed February 27, 2008); J. J. Molnar, "Using the Internet for Instruction: Experiences, Possibilities, and Considerations," *North American Colleges and Teachers of Agriculture (NACTA) Journal* (available at http://find articles.com/p/articles/mi_qa4062/is_200412/ai_n9472420/print (accessed February 17, 2008); E. Nowick and M. Gardner, "Getting It out There: A Cooperative Agricultural Network for Information Sharing," *Technical Services Quarterly* 19, no. 3 (2002): 41–49, available at https://www.haworthpress.com/store/ArticleAb stract.asp?sid=2HRFU386L3SV9HJ7XSM8B4M8L82QB358&ID=4081 (accessed February 17, 2008); Amy T. Wells, Susan Calcari, and Travis Koplow (eds.), *The Amazing Internet Challenge: How Leading Projects Use Library Skills to Organize the Web* (Chicago, IL: American Library Association, 1999).

13. National Agricultural Library, Agriculture Network Information Center, AgNIC: Concept and Prototype Pilot Project (1994), available at http://www.agnic.nal.usda.gov/agnic/agnic.html (accessed February 16, 2008); National Agricultural Library, Project Proposal for Iowa Communications Network Pilot Project (Submitted to the General Services Administration). (Beltsville, MD: USDA National Agricultural Library, October 21, 1994).

14. These include Iowa State University, Cornell University, Michigan State University, Purdue University, St. Joseph's College, and from U.S. Department of Agriculture: National Agricultural Library, Cooperative State Research and Extension Service (CSREES), Economic Research Service (ERS), and National Agricultural Statistics Service (NASS), and the American Distance Education Consortium (ADEC); also participating was the Canadian Agriculture Library and private associations: Clearinghouse for Networked Information Discovery and Retrieval (CNDIR) and American Society for Horticultural Science (ASHS).

15. National Agricultural Library, Managing Electronic Information in Agriculture toward an Agriculture Network Information Center: A Model for Distributed Access, 2. Summary Report of AgNIC Planning Workshop December 4, 5, and 6, 2004 (Washington, DC: National Agricultural Library, 1995). Available at http://www.agnic.org/about/proceedings/reports/agnicreports1294.html (accessed February 16, 2008).

16. He is currently the Chief Information Officer for the NSF Office of Information and Resource Management.

17. National Agricultural Library, Managing Electronic Information in Agriculture toward an Agriculture Network Information Center, 4.

18. Ibid.

19. National Agricultural Library, University of Arizona, Cornell University, Iowa State University, and University of Nebraska–Lincoln.

20. For a current version, see Agriculture Network Information Center, By-Laws and Governance (2007). Available at http://www.agnic.org/about/facts/gover nance_2006_rev_2007.pdf (accessed February 17, 2008).

21. Agriculture Network Information Center, By-Laws and Governance.

22. Hutchinson, *Major Agricultural Information Initiatives*.

23. Agriculture Network Information Center, By-Laws and Governance (2007).

24. Ibid.

25. Interagency Panel for Assessment of the National Agricultural Library, *Report on the National Agricultural Library* (Beltsville, MD: National Agricultural Library, 2001). Available at http://www.nal.usda.gov/assessment/contents.html (accessed February 17, 2008).

26. Barbara Hutchinson et al., *Collaboration and Cooperation among Libraries, Cooperative Extension and Agricultural Experiment Stations in Land-Grant Universities: The Results of a 2004–05 Survey* (2005). One of three reports prepared for the Planning Group for a Leadership Council for Agricultural Information and Outreach (USDA). Available at http://www.usain.org/library_extensioncollab/Collaboration ReportFinal6–05.pdf (accessed February 27, 2008).

27. In particular, these meetings would not have been possible without the assistance of University of Arizona Dean of Libraries, Carla Stoffle, and Director of Arizona Cooperative Extension, James Christenson.

28. Planning Group, Meeting Summary, and Draft Plan (Beltsville, MD: National Agricultural Library, Planning Group for the Leadership Council for Agricultural Information and Outreach, 2006). Available at http://www.agnic.org/about/leadership/january-2006-meeting-beltsville-md/meeting-notes-and-draft-plan-jan-2006.doc (accessed February 17, 2008).

29. Hutchinson et al., *Collaboration and Cooperation among Libraries, Cooperative Extension and Agricultural Experiment Stations in Land-Grant Universities.*

30. Ibid.; Gardner et al., *Partnering for Improved Access to Agricultural Information.*

31. Further details on AgNIC collaborations are available on the AgNIC Web site, http://www.agnic.org/about/.

32. Jones, Ruyle, and Hutchinson, "Building a Collaborative AgNIC site as an Outreach Model."

33. National Agricultural Library, Project Proposal for Iowa Communications Network Pilot Project.

34. General Services Administration, Memorandum of Understanding between The General Services Administration and The Arizona Board of Regents, on behalf of Arizona State University (Washington, DC: General Services Administration, March 9, 1995).

35. General Services Administration, Interagency Agreement between the General Services Administration and The U.S. Department of Agriculture National Agricultural Library (Washington, DC: General Services Administration, April 14, 1995).

36. National Agricultural Library, Cooperative Agreement: Develop More Advanced Approaches to Disseminating Electronic Information (Beltsville, MD: National Agricultural Library, September 29, 1995).

37. Ibid, 4.

38. National Agricultural Library, *Progress Report on the Agriculture Network Information Center Project* (Beltsville, MD: National Agricultural Library, 1996); Jeanne L. Pfander, Y. Han, L. Wyatt, and M. S. Bracke. "Full-text Online Access to Society for Range Management Journals," *Rangelands* 28, no. 1 (2006): 46–48; Society for Range Management, Memorandum of Agreement between The Society for Range Management and The Arizona Board of Regents on behalf of The University of Arizona Library (Wheat Ridge, CO: Society for Range Management, 1996).

39. National Agricultural Library, Cooperative Agreement.

40. Barbara S. Hutchinson and George B. Ruyle, "Wired without the Barbs: Using the Internet for Rangeland Information," *Rangelands* 22, no. 6 (2000): 19–22; Barbara Hutchinson and George B. Ruyle, "Partnering for Better Management of Western Rangelands: Using Web Technologies to Get the Word out," *Journal of Agricultural and Food Information* 4, no. 3 (2003): 75–89; Jones, Ruyle, and Hutchinson, "Building a Collaborative AgNIC Site as an Outreach Model."

41. Barbara Hutchinson, Jeanne Pfander, and M. Haseltine, "Rangeland Management Information on the Web," *Arizona's Ranchers Guide* (Tucson, AZ: Cooperative Extension, 2001).

42. Arizona Rangelands, About Section (2008). Available at http://rangeland swest.org/jsp/module/az/about/about.jsp# (accessed February 27, 2008).

43. Jones, Ruyle, and Hutchinson, "Building a Collaborative AgNIC Site as an Outreach Model"; Hutchinson and Ruyle, "Wired without the Barbs."

44. Jones, Ruyle, and Hutchinson, "Building a Collaborative AgNIC Site as an Outreach Model," 132.

45. Ibid.

46. Colorado State University, Idaho State University, Kansas State University, Montana State University, New Mexico State University, North Dakota State University, Oklahoma State University, Oregon State University, South Dakota State University, Texas A&M; University of Alaska; University of Arizona; University of California, Davis and Berkeley; University of Hawaii, University of Nebraska-Lincoln, University of Nevada-Reno, University of Wyoming, Utah State University, and Washington State University.

47. See Annual Reports for 2006 and 2007 at http://rangelandswest.org/jsp/about/meetings/2007/index.jsp (accessed February 27, 2008).

48. Note that two respondents indicated both academic and extension affiliation and another two indicated both academic/library affiliation.

49. Word Spy (http://www.wordspy.com/words/born-digital.asp) defines "born-digital" as "relating to a document that was created and exists only in a digital format."

50. Reborn digital content is defined here as content that was first incarnated in physical, typically print, format and has been converted to digital format via a scanning (often with OCR software) process.

51. L. Eells, "Born-Digital Agricultural Resources: Archives and Issues," *Agricultural Information Worldwide* 52, no. 3 (2008): 67–82; R. Heatley, *Plan to Develop a Digital Information Infrastructure to Manage Land Grant Information* (Michigan State University, 2007), available at http://www.adec.edu/whats-new.html (accessed February 17, 2008); R. Heatley, *Potential Areas for Collaboration within a Digital Land Grant Information System* (Michigan State University, 2005), available at http://www.usain.org/library_extensioncollab/Heatleycollab.html (accessed February 17, 2008).

52. Austin, *The Collaboration Challenge*; Linden, *Working across Boundaries*.

CONCLUSION

12

OTHER PERSPECTIVES AND CONCLUDING THOUGHTS

Peter Hernon, Ronald R. Powell, and Amy F. Fyn

As this book highlights, convergence and collaboration can occur within libraries and involve different units on campus and beyond. Such cooperation need not be focused exclusively on technology and can, for example, represent a dedication of library space to an activity such as a poetry center that builds on historical links to an academic department (Chapter 10). In an innovative publishing strategy, the University of Michigan Library, Press, and Scholarly Publishing Office recently announced a collaborative program in which the Press's *Digital Culture* imprint will both sell books and offer the full text of those books on its Web site. Chapter 11 offers yet another perspective, that of libraries collaborating with other university libraries and the national government. Convergence and collaboration underscore the evolution of libraries from the historical perspective that is collection focused to a blending of services and roles that help the institution better accomplish its mission. The library becomes a facilitator and dedicates space and resources to, in effect, provide one-stop shopping that enables students to gain the academic support they need to complete their programs of study and to graduate. Convergence and collaboration can change the perspective of a library while at the same time reinforcing the view of library as a place—"a place for students and faculty to read and study, to gather and deliberate, and to question, challenge and support one another."[1]

Convergence and collaboration have also appeared in the integration of communications and computing resources and services. In an article considering this model of convergence, the authors identify reasons for pursuing convergence, most of which apply to the other models treated in this book. They conclude that the "primary reasons for pursuing convergence are to achieve operational efficiencies and to provide additional or enhanced services,"[2] and that "cost and infrastructure requirements are the top inhibitors."[3]

From the perspective of information literacy, defined as "an intellectual framework for identifying, finding, understanding, evaluating and using information" ethically and legally,[4] academic libraries have been collaborating with other campus units for some time. In *Developing Research and Communication Skills: Guidelines for Information Literacy in the Curriculum*, the Middle States Commission on Higher Education sees that framework as having "relevance for faculty members, librarians, students, administrators, and the institution as a whole." Furthermore, "information can serve as a framework for linking together and enhancing the various expectations for student learning at the institution, program, and classroom levels."[5] In addressing technologies, this overview document explains,

As technologies continue to transform learning, it is important to separate the technological tools used to access information from the skills of understanding and using the content of that information. Technology is a part of the overall process but not an endpoint.[6]

The Middle States Commission on Higher Education views information literacy as an evolving concept, one that individual institutions can define, and as a shared responsibility between teaching faculty and librarians. The Commission encourages faculty members to collaborate with each other and librarians. This collaboration is integral to the effectiveness of information literacy as a student learning outcome. It is this collaboration that must be nurtured and the evidence gathered used to improve the learning process.

PERSPECTIVES OF NON-LIBRARIANS

Since convergence does involve many units on campus besides the library; an examination of this topic from the perspective of non-library units should provide a more balanced understanding of the trends, underlying issues, and concerns. Some libraries included in the survey reported in the first chapter are engaged in partnerships with other campus units. Ten individuals from those other units were surveyed via e-mail with the aim of learning more about convergence from the perspective of non-library units, why the collaboration was initiated, and how they think it is faring. Two of the non-librarians contacted were no longer affiliated with the institutions, and five of the remaining eight individuals responded to three questions:

1. For what reasons did your campus unit decide to collaborate with the campus library?
2. How would you describe and assess that collaboration thus far?
3. Do you have any other comments on the issue of academic libraries' converging and collaborating with other campus units/services?

Why Collaborate?

Given the perspective of this book and the survey, much of the collaboration involves libraries and information technology (IT) units. Collaboration might require pooling resources to purchase microcomputers in a bulk sale, but it is not undertaken solely to produce cost efficiencies. Both partners want their constituent groups to be able to use different technologies and software packages, be able to locate and retrieve information in different formats, and use IT support services for their teaching, research, and completion of assignments. A motive for collaboration might be pedagogical and helping students to learn. Those students might have disabilities, might use technology to relax or communicate with their friends and others, and might engage in group activities. Both the teaching faculty and librarians must be aware of how students learn and be responsive.

Hamilton College

David Smallen, Hamilton College's Vice President for Information Technology, explains the motive for collaboration thusly:

> Knowledge is a critical resource. Leaders must know how to collaborate with others to access, evaluate, synthesize, and analyze information to create knowledge. They must then make decisions based upon that knowledge and communicate those decisions in a compelling manner. This ability to transform information into knowledge is the basis of an information-literate citizen. Librarians and technologists have critical roles to play in assisting students to develop this literacy. We recognized this and believed that together we could do more than we can independently. Thus, [this is the reason for] our strategic partnership with the library. This partnership is focused on achieving Hamilton's goals of developing excellence in students' communication skills and providing them with the necessary skills to be information literate citizens.

The recognition of the similarity of the roles played by both librarians and members of IT departments to increase students' abilities in processing and synthesizing information and knowledge encourages a strong partnership at Hamilton College. Smallen clearly expressed the rationale behind joint ventures of libraries and Information Technology: "I think that library/IT partnerships are essential for delivering the highest level of support to faculty and students." As the two major academic support organizations on campus, finding ways to work effectively together is in the best interests of the institution and the constituents it serves.

Hamilton College's Instructional Technology Support Services Director, Nikki Reynolds, adds that, beyond the physicality of shared space, the sharing of skills and functions led to collaboration. Further,

> Hamilton College ITS has always been located within the library. As computer use changed and spread through the years, we began to notice functional overlaps between

the Library and ITS. Ultimately, the Director of the Libraries and the Vice President for IT jointly decided that faculty and students would benefit [if] we collaborated, particularly at the level of the Reference Librarians and the Instructional Technology team. We began by trying to offer coordinated support to faculty in course design, and design of student assignments within courses. We moved from there to coordinated support for student work, particularly through our Multimedia Presentation Center (MPC). Most recently, we have moved to create an Information Commons, to provide a single point of contact for information support needs of all types.

The collaboration centered on the faculty and their views on what they wanted the students in their classes to do and accomplish.

Vanderbilt University

Patricia Armstrong, Assistant Director of the Center for Teaching at Vanderbilt University, built on the comments made at Hamilton College by mentioning

There are many reasons why the Center for Teaching (CFT), a faculty, TA, and instructional development center, chose to collaborate with the Vanderbilt University Library. First, we are deeply committed to collaboration at the individual, departmental, and institutional levels and enjoy working with other units on campus to provide quality programming and services to the University community and to foster growth and change. Second, the kinds of support services that the CFT provides to faculty members, in particular, as well as graduate students complement those provided by the Library to those same constituencies. Third, as more and more libraries are exploring alternative models such as a learning commons, it is important that pedagogical centers such as ours participate as partners in that exploration given that academic support units are "natural neighbors" with library units in such learning commons. Finally, as librarians are called upon more and more to provide instructional services, the CFT is committed to serving librarians—as we do faculty and graduate students—in their instructional roles.

The CFT's commitment to collaborate with other campus partners at any level was part of the motivation to work with the university library. The two units have a similar service perspective that facilitated collaborative projects.

Active interest and involvement in transforming the library to serve faculty and students better as scholarly communication and information-seeking behavior change has shown that both the CFT and the library do not want to be static in how they support their constituent groups. Recognizing that librarians are also instructors, the CFT offered its instructional support services to the librarians.

Johns Hopkins University

From its inception, the Center for Educational Resources (CER) has partnered with campus librarians to provide service to faculty. As more schools on campus joined with the CER, the Center shifted focus as Mike Reese, Assistant Director of the Center for Educational Resources, explains:

When the Center for Educational Resources was founded 5 years ago, we employed 3 staff to support over 400 faculty in Krieger School of Arts and Science at Johns Hopkins. To provide excellent service to such a large number of faculty we knew we would need to partner with other groups. We began working with librarians because of their existing relationship with faculty. Three years later, the Whiting School of Engineering requested to become a full partner of our Center so engineering faculty could access CER services. Our Center changed its administrative reporting from the Krieger School of Arts and Sciences to the Library so that we reported to a central division that already supported both schools. We transitioned smoothly to this new reporting arrangement because we had already developed a strong working relationship with our librarian and library staff colleagues.

The CER successfully capitalized on the relationships that librarians built as part of their effort to support learning.

University of Michigan–Dearborn

The challenges of student retention are addressed by combining efforts between the library and Enrollment Services. Linda Brown, Assistant Vice Chancellor of the Office of the Registrar, notes that:

First you must understand that we have a "non traditional" Library and Library Staff. Our library is more focused on "student retention" than most libraries. When attempting to "shock" our students by "exceeding their expectations" we think first of the Library Staff. Most of what we in Enrollment services collaborate with the Library with includes new student arrival and continuing student services... [S]ome of the things we are working on with the Library including the "new admit Library access," "help with H.S. Senior research papers," etc. The Library is the number 1 collaborator in the SummerPathways (new student employment initiative).

By partnering with the library, the Enrollment Services department is able to offer students a tangible way to increase their likelihood of doing well in their classes. Focusing on retaining students by giving them the tools they need to succeed in classes demonstrates how cooperation between disparate units can have a significant impact on a campus. Highlighting the library staff as a front-line service provider and relating library experiences with retention recognizes the customer-service aspects of library service, and effectively ties them into recruiting and retaining students. The university administration recognizes the support offered by the library and found ways to enhance students' experiences.

The School of Education partnered with the library in a bid to receive a collection of children's books from the Grand Rapids (MI) Public Library. The partnership with the library lent additional credibility to the School of

Education's request to receive the collection, and the university won the bid. The collection, known as The May G. Quigley Collection of Children's Literature, is housed in Mardigian Library. The research librarians aided in the introduction of this collection, and cataloging staff processed the materials, making them available for use in the library.

Assessment of Collaboration

Overwhelmingly, non-librarians responded positively when evaluating their collaboration with their campus library. Several participants mentioned unexpected benefits resulting from the partnerships with the library.

Hamilton College

Smallen describes the collaboration between the departments on campus as a partnership, demonstrating the equal input each unit has in joint projects. The joint venture has led to increased opportunities to serve the campus community;

This partnership has been very successful, both in terms of the support provided to faculty and students and the development of collaboratively supported facilities (the Multimedia Presentation Center and the Information Commons). I think the hard work that individuals in these two organizations have done over the last five years has put us far ahead of our peers in the quality of the collaborative support librarians and technologists provide. This support has been institutionalized through joint working committees and processes.

Vanderbilt University

Collaboration has been an asset to the Center for Teaching. Interaction between the staff of the two campus units has increased and offered more opportunities to work together in other ventures as well as to create new professional opportunities. Armstrong describes the current collaboration as:

Active and fruitful! The director of the Center for Teaching has collaborated for many years with the University Librarian to develop a plan for a learning commons at Vanderbilt. The University Librarian sits on the CFT advisory board and is in frequent contact with the director of the CFT about library initiatives. One of the assistant directors at the CFT has worked closely for 18 months with an area and now instructional librarian at our central library. They have developed and facilitate pedagogical workshops both at Vanderbilt and for a national conference and are co-chairing the newly-founded Committee on Undergraduate Information Literacy. With this committee they are spearheading information literacy initiatives on campus that support and deepen such initiatives already in place in the Peabody College of Education and Human Development at Vanderbilt.

Additional benefits gained by the library in working with other campus departments are the goodwill of non-library departments and the heightened awareness of the usefulness of the library on campus. As Armstrong comments,

It is not unheard of for the hard work of librarians to remain invisible and so unheralded at research universities. We at the CFT are hopeful that our collaborations with Vanderbilt's librarians will help them to gain more exposure and recognition for the valuable contributions they make to the intellectual life of our campus.

As the units continue to work together, there are more opportunities to work cooperatively on other projects and to develop new sets of goals. The familiarity gained from working as a group can make the next project or undertaking easier. A string of successful ventures, she notes, makes the next goals more attainable.

Johns Hopkins University

The collaboration between the Center for Educational Resources and the library has provided further opportunity for working together with colleagues across departmental lines. Reese, who is enthusiastic about the continued opportunities for staff from both units, points out that:

The success to date has been overwhelming. The Center for Educational Resources staff have presented with their librarian colleagues at several conferences (both library and teaching-oriented) on the effectiveness of a project development model that includes staff from both departments. In addition, the CER is currently pursuing grant opportunities with our library colleagues to support technology development that will support both research and teaching.

The attainment of the educational mission of universities and colleges depends, in part, on the support of departments. By creating a continuum among support services, the faculty and students receive the best service possible. Studying and implementing ways to complement the services of another department enhances the services that each department offers individually. Reese goes on to state:

Teaching and learning centers, like the CER, and librarians share a common mission of supporting faculty. In addition, both groups must meet the challenge of a study cohort that continually becomes more sophisticated users of information and expect more engaging learning environments. While staff expertise differs, it is complementary. Librarians, instructional designers, and educational technologists can work better by working together. In the end, the faculty and students benefit by receiving more integrated, well-designed service and resources.

The University of Michigan–Dearborn

The benefits of collaboration have also spread beyond the two campus units. According to Brown, "The collaboration has greatly benefited Enrollment Services in our efforts to impact student retention but I think the collaboration has benefited our entering and continuing students more." She believes the library has undergone many changes during her tenure at the university, and she adds:

When I first came to U of M Dearborn in 1975 a student could be "expelled" for bringing a candy bar into the Library. Listening to the Student Affairs Directors and hearing what students need, the Head Librarian (Director of Services, Tim Richards) changed everything we thought we knew about Libraries. He and his staff are involved in [working with] students and student success far beyond providing books and periodicals. They are involved in all aspects of our campus.

Other Comments

Additional opportunities to build on prior collaborations also help to promote student success at Hamilton College. Reynolds notes that:

The collaboration is going well, and is gradually becoming deeper. For example, for some courses we now offer "open labs" in which the students in the course come to the MPC [Multimedia Presentation Center] to work on the project during a particular time. During that time, both an Instructional Technologist and a Reference Librarian will be on hand to answer questions about the development of the student's project. Most of the time, the faculty member is also present, making for an ideal collaboration in support of the students' successful completion of the project.

The Hamilton model clearly expresses the interplay between the instructional technologist and the reference librarian, indicating both play important roles in furthering student learning. Another benefit is the increased contact with faculty and opportunities to work collaboratively with them.

Collaborations are often not simple, easy, or seamless, however. Reynolds offered an honest assessment of the behind-the-scenes efforts that must be expended when working with outside groups:

Of course, there have been bumps along the way, and in the early days, moments when the Librarians or the Technologists wanted to give up the idea of collaboration. We have persistently worked through these stressed periods, and the collaboration continues to improve and deepen with each joint project. We still expect some cultural clashes, or differences in particular goals between units, but we also expect we can talk our way through to some compromise.

Understandably, collaboration among departments whose tasks and mission are not identical may result in some friction. Misunderstandings and

OTHER PERSPECTIVES AND CONCLUDING THOUGHTS 209

misconceptions must be addressed and resolved before the units can move forward. Realistic expectations about the level of support paraprofessionals and student workers can provide are also important. As Reynolds points out, the common denominators for these specific groups may be knowledge and technology, but the ways in which each group uses those denominators differ. She thinks that:

> The degree to which the librarians are deep users of technology has a significant effect on the discussions between the two units. Being proficient at using the Microsoft Office products is usually not enough to allow librarians to understand some of the support challenges their IT counterparts face. Getting to the point where librarians are willing to accept the statement that "I'm sorry, but I can't fix that" about some technology problems is important. Also, the extent to which models of using students to augment professional staff are aligned has a significant impact on working relationships. If these two areas can be bridged early in the process, a few "bumps" can be reduced or eliminated.

Each group must recognize that the other has limitations, whether it is staff hours, budgetary constraints, or spheres of knowledge. To keep everyone involved and invested, collaborations often take a little more care to smooth over trouble spots. Staffing is a key consideration. If two departments collaborate but leave the implementation to under- or untrained student employees working alone on evening and weekends, the venture has less opportunity to succeed.

Summary

The reasons to collaborate with the library are many; however, the desired results are similar. All campus units want to improve and enhance the services they offer. Libraries want to support other campus units and departments in their efforts. They both want to further the educational mission of the parent institution. Collaborative efforts develop from these overlapping needs. According to several study participants, two ingredients needed in a successful collaboration are respect and recognition. Each unit must have respect for the work that the other unit does, both separately and within the partnership. Recognition of the ability of librarians to enhance the services of other support units is often overlooked. If the contributions of each partner are acknowledged, a more respectful approach to collaboration that places the collaborative partners on equal footing can develop.

CONCLUSION

Table 12.1 serves as a reminder that there has been interest in convergence and collaboration, as defined and illustrated in this book, for more than a decade. The literature will continue to grow and libraries will remain

Table 12.1
Selected Readings on Convergence and Collaboration

Bailey, D. Russell, and Barbara G. Tierney. *Transforming Library Services through Information Commons: Case Studies for the Digital Age.* Chicago: American Library Association, 2008.

Beagle, Donald R. *The Information Commons Handbook,* with contributions by Donald R. Bailey and Barbara Tierney. New York: Neal-Schuman Publishers, 2006.

Bhatt, Jay, Joanne Ferroni, Bob Kackley, and Dorilona Rose. "Drexel University, the University of Maryland and Their Libraries' Experiences Collaborating with Various Research Programs." *New Review of Information Networking* 11, no. 1 (2005): 83–98.

Bishoff, Liz. "The Collaboration Imperative: If Librarians Want to Lead in Creating the Digital Future, They Need to Learn How to Work with Their Colleagues in Museums and Archives." *Library Journal* 129, no. 1 (2004): 34.

Boxall, James. "Geographers, Librarians and Spatial Collaboration." *The Canadian Geographer* 47, no. 1 (2003): 18–27.

Dallis, Diane, and Carolyn Walters. "Reference Services in the Commons Environment." *Reference Services Review* 34, no. 2 (2006): 248–60.

Davenport, Nancy. "Place as Library?" *Educause Review* 41, no. 1 (2006): 12–13.

Diedriech, David, and Lynda LaRoche. "Creating a Collaborative Environment: Instructional and Learning Services." *Proceedings of the 2005 ASCUE Conference* (2005): 94–98. Available at http://www.juniata.edu/faculty/fusco/ascue2005/papers/p94.pdf (accessed November 15, 2007).

Furlough, Michael. "University Presses and Scholarly Communication; Potential for Collaboration." *College & Research Libraries News* 69, no. 1 (January 2008): 32–36.

Hess, Charlotte, and Garald Bernbom. "INforum: A Library/IT Collaboration in Professional Development at Indiana University." *Cause/Effect* 17, no. 3 (1994): 13–18.

Hope, Charity B., and Christina A. Peterson. "The Sum Is Greater than the Parts: Cross-Institutional Collaboration for Information Literacy in Academic Libraries." *Journal of Library Administration* 36, nos. 1–2 (2002): 21–38.

Hutchins, Elizabeth O., Barbara Fister, and Kris MacPherson. "Changing Landscapes, Enduring Values: Making the Transition from Bibliographic Instruction to Information Literacy." *Journal of Library Administration* 36, nos. 1–2 (2002): 3–19.

Jackson, Shaun, Carol Hansen, and Lauren Fowler. "Using Selected Assessment Data to Inform Information Literacy Program Planning with Campus Partners." *Research Strategies* 20, nos. 1–2 (2004): 44–56.

Lippincott, Joan K. "New Library Facilities: Opportunities for Collaboration." *Resource Sharing and Information Networks* 17, nos. 1/2 (2004): 147–57.

Marshalsay, Barbara. "Convergence and Resurgence: The Integration of Academic Libraries and Computing Centres." *Canadian Journal of Information and Library Science* 23, no. 4 (1998): 28–61.

Sayers, Richard. "Open Relationships, de-facto Marriages, or Shotgun Weddings? The Convergence and Integration of Libraries and Computing/information Technology Services within Australian Universities." *Australian Library Journal* 50, no. 1 (2001): 53–71.

Table 12.1
(Continued)

Swartz, Pauline S., Brian A. Carlisle, and E. Chisato Uyeki. "Libraries and Student Affairs: Partners for Student Success." *Reference Services Review* 35, no. 1 (2007): 109–22.
Wilson, Kerry, and Eddie Halpin. "Convergence and Professional Identity in the Academic Library." *Journal of Librarianship and Information Science* 38, no. 2 (2006): 79–91.
Young, Arthur P. "Information Technology and Libraries: A Virtual Convergence." *Cause/Effect* 17, no. 3 (1994): 5–6, 12.

---

complex organizations that assume new roles, services, and responsibilities. Jerry D. Campbell, in his highly regarded "Changing a Cultural Icon: The Academic Library as a Virtual Destination," writes,

Numerous creative and useful services have evolved within academic libraries in the digital age: providing quality learning spaces; creating metadata; offering virtual reference services; teaching information literacy; choosing resources and managing resource licenses; collecting and digitizing archival materials; and maintaining digital repositories. For the most part, these services are derivative and diffuse. They grew out of the original mission of the academic library. As a group, they do not constitute a fundamental purpose for the future library, and they lack the ringing clarity of the well-known historic mission in which they are rooted. However, considered individually and investigated more closely, some or one of them may indeed prove to hold the key to the future of the academic library.[7]

He concludes, "the academy may be able to maintain much of the ineffable, inspirational value associated with academic libraries while retaining their practical value through altogether transformed activities and functions built upon a new mission designed for a more digital world."[8]

This book addresses some of those transformed activities and functions and the editors invite a discussion of what comprises a library, a topic that students in schools of library and information science, as well as others, need to understand. Yet what is truly exciting is that this new perspective of the library does not fully represent what academic libraries have become. Undoubtedly, as this century progresses, the foundations identified in this book will expand and demonstrate new strategic directions—ones that will make the library even more integral to campus life.

NOTES

1. Suffolk University, Sawyer Library, "Long-Range Plan: Strategic Directions July 1, 2005—June 30, 2010" (Boston: Sawyer Library, 2005). Available at http://www.suffolk.edu/files/SawLib/2005–2010-strat-plan.pdf (accessed February 28, 2008).

2. Mike Enyeart, E. Michael Staman, and Jose J. Valdes Jr., "Convergence Is Real," *EDUCAUSE Review* 42, no. 2 (March/April 2007), 47.
3. Ibid., 49.
4. Middle States Commission on Higher Education, *Developing Research and Communication Skills: Guidelines for Information Literacy in the Curriculum* (Philadelphia, PA: Middle States Commission on Higher Education, 2003), 1.
5. Ibid.
6. Ibid., 5.
7. Jerry D. Campbell, "Changing a Cultural Icon: The Academic Library as a Virtual Destination," *EDUCAUSE Review* 41, no. 1 (January/February 2006): 16–30.
8. Ibid., 31.

BIBLIOGRAPHY

ARTICLES

Albanese, Andrew Richard. "Campus Library 2.0," *Library Journal* 129, no. 7 (April 15, 2004): 30–33.

Bailey, Russell, and Barbara Tierney. "Information Commons Redux: Concept, Evolution, and Transcending the Tragedy of the Commons," *The Journal of Academic Librarianship* 28, no. 5 (September 2002): 277–86.

Beagle, Donald. "Learning Beyond the Classroom: Envisioning the Information Commons' Future: Conference Report," *Library Hi Tech News* 21, no. 10 (2004): 4–6.

Beagle, Donald. "Extending the Information Commons: From Instructional Testbed to Internet2," *The Journal of Academic Librarianship* 28, no. 5 (September 2002): 287–96.

Bolin, Mary. "The Library and the Computer Center: Organizational Patterns at Land Grant Universities," *The Journal of Academic Librarianship* 31, no. 1 (2005): 3–11.

Brewer, Gordon. "Convergence for the Right Reasons," *Multimedia Information and Technology* 29, no. 4 (November 2003): 107–109.

Campbell, Jerry D. "Changing a Cultural Icon: The Academic Library as a Virtual Destination," *EDUCAUSE Review* 41, no. 1 (January/February 2006): 16–30.

Campbell, Nancy F., and Threasa L. Wesley. "Collaborative Dialogue: Repositioning the Academic Library," *portal: Libraries and the Academy* 6, no. 1 (2006): 93–98.

Church, Jennifer. "The Evolving Information Commons," *Library Hi Tech* 23, no. 1 (2005): 75–81.

Cowgill, Allison, Joan Beam, and Lindsey Wess. "Implementing an Information Commons in a University Library," *The Journal of Academic Librarianship* 27, no. 6 (November 2001): 432–39.

Coyle, Karen. "The Future of Library Systems, Seen from the Past," *The Journal of Academic Librarianship* 33, no. 1 (2007): 138–40.

Dewey, Barbara I. "The Embedded Librarian: Strategic Campus Collaborations," *Resource Sharing and Information Networks* 17, nos. 1/2 (2004): 5–17.

Eells, L. "Born-Digital Agricultural Resources: Archives and Issues," *Agricultural Information Worldwide* 52, no. 3 (2008): 67–82.

Enyeart, Mike E., Michael Staman, and Jose J. Valdes Jr. "Convergence Is Real," *EDUCAUSE Review* 42, no. 2 (March/April 2007): 46–66.

Feng, Cyril C.H., and Frieda O. Weise. "Library/Computer Center Partnership," *Journal of the American Society for Information Science* 39, no. 2 (1988): 126–30.

Fliss, Susan. "Collaborative Creativity: Supporting Teaching and Learning on Campus," *College & Research Libraries News* 66, no. 5 (May 2005): 378–80.

Hattwig, Denise L. "The UW Image Bank: A Libraries and Visual Resources Digital Image Collaboration at the University of Washington, Part I," *Visual Resources Association Bulletin* 31, no. 3 (Spring 2005): 31–34.

Holmes, Gerald V., and Charna K. Howson. "Grants: Interdepartmental Collaboration to Teach Grantsmanship Skills," *The Bottom Line: Managing Library Finances* 13 (2000): 146–49.

Hutchinson, Barbara, and George B. Ruyle. "Partnering for Better Management of Western Rangelands: Using Web Technologies to Get the Word Out," *Journal of Agricultural and Food Information* 4, no. 3 (2003): 75–89.

Hutchinson, Barbara S., and George B. Ruyle. "Wired without the Barbs: Using the Internet for Rangeland Information," *Rangelands* 22, no. 6 (2000): 19–22.

Jacobson, Trudi E. "Partnerships between Library Instruction Units and Campus Teaching Centers," *The Journal of Academic Librarianship* 27, no. 4 (July 2001): 311–16.

Jones, Douglas E., George Ruyle, and Barbara Hutchinson. "Building a Collaborative AgNIC Site as an Outreach Model: Rangelands of the Western U.S.," *The Reference Librarian* 39, no. 82 (2003): 125–40.

Kratz, Charles. "Transforming the Delivery of Service," *College & Research Libraries News* 64, no. 2 (February 2003): 100–101.

Lippincott, Joan K. "New Library Facilities: Opportunities for Collaboration," *Resource Sharing and Information Networks* 17, nos. 1/2 (2004): 147–57.

MacWhinnie, Laurie A. "The Information Commons: The Academic Library of the Future," *portal: Libraries and the Academy* 3, no. 2 (April 2003): 241–57.

Miller, Rush. "What Difference Do We Make?" *The Journal of Academic Librarianship* 33, no. 2 (2007): 1–2.

Miller, William. "Introduction: Cooperation within Institutions," *Resource Sharing and Information Networks* 17, nos. 1/2 (2004): 1–3.

Mullins, James L., Frank R. Allen, and Jon R. Hufford. "Top Ten Assumptions for the Future of Academic Libraries and Librarians: A Report from the ACRL Research Committee," *College & Research Libraries News* 68, no. 4 (2007): 240–41, 246.

Pfander, Jeanne L., Y. Han, L. Wyatt, and M. S. Bracke. "Full-text Online Access to Society for Range Management Journals," *Rangelands* 28, no. 1 (2006): 46–48.

Riggs, Donald E. "New Libraries Remain an Excellent Investment," *College & Research Libraries* 63, no. 2 (March 2002): 108–109.
Rutherford, Shauna, K. Alix Hayden, and Paul R. Pival. "WISPR (Workshop on the Information Search Process for Research) in the Library," *Journal of Library Administration* 45, no. 3–4 (2006): 427–43.
Walters, Tyler O. "Reinventing the Library—How Repositories Are Causing Librarians to Rethink Their Professional Roles," *portal: Libraries and the Academy* 7, no. 2 (2007): 213–25.

BOOKS

Association of Research Libraries. SPEC Kit 292: *Institutional Repositories*. Washington, DC: ARL, 2006.
Austin, James E. *The Collaboration Challenge: How Non-Profits and Businesses Succeed through Strategic Alliances*. San Francisco: Jossey-Bass, 2000.
Brown, John Seely, and Paul Duguid. *The Social Life of Information*. Boston: Harvard Business School Press, 2000.
Elmborg, James K., and Sheril Hook (Ed.). *Centers for Learning: Writing Centers and Libraries*, ACRL Publications in Librarianship no. 58. Chicago: Association of College and Research Libraries, 2005.
Franklin, Stephen D., and Ellen Stenski. *Building University Electronic Educational Environments*. Norwell, MA: Kluwer Academic Publishers, 1999.
Hanson, Terry, ed. *Managing Academic Support Services in Universities: The Convergence Experience*. London: Facet, 2005.
Kuhlthau, Carol C. *Seeking Meaning: A Process Approach to Library and Information Services*, 2nd ed. Westport, CT: Libraries Unlimited, 2004.
Linden, Russell M. *Working across Boundaries: Making Collaboration Work in Government and Nonprofit Organizations*. San Francisco: Jossey-Bass, 2002.
Shapiro, Debra. *E-Scholarship*. A LITA [Library and Information Technology Association] Guide No. 12. Chicago: American Library Association, 2005.
Wells, Amy T., Susan Calcari, and Travis Koplow, eds. *The Amazing Internet Challenge: How Leading Projects Use Library Skills to Organize the Web*. Chicago: American Library Association, 1999.
Zieman, Irving Pergament. *Founders to Bounders: Boston in Rhyme*. Cambridge, MA: Starr Books, 1961.

BOOK CHAPTERS

Hutchinson, Barbara, Jeanne Pfander, and M. Haseltine. "Rangeland Management Information on the Web," In *Arizona's Ranchers Guide*. Tucson, AZ: Cooperative Extension, 2001.
Nitecki, Danuta A., and William Rando, "Evolving an Assessment of the Impact on Pedagogy, Learning, and Library Support of Teaching with Digital Images," In *Outcomes Assessment in Higher Education: Views and Perspectives,* edited by Peter Hernon and Robert E. Dugan. Westport, CT: Libraries Unlimited, 2004.

DISSERTATIONS

Lippincott, Joan K. *Collaboration between Librarians and Information Technologists: A Case Study Employing Kolb's Experiential Learning Theory.* College Park, MD: University of Maryland, Department of Education Policy, Planning, and Administration, 1999.

REPORTS

Hawkins, Brian L., and Patricia Battin, eds. *The Mirage of Continuity: Reconfiguring Academic Information Resources for the 21st Century.* Washington, DC: Council on Library and Information Resources and Association of American Universities, 1998.

WEB RESOURCES

Adams, Michael. "State of the University Address." Athens, GA: University of Georgia, 2004. Available at http://www.uga.edu/news-bin/artman/exec/view.cgi?archive=7&num=977 (accessed March 5, 2008).

Adams, Michael. "State of the University Address." Athens, GA: University of Georgia, 2008. Available at http://www.uga.edu/news/artman/publish/080117SOTU2008_text.shtml (accessed March 5, 2008).

Agriculture Network Information Center. *About Section* (2008). Available at http://www.agnic.org/about (accessed February 17, 2008).

Agriculture Network Information Center. *Draft Concept and Prototype Pilot Project* (1994). Available at http://www.agnic.org/about/leadership/background/DraftVision (accessed February 17, 2008).

Agriculture Network Information Center. By-Laws and Governance (2007). Available at http://www.agnic.org/about/facts/governance_2006_rev_2007.pdf (accessed February 17, 2008).

American Heritage Dictionary of the English Language. "Collaborate." 4th ed. Boston: Houghton Mifflin, 2000. Available at http://www.bartleby.com/61/ (accessed February 25, 2008).

Arizona Rangelands. About Section (2008). Available at http://rangelandswest.org/jsp/module/az/about/about.jsp# (accessed February 27, 2008).

Askren, Mark, and Marina Arseniev. "Combating Stovepipes: Implementing Workflow in uPortal," *EDUCAUSE Quarterly* 27, no. 2 (2004). Available at http://www.educause.edu/pub/eq/eqm04/eqm0429.asp (accessed August 17, 2007).

The Carnegie Classification of Institutions of Higher Education. Stanford, CA: The Carnegie Foundation for the Advancement of Teaching, 2006. Available at http://www.carnegiefoundation.org/classifications/ (accessed August 21, 2006).

Casey, Michael E., and Laura C. Savastinuk. "Library 2.0: Service for the Next-generation Library," *Library Journal.com* (September 1, 2006). Available at http://www.libraryjournal.com/article/CA6365200.html (accessed September 1, 2006).

Cloonan, Michele V., and John G. Dove. "Ranganathan Online: Do Digital Libraries Violate the Third Law?" *Library Journal.com* (April 1, 2005). Available at http://www.libraryjournal.com/article/CA512179.html (accessed August 17, 2007).

"Collaborative Facilities." Hanover, NH: Dartmouth College. Available at http://www.dartmouth.edu/~collab/ (accessed June 21, 2006).

"*Collections of Materials on Collaborative Spaces*," Planning Collaborative Spaces in Libraries: An ACRL/CNI Preconference, June 20, 2003. Available at http://www.cni.org/regconfs/acrlcni2003/resources.html (accessed June 21, 2006).

"Convergence," *Oxford English Dictionary*. Available at http://0-dictionary.oed.com.library.simmons.edu/cgi/entry/50049149?single=1&query_type=word&queryword=convergence&first=1&max_to_show=10 (accessed June 21, 2006).

Dempsey, Lorcan. "Lifting out the Catalog Discovery Experience." *Lorcan Dempsey's blog*. Available from http://orweblog.oclc.org/archives/001021.html (accessed May 14, 2006).

Dempsey, Lorcan. "Networkflows," *Lorcan Dempsey's blog*. Available at http://orWeblog.oclc.org/archives/000933.html (accessed January 28, 2006).

Duncan, Jim. "Convergence of Libraries, Digital Repositories and Management of Web Content" (October 11, 2004). Available at http://connect.educause.edu/library/abstract/convergenceoflibrari/37263 (accessed August 18, 2007).

Eberle-Sinatra, Michael. "Synergies: The Canadian Information Network for Research in the Social Sciences and Humanities" (poster presented at Digital Humanities 2007, Urbana-Champaign, IL) Abstract available at http://www.digitalhumanities.org/dh2007/abstracts/xhtml.xq?id=263 (accessed January 2008).

"eScholarship Repository" (California Digital Library, 2007). Available at http://repositories.cdlib.org/escholarship/more_about.html (accessed August 17, 2007).

Final Report of the Chancellor's Educational Technology Task Force. Irvine, CA: University of California, Irvine, 1996. Available at http://eee.uci.edu/about/_assets/EdTechTF.FR.html (accessed August 18, 2007).

Gardner, Melanie, Jean Gilbertson, Barbara Hutchinson, Tim Lynch, Janet McCue, and Amy Paster. *Partnering for Improved Access to Agricultural Information: The Agriculture Network Information Center (AgNIC) Initiative. ARL Bimonthly Report* 223 (2002). Available at http://www.arl.org/bm~doc/agnic1.pdf (accessed February 27, 2008).

"Georgia's Five Little Acres: The Student Learning Center at the University of Georgia." A PowerPoint presentation by William Gray Potter, presented at the Coalition of Networked Information Meeting, Spring 2004. Available at http://www.cni.org/tfms/2004a.spring/abstracts/PB-georgia-potter.html (accessed July 31, 2008).

Heatley, R. *Plan to Develop a Digital Information Infrastructure to Manage Land Grant Information*. Michigan State University, 2007. Available at http://www.adec.edu/whats-new.html (accessed February 17, 2008).

Heatley, R. *Potential Areas for Collaboration within a Digital Land Grant Information System*. Michigan State University, 2005. Available at http://www.usain.org/library_extensioncollab/Heatleycollab.html (accessed February 17, 2008).

Hutchinson, Barbara. *Major Agricultural Information Initiatives: With Emphasis on Developing Country Services*, prepared for Cornell University and the Gates Foundation for the WorldAgInfo Symposium, October 2007. Available at http://worldaginfo.org/files/Agricultural%20Information%20Initiatives.pdf (accessed February 17, 2008).

Hutchinson, Barbara, et al. *Collaboration and Cooperation among Libraries, Cooperative Extension and Agricultural Experiment Stations in Land-Grant*

Universities: The Results of a 2004–05 Survey (2005). One of three reports prepared for the Planning Group for a Leadership Council for Agricultural Information and Outreach (USDA). Available at http://www.usain.org/library_extensioncollab/CollaborationReportFinal6–05.pdf (accessed February 27, 2008).

Hutchinson, Barbara, et al. *Making the Case for a Next-Generation Digital Information System to Ensure America's Leadership in Agricultural Sciences in the 21st Century*. A Background Document. Commissioned by the United States Agricultural Information Network (USAIN). October 2006 (updated December 2007) (now available at http://www.usain.org/whitepaperfinal.pdf).

Interagency Panel for Assessment of the National Agricultural Library. *Report on the National Agricultural Library*. Beltsville, MD: National Agricultural Library, 2001. Available at http://www.nal.usda.gov/assessment/contents.html (accessed February 17, 2008).

Johnson, Richard K. "Institutional Repositories: Partnering with Faculty to Enhance Scholarly Communication," *D-LIB Magazine* 8, no. 11 (2002). Available at http://www.dlib.org/dlib/november02/johnson/11johnson.html (accessed August 17, 2007).

Kratz, Charles. "Transforming the Delivery of Service: The Joint-use Library and Information Commons," *College & Research Libraries News* 64 (February 2003). Available at http://www.ala.org/ala/acrl/acrlpubs/crlnews/backissues2003/february1/transforming.htm (accessed June 21, 2006).

Lippincott, Joan K. Homepage. Available at http://www.cni.org/staff/joan_publications.html (accessed June 21, 2006).

Lonsdale, M. *Global Gateways: A Guide to Online Knowledge Networks* (Australian Council for Educational Research, 2003). Available at http://www.educationau.edu.au/jahia/webdav/site/myjahiasite/shared/papers/global_gateways_v3.pdf (accessed February 27, 2008).

Molnar, J. J. "Using the Internet for Instruction: Experiences, Possibilities, and Considerations," *North American Colleges and Teachers of Agriculture (NACTA) Journal*. Available at http://findarticles.com/p/articles/mi_qa4062/is_200412/ai_n9472420/print (accessed February 17, 2008).

Multicultural Canada. "Canada's Multicultural Historical Resources Online." Available at http://www.multiculturalcanada.ca/ (accessed January 2008).

National Agricultural Library, Agriculture Network Information Center. AgNIC: Concept and Prototype Pilot Project (1994). Available at http://www.agnic.nal.usda.gov/agnic/agnic.html (accessed February 16, 2008).

National Agricultural Library. *Managing Electronic Information in Agriculture toward an Agriculture Network Information Center: A Model for Distributed Access*, 2. Summary Report of AgNIC Planning Workshop December 4, 5, and 6, 2004 (Washington, DC: National Agricultural Library. 1995). Available at http://www.agnic.org/about/proceedings/reports/agnicreports1294.htmlc (accessed February 16, 2008).

Nowick, E., and M. Gardner. "Getting It out There: A Cooperative Agricultural Network for Information Sharing," *Technical Services Quarterly* 19, no. 3 (2002): 41–49. Available at https://www.haworthpress.com/store/ArticleAbstract.asp?sid=2HRFU386L3SV9HJ7XSM8B4M8L82QB358&ID=4081 (accessed February 17, 2008).

Planning Group, Meeting Summary, and Draft Plan. Beltsville, MD: National Agricultural Library, Planning Group for the Leadership Council for Agricultural Information and Outreach, 2006. Available at http://www.agnic.org/about/leadership/january-2006-meeting-beltsville-md/meeting-notes-and-draft-plan-jan-2006.doc (accessed February 17, 2008).

Ricker, Shirley, and Isabel Kaplan. "Are We Crossing the Line? A Survey of Library and Writing Program Collaboration." PowerPoint presentation. Available at http://docushare.lib.rochester.edu/docushare/dsweb/Get/Document-22020 (accessed June 23, 2006).

"The 2003 OCLC Environmental Scan: Pattern Recognition: What Haven't You Noticed Lately?" Dublin, OH: OCLC, Inc., 2003. Available from http://www.oclc.org/reports/escan/toc.htm (accessed August 18, 2007).

"Top Technology Trends for Libraries: Y2K." Chicago, Library Information Technology Association, 2000. Available at http://www.ala.org/ala/lita/litaresources/toptechtrends/midwinter2000.cfm (accessed August 18, 2007).

University of Calgary. "Faculty Technology Days 2007." Available at http://www.ucalgary.ca/ftd/courses (accessed January 2008).

University of Calgary. Effective Writing Program, "Workshops." Available at http://www.efwr.ucalgary.ca/efwr/workshopsmain (accessed January 2008).

University of Calgary. Information Hub Planning Committee, "Information Hub Planning Document." Calgary, Canada: University of Calgary, 1998. Available at http://www.ucalgary.ca/IR/infocommons/(accessed January 2008).

University of Calgary. Library of the Future Task Force. Accelerating the Transformation of Information Resources, Section 2, The Transformation of the Library. Available at http://www.ucalgary.ca/lib-old/lftf/finalreport/transformation1.html (accessed January 2008).

University of Calgary. Library of the Future Task Force. "Accelerating the Transformation of Information Resources," Section 5. The Transformed Library. Available at http://www.ucalgary.ca/lib-old/lftf/finalreport/translibrary.html (accessed January 2008).

University of Calgary. Library Task Force. "Final Report: Section 1—Executive Summary and Recommendations." Available at http://www.ucalgary.ca/lib-old/ltf/report/recommend.html (accessed January 2008).

University of Calgary. Library Task Force. "Final Report—September 30 1997." Available at http://www.ucalgary.ca/lib-old/ltf/report/index.html (accessed January 2008).

University of Calgary. Office of the Provost and Vice-President (Academic). "Announcement: Changes in the Provost's Portfolio." Calgary, Canada: University of Calgary, n.d. Available at http://www.ucalgary.ca/provost/about/portfolio-changes (accessed January 2008).

University of Calgary. Strategic Transformation Coordination Task Force, "Design Teams Drafted." Available at http://www.ucalgary.ca/Transformation/Designteams.html (accessed January 2008).

University of Calgary. Strategic Transformation Coordination Task Force, "Situation Assessment." Available at http://www.ucalgary.ca/Transformation/insert1/Page4.html (accessed January 2008).

University of Kansas. "Collaborative Learning Spaces." Lawrence: University of Kansas. Available at http://www.ku.edu/~hvc2/colloblearning.shtml (accessed June 21, 2006).

University of Southern California, Annenberg School for Communication. "Convergence," in *USC Annenberg Online Journalism Review*. Available at http://www.ojr.org/ojr/business/1068686368.php (accessed June 21, 2006).

van Westrienen, Gerhard, and Clifford A. Lynch. "Academic Institutional Repositories: Deployment Status in 13 Nations as of mid 2005," *D-LIB Magazine* 11, no. 9 (2005). Available at http://www.dlib.org/dlib/september05/westrienen/09westrienen.html (accessed August 17, 2007).

Wetzel, Karen A., and Mary E. Jackson. *Portal Functionality Provided by ARL Libraries: Results of an ARL Survey*. ARL Bimonthly Report 222 (June 2002). Available at http://www.arl.org/newsltr/222/(accessed June 21, 2006).

Yale University. "Library Teaching and Learning Experimental Space." New Haven, CT: Yale University. Available at http://www.library.yale.edu/cclexp/(accessed June 21, 2006).

UNPUBLISHED RESOURCES

de Farber, Bess. *Collaboration Basics*. Unpublished presentation delivered at the University of Arizona, September 1, 2006.

General Services Administration. Interagency Agreement between The General Services Administration and The U.S. Department of Agriculture National Agricultural Library. Washington, DC: General Services Administration, April 14, 1995.

General Services Administration. Memorandum of Understanding between The General Services Administration and The Arizona Board of Regents, on behalf of Arizona State University. Washington DC: General Services Administration, March 9, 1995.

Georgia Institute of Technology. "Library Commons; Memo of Understanding." Atlanta: Library and Information Center, Georgia Institute of Technology, n.d.

Kearns, Julie, and Scharnau, Keith. *Learning Support Needs: What U of C Students Need to be More Effective Learners*. Joint Research Project Final Report. Calgary, Canada: University of Calgary, 1999.

National Agricultural Library. Cooperative Agreement: Develop More Advanced Approaches to Disseminating Electronic Information. Beltsville, MD: National Agricultural Library, September 29, 1995.

National Agricultural Library. Progress Report on the Agriculture Network Information Center Project. Beltsville, MD: National Agricultural Library, 1996.

National Agricultural Library. Project Proposal for Iowa Communications Network Pilot Project (Submitted to the General Services Administration). Beltsville, MD: USDA National Agricultural Library, October 21, 1994.

Palmer, Catherine. "EEE Operational Group Report," e-mail message to Carol Ann Hughes (December 1, 2003).

Society for Range Management. Memorandum of Agreement between The Society for Range Management and The Arizona Board of Regents on behalf of The University of Arizona Library. Wheat Ridge, CO: Society for Range Management, 1996.

Stuart, Crit. "Collaborative Learning Space: A Partnership between Information Technology and the Library. Atlanta: Library and Information Center, Georgia Institute of Technology, 2005.
Suffolk University. "Library Granted New Collection," *The Suffolk Journal* (Fall 1956) (unpublished).
University of Calgary. *Strategic Transformation Report Summaries: September 1998.* (unpublished report). Calgary: Strategic Transformation Coordination Task Force, University of Calgary, 1998.

INDEX

Adams, Michael, 135, 139
Ad Hoc Committee on Student Plagiarism, University of Massachusetts, 109–10
Agricultural Information and Documentation System for America (SIDALC), 181
Agriculture Network Information Center (AgNIC): as alliance model, 179–80; characteristics of, 180–81; collaboration characteristics, 184–85; digital media services, 192–93; Organization Work Group, 180; partner expectations, 181–82; strengthen support for, 183–84; University of Arizona experience, 185–94; Web sites for, 186
Alberta Heritage Digitization Project, 83
Albion College, IT collaboration, 16–17
Allison, Robert, 166
American Library Association (ALA), 36, 183
Andrew W. Mellon Foundation, 155
Arabic and Middle Eastern Electronic Library (AMEEL), Yale University, 153
ARC. *See* Armenian Research Center

Archives: Columbia University records, 145; convergence of, 82–84; digital, 144, 184; Georgia Tech, 58; Henry Ford Estate, 26, 70; of human rights organizations, 147; institutional digital, 18; library responsibility for, 27; Mardigan Library, 68–69, 72–73, 77; NEH participation, 69; UCU Yale project, 160; University of Calgary mergers, 97; University of Massachusetts, 106, 112; Wayne State University, 29
Arid Lands Information Center (ALIC), University of Arizona, 186
Arizona Remote Sensing Center (ARSC), 187
Arizona State University (ASU), 185
ARL Directors Discussion List, 4
Armenian Research Center (ARC), Mardigan Library, 26, 73, 77
Armstrong, Patricia, 204, 206–7
Art gallery collaboration, Mardigan Library, 73–74
Art programs, University of Georgia, 136
Association for Research Libraries (ARL), 183

Association of College and Research Libraries (ACRL), 36
ASU. *See* Arizona State University
Audiovisual services, 69–70, 171–72
Austin, James E., 178–79
Auxiliary services, University of Massachusetts, 104–5

Battin, Patricia, 37
Blue Ribbon Panel, USDA, 183
Bolin, Mary, 36–37
Brown, Linda, 205, 208
Brown University, 17–19
BudigOne (digital media lab), 9
Buss, Carla Wilson, 125–39

Campbell, Jerry D., 1–2, 211
Campus Media Services (CMS), Mardigan Library, 67, 78
Campus police, University of Massachusetts, 106
Campus Web sites: for AgNIC, 186; for course planning, 144; Our Future Our Past, 83; social networking, 148; strategy team, Mardigan Library, 74–75; UCI look and feel, 40–41; usability testing, 74–75; Western Rangelands management, 185–89. *See also* Digital media services; Online systems
Canadian Agriculture Library, 181
The Canadian Research Network for Research in the Social Sciences and Humanities, 84
Career services: with learning commons, 6; student success, 45, 79; University of Georgia, 138; University of Massachusetts, 25, 118
The Carnegie Classification of Institutions of Higher Education, 4
Cataloging systems: for ARC collection, 26, 73, 77; for archive staff, 26; institutional repository, 122–23; Library of Congress cooperative, 182; metadata applications, 12, 18–19, 51, 113, 122–23; online services, 12, 42, 116, 166; OPAC system, 65

CCNMTL. *See* Columbia Center for New Media Teaching and Learning
Center for Digital Initiatives, Brown University, 17–18
Center for Digital Research and Scholarship (CDRS), Columbia University libraries, 143
Center for Educational Resources (CER), Johns Hopkins University, 204–5, 207
Center for Educational Technology (CET), Emory University, 20
Center for Enhancement of Teaching and Learning (CETL), Georgia Tech, 20
Center for Teaching (CFT), Vanderbilt University, 204
Center for Teaching, University of Massachusetts, 107
Center for Teaching and Learning (CTL), University of Georgia, 125–26
Center for the Enhancement of Teaching and Learning (CETL), Georgia Tech, 61
Center for Undergraduate Research Opportunities (CURO), University of Georgia, 137
CEP. *See* Civic Engagement Project
Chief Information Officer (CIO), 82, 142
China, resources to, 50
CIAO. *See* Columbia International Affairs Online
CIO. *See* Chief Information Officer
Circulation departments: course reserves, University of Massachusetts, 122; in space configurations, 53–54; system replacement, Mardigan Library, 65–66; technology influences on, 122; when inadequate, 65–66
Civic Engagement Project (CEP), Mardigan Library, 74
Client Needs Group, University of Calgary, 96
CMS. *See* Campus Media Services

Cohen, Nadine, 125–39
CoLAB Planning Series, 178
Collaboration/collaborative programs: for agricultural information, 177–97; assessment of, 206–8; decentralized, Brown University, 17–19; dialogue with teaching faculty, 3, 89; at Georgia Tech, 49–61; with information technology, 1, 16–17, 203; with non-librarians, 203; rangeland management Web site, 185–88; structural changes, Mardigan Library, 77–78; as tricky proposition, 29; at UCI, 35–47; University of Calgary, 84–91; University of Georgia, Student Learning Center, 125–27, 135–37; virtual *vs.* official, 77–78; at Yale University, 30–31
Collaborative Learning Environment (CLC), 8
College libraries (COLLIB-L), 4
College of Agriculture and Life Sciences (CALS), University of Arizona, 186
College of Arts, Sciences, and Letters (CASL), Mardigan Library, 77
Columbia Center for New Media Teaching and Learning (CCNMTL), 144–45
Columbia International Affairs Online (CIAO), 143
Columbia's Center for New Media Teaching and Learning (CCNMTL), 19
The Columbia University libraries: the 3 C's, 19; CIO administration, 142; converging units, 143–45; future trends for, 145–49; medical/science research community, 148; organizational context, 141–43; student needs, 149
Committee on Yale College Education (CYCE), 152–53
Community and junior colleges (CJC-L), 4
Computer software, course management, 5–6

Computing and Information Services (CIS), 17
Content management system, UCI, 40–41
Convergence: advantages, 9–10, 13, 52, 202; among stakeholders, 38; of archives, 82–84; common drivers, 3; defined, 1–2; disadvantages/difficulties, 10–11, 13, 47; for faculty, 3, 8, 10; future areas for, 11–12; literature review of, 2–3; multifaceted, 7–8; non-librarians and, 202; procedures used for, 3–4; programmatic, 44–46; questionnaire findings, 5–6; study objectives, 3; Suffolk University, Poetry Center, 167–70, 173–74; technological, 37–40, 202; as top strategy, 36; as traditional library offerings, 12–14; University of Calgary, 6–7, 81–100; virtual *vs.* official, 77–78; Yale libraries, 151–61
Convergence, collaboration, and competition (3 C's), 19
Cooperative State Research and Extension Service (CSREES), 180
Coordination Task Force, University of Calgary, 91–93
Copyright Advisory Office, Columbia University libraries, 144
Core Operations Group (COG), Mardigan Library, 72
Creative writing program, Suffolk University, 165–67, 169, 173–74
Curriculum reform, Yale University, 152–54
Custodial services, University of Massachusetts, 105–6

Dewey, Barbara I., 10
Digital Culture imprint, University of Michigan, 201
Digital media services: for AgNIC, 192–93; archives, 144, 184; CDRS cyberscholarships, 143; Columbia University libraries, 145; metadata applications, 155; University of

Calgary, 83; University of Georgia, 136, 138; Yale University, 153. *See also* Campus Web sites; Online systems
Disability services, University of Massachusetts, 118
Distance learning: CMS, Mardigan Library, 67; Georgia Tech, 49–50, 59; University of Calgary, 90; University of Michigan, 27
Distance Learning and Professional Education (DLPE), Georgia Tech, 59
Distinguished Faculty Friend Award, Mardigan Library, 75
Distributed Learning Task Force, University of Michigan, 64
Document Delivery Services, University of Calgary, 88
Drucker Foundation, 177
Du Bois, W.E.B., 112
Dugan, Robert E., 163–75
Duncan, Jim, 36–37

Earthscape knowledge center, Columbia University libraries, 143
Eaton, Nancy L., 9–11
Edwards, Mike, 102
EEE. *See* Electronic Educational Environment
Electrical and Computer Engineering's (ECE) Digital Media Lab, Georgia Tech, 59
Electronic Educational Environment (EEE), 7, 37–40
Electronic library, University of Georgia, 129, 133–35
Electronic Library Initiatives (ELI/Davis program), Yale University, 153
Electronic Press (EPAGE services), Georgia Tech), 57–59
Electronic Publishing Initiative at Columbia (EPIC), Columbia University libraries, 143
Electronic reserves, University of Massachusetts, 111
Electronic Text Center and the Electronic Data Service (EDS), Columbia University, 19

Emory Center for Interactive Teaching (ECIT), 20
Emory University, 19–20
Enrollment services, University of Michigan, 205
Enterprise Information Technology Services (EITS), University of Georgia, 125
EPAGE services. *See* Electronic Press

Faculty/faculty needs: AV services, 69–70; collaborative dialogue with, 3, 89; convergence for, 3, 8, 10; Distinguished Faculty Friend Award, 75; EEE web technology, 39; information technology assistance, 68; institutional repository for, 43–44; of libraries, 28; orientation, 75–76; pedagogy and, 107–14; staff development, 70–72; teaching commons, 123; Tegrity software, 60; University of Georgia, 132; writing facility, 109
Faculty Outreach Committee, Mardigan Library, 76
Faculty Salon, Mardigan Library, 73
Faculty Senate Scholarship Committee, University of Michigan, 27
de Farber, Bess, 178–79
Feng, Cyril C. H., 37
Fine Arts and Visual Resources, University of Calgary, 82
Focus Action Committee, Mardigan Library, 76–77
Follett University Bookstore, University of Massachusetts, 106–7
Formative Evaluation Research Associates (FERA), Mardigan Library, 70–71
Freshman Advising and Mentoring (FAME), Emory University, 20
Fyn, Amy F., 201–12

General Services Administration (GSA), 185
GENIUS. *See* Global Expertise Network for Industry, Universities, and Scholars

INDEX 227

Georgia Institute of Technology (Georgia Tech): EPAGE services, 57–59; facilities, for student success, 51–57; learning commons, 13, 21–22; library collaboration at, 49–50; OIT at, 20–22, 49, 52–56; print *vs.* digital media, 51; resources to China, 50; Sakai usage, 60; SMARTech institutional repository service, 57–59; undergraduate retention, 56
Gherman, Paul, 9–10
Global Expertise Network for Industry, Universities, and Scholars (GENIUS), 147
Gloss, Ken, 167, 174
GSA. *See* General Services Administration

Hamilton College, 203–4, 206, 208–9
Hawkins, Brian L., 37
Hemmasi, Harriette, 12
Henry Ford Estate, University of Michigan, 26, 70
Hernon, Peter, 1–14, 201–12
Hewitt, Ken, 92
Hughes, Carol Ann, 10, 35–47
HumaniTech program, 8
Human rights organizations, archives, 147
Hutchinson, Barbara S., 177–97

Image Collection Library, University of Massachusetts, 113
Indiana University-Purdue University Columbus (IUPUC), 7
Information Commons, University of Calgary, 84–88, 95–97
Information services enterprises, 141–49
Information Technologies and International Development (journal), 58
Information technology (IT): collaboration and, 1, 16–17, 203; faculty help with, 68; Hamilton College, 203–4; Mardigan Library, services, 67–68; as strategic motivator, 50; sustainability of, 37; University of Calgary, 86–87, 95; Yale University, 154
Information Technology Services (ITS), 154
Inquiry through blended learning (ITBL), University of Calgary, 90
Institutional digital archive, Brown University, 18
Institutional repositories, 5–6, 13, 43–44
Instructional technology (IT): Albion College collaboration, 16–17; Brown University support, 18; CCNMTL leadership in, 144; Hamilton's College, 203–4; University of Georgia, 136
Intellectual asset management, libraries, 51
Interdisciplinary studies, Yale University, 152–54
Interlinked cross-silo world, libraries, 49
International Programs Office (IPO), University of Massachusetts, 118–19
International Rice Research Institute (IRRI), 181
The Internet, collaborative library services, 51
Iowa Communications Network (ICN) Pilot Project, 185
Irving Zieman Poetry Library. *See* Suffolk University, Poetry Center
Ivy Tech Community College of Columbus, 7

Johns Hopkins University, 204–5, 207
Juvenile Historic Collection, Mardigan Library, 74

Kennedy, Scott E., 9, 11
King, Florence E., 125–39
Kriigel, Barbara J., 63–79

Larry L. Sautter Award for Innovation in Information Technology, 39
LCR. *See* Libraries and Cultural Resources

Leadership cultivation, Mardigan Library, 71–72
Learning collaborative technology, 59–61
Learning commons/resource center: career services with, 6; establishment of, 5–6, 13; Georgia Tech, 13, 21–22; library role in, 123–24; University of Calgary, 96–98; University of Connecticut–Storrs, 12; University of Massachusetts, 25–26, 102–8, 114–20, 122–23; Vanderbilt University, 204, 206; Yale University, 154
Learning organization principles, Mardigan Library, 70
Liaison programs, University of Massachusetts, 112–13
Librarians: campus partners for, 11; data, 91; information technology and, 89; larger role of, 36–37, 45, 153, 193; as liaison, 90, 112–13, 122–23; metadata applications for, 36, 187; network resource position, 68–69; outside activities, involvement in, 28; promotion of, 65; skills needed, 133–34; *vs.* non-librarians, 202–9
Libraries: archive responsibility of, 27; convergence, traditional offerings, 12–14; digital, 145; electronic services, 129, 133–35; faculty needs for, 28; as information services enterprise, 141–49; in learning commons creation, 123–24; proactive roles of, 29; purpose of, 1, 201; R&D agendas, 146; RSS Feeds in, 42, 148; UROP Research Fellowship for, 45
Libraries, collaborative services: evolution of, 201; facilities, for student success, 51–57; intellectual asset management, 51; interlinked cross-silo world, 49; the Internet, 51; learning technology, 59–61; motivators for strategic mission, 50–52; and OIT, 49, 52–56; refocusing services, 57–59

Libraries and Cultural Resources (LCR), University of Calgary, 81–84
Libraries' Information Literacy Initiative, 8
Library East Commons (LEC), Georgia Tech, 53, 55
Library Information Technology Association (LITA), 36
Library of the Future Task Force (LFTF), University of Calgary, 94–95
Library Situation Assessment Task Force, University of Calgary, 93–94
Library West Commons (LWC), Georgia Tech, 54–55
Lippencott, Joan K., 2, 102
Literacy services: Center for Teaching, 107; information skills/perspective, 90, 96, 202; by liaison librarians, 90, 113; peer tutoring program, 45–46; University of Georgia, 138
Literature review of convergence, 2–3

MacMillan Center for International and Area Studies, Yale University, 152, 157
Maps, Academic Data, and Geographic Information Centre (MADGIC), University of Calgary, 88, 91
Marchant, Fred, 163–75
Mardigan Library, University of Michigan. *See* University of Michigan, Mardigan Library
Medical Library, Yale University, 160
Medical/science research community, Columbia University libraries, 148
Memorandum of Understanding (MOU), GSA *vs.* ASU, 185
Metadata applications: cataloging systems, 12, 18–19, 51, 113, 122–23; Columbia University, 154–56; of digital data, 155; for librarians, 36, 187; resources for, 181; Yale University, 30–31
Meyer, Richard W., 49–61
Michigan Library Association Leadership Academy, 72

Middle States Commission on Higher Education, 202
Mildred F. Sawyer Library, 165–66, 171. *See also* Suffolk University, Poetry Center
Miller, Rush, 35
Moore, Anne C., 101–24
Motivators, collaborative library services, 50–52
Multicultural Canada project, digitization, 84
Multifaceted convergence, UCI, 7–8
Multimedia Presentation Center (MPC), Hamilton College, 208
MyDropBox plagiarism detection software, 110

NACS. *See* Network and Academic Computing Services
National Agricultural Library (NAL), 180–83
National Endowment for the Humanities (NEH), 69
National Science Foundation (NSF), 180
Natural Resources Conservation Service (NRCS), Arizona, 187
Neal, James, 141–49
NEH. *See* National Endowment for the Humanities
Network and Academic Computing Services (NACS), 7, 38, 43–44
Network resource librarian, Mardigan Library, 68
New Haven campus acquisition, Yale University, 152, 158–59
New Student Orientation (NSO), University of Massachusetts, 120
Nongovernmental organizations (NGOs), 189
Non-librarians, 202–9

Office for Information Technology (OIT): Georgia Institute of Technology, 20–22, 49, 52–56; University of Massachusetts, 117–18
Office for Teaching and Learning (OTL), Wayne State University, 28

Office of Faculty Development, University of Massachusetts, 107–9
Online public access catalog (OPAC), Mardigan Library, 65
Online systems: catalog services, 12, 42, 116, 166; CIAO resources, 143; Earthscape knowledge center, 143; EEE course management system, 7, 37–40; references/acquisitions, 120, 122; RSS Feeds, 42, 148; streaming audio/video, 111–12. *See also* Campus Web sites; Digital media services
OPAC. *See* Online public access catalog
Organizational structure/context, 66–70, 70–72
Organizational structure/context, libraries, 141–43
Our Future Our Past, web site, 83

Pedagogy and faculty, University of Massachusetts, 107–14
Peer tutoring program, UCI, 45–46
PeopleSoft student system (SPIRE), University of Massachusetts, 120
Pfander, Jeanne L., 177–97
Plagiarism issues, University of Massachusetts, 109–10
Pluralism Project, religious music, 75
Poetry Center. *See* Suffolk University, Poetry Center
Powell, Ronald R., 1–14, 201–12
Print *vs.* digital media, Georgia Tech, 51
Prochaska, Alice, 11, 151–61
Programmatic convergence, UCI, 44–46
Programs in International Educational Resources (PIER), Yale University, 153
Promotion policy, Mardigan Library, 65
Provost's Learning Commons Committee (PLCC), University of Massachusetts, 103–4
Public Affairs and Alumni Relations (PAUR), Brown University, 18

INDEX

Ranganathan's Five Laws, 47
Rangeland management. *See* Western Rangelands
R&D. *See* Research and development
Recognizing the Actual Desires And Requirements (RADAR), Mardigan Library, 70
Reese, Mike, 205, 207
References/acquisitions, online systems, 120, 122
RefWorks, bibliography management, 110–11
Regional Data Centre (RDC), University of Calgary, 91
Research and development (R&D), Columbia University, 146
Research commons, University of Massachusetts, 123
Research support, Yale University, 155–57
Reynolds, Nikki, 203–4, 208–9
Richards, Timothy F., 63–79
Ronayne, Michael, 165
RSS Feeds (Really Simple Syndication), 42, 148
Ruyle, George B., 177–97

Sakai open source collaboration, Georgia Tech, 60
Sargent, David, 166–68
Satellite help services, 5–6
Sautter Award. *See* Larry L. Sautter Award for Innovation in Information Technology
Schafer, Jay, 101–24
School of Medicine, Yale University, 156, 160
SIS. *See* Student information system
Smallen, David, 203, 206
SMARTech institutional repository service, Georgia Tech, 57–59
Space configurations: circulation departments, 53–54; Suffolk University, 168–73; Yale University, 157–59
Staff development. *See* Faculty/faculty needs
Stakeholders convergence, 38

Stanley, Deborah, 125–39
Statistics Canada, University of Calgary, 91
St. Bonaventure University, 7
Strawn, George, 180
Streaming audio/video, 111–12
Stuart, Crit, 13–14
Student information system (SIS), Mardigan Library, 65–66
Student Learning Center (SLC), University of Georgia, 23–25
Student needs: academic support enterprise, 101–24; career services, success, 45, 79; Columbia University, 149; University of Georgia, Student Learning Center, 130–32. *See also* Learning commons/resource center
Suffolk University, Poetry Center: academic objectives, 174; audiovisual services, 171–72; convergence of, 167–70, 173–74; creative writing program, 165, 167; Mildred F. Sawyer Library, 165–66, 171; space configurations, 168–73; strategies for creation, 170–71; Zieman gift for, 163–64, 167–69

Teachers. *See* Faculty/faculty needs
Teaching commons, University of Massachusetts, 123
Technological convergence, 37–40, 202
Technology Resource Center (TRC), Wayne State University, 28
Technology Task Force (TTF), University of Calgary, 92
Tegrity Course Capture Software Pilot Team, Georgia Tech, 60
Tenglund, Ann M., 7
3 C's. *See* Convergence, collaboration, and competition
Turnitin Plagiarism Detection Service, University of Massachusetts, 109–10
Tutoring, University of Georgia, 136–38

UA. *See* University of Arizona
UCI. *See* University of California, Irvine

INDEX 231

Uganda Christian University (UCU), Yale University, 160
Undergraduate Research Opportunity Program (UROP), 8, 44–45
Undergraduate Research Option (URO), Georgia Tech, 59
Undergraduate retention, Georgia Tech, 56
University libraries (ULS-L), 4
University of Arizona, AgNIC experience, 185–94
University of Arizona Libraries (UAL), 186
University of Calgary: archive mergers, 97; budget cuts, 93–94; CIO position, 82; collaborations, 84–91; convergence at, 6–7, 81–100; digitizing materials, 83; LCR at, 81–82; learning commons at, 97–98; MADGIC at, 88, 91; planning/strategic transformation, 91–97; Statistics Canada employees, 91; training/staff development, 88
University of California, Irvine (UCI): Administrative Computing, 42; collaboration at, 35–47; content management system, 40–41; convergence at, 37–38; EEE at, 7, 37–40; eScholarship Repository, 43; institutional repository, 43–44; multifaceted convergence, 7–8; NACS staff proposals, 43–44; peer tutoring program, 45–46; programmatic convergence, 44–46; student portal, 42–43; technological convergence at, 38–40; UROP program at, 44–45
University of Connecticut, 12, 22–23
University of Georgia, Student Learning Center: academic impact, 135; building description, 128–29; collaboration in, 125–27, 136–37; electronic library, 129, 133–35; faculty needs, 132; focus group interviews, 133; history and development, 23–25, 127–37; planning of, 127–28; primary partners in, 125; student needs, 130–32; usage traffic, 129–30
University of Kansas, 8–9
University of Massachusetts, W.E.B Du Bois Library: auxiliary services, 104–5; campus police, 106; career services, 25–26, 118; Center for Teaching, 107; custodial services, 105–6; disability services, 118; electronic reserves, 111; faculty writing facility, 109; first-year experience programs, 113–14; Follett University Bookstore, 106–7; future initiatives, 123; Image Collection Library, 113; internal library operations, 120–23; IPO integration, 118–19; learning commons creation, 25–26, 102–4, 107–8, 122; learning resource center, 114–15; liaison programs, 112–13; Office of Faculty Development, 107–9; OIT collaboration, 117–18; other campus agencies, 104–7; pedagogy and faculty, 107–14; RefWorks, bibliography management, 110–11; streaming audio/video, 111–12; student academic support, 114–20; Turnitin Plagiarism Detection Service, 109–10; University Archives Department, 106, 112; writing center, 115–16
University of Michigan, Mardigan Library: archives, 68–69; audiovisual services, 69–70; campus web strategy team, 74–75; CEP, for student participation, 74; CMS services, 67; collaboration at, 26–28, 208; conditions for success, 63–66; as engaged entity, 63; enrollment services, 205; faculty salons, 73; Henry Ford Estate, 26, 70; ITS for, 67–68; leadership cultivation, 71–72; mission/vision/goals of, 64–65, 78–79; network resource librarian, 68; OPAC replacement, 65–66; organizational structure/development, 66–72; promotion

policy, 65; SIS replacement, 65–66; TV studio, 66–67
University of Pittsburgh, 35
UROP. *See* Undergraduate Research Opportunity Program
U.S. Agricultural Information Network (USAIN), 182
U.S. Department of Agriculture (USDA), 180, 183

Vanderbilt University, 9, 204, 206–7
Virtual *vs.* official, convergence/collaboration, 77–78
Voice/Vision Holocaust Survivor Oral Histories Archive, Mardigan Library, 72–73, 77

Walter, Scott, 8
Walters, Tyler O., 49–61
Warren, Darlene, 81–100
Wayne State University (WSU), 28–30
WebCT (learning management system), 22
W.E.B. Du Bois Library. *See* University of Massachusetts, W.E.B Du Bois Library
Web sites, 185–88. *See also* Campus Web sites
Weise, Frieda, 37
Western Coordinating Committee (WCC), University of Arizona, 189
Western Council for Agricultural Research, Extension, and Teaching (WCARET), 188

Western Rangelands, University of Arizona: AgNIC experience, 188–92; lessons learned, 192–94; operating structure, 189; rangeland management Web site, 185–88; survey results, 189–92
White, Elizabeth, 125–39
Workshop on the Information Search Process for Research (WISPR), University of Calgary, 90
Writing and Library Research Peer Tutor Program, 8
Writing centers, 115–16, 136–38, 152

Yale Collections Collaborative, 155–56
Yale University: collaborative programs at, 30–31; curriculum reform, 152–54; information technology at, 154; interdisciplinary studies, 152–54; Medical Library, 160; New Haven campus acquisition, 152, 158–59; and outside communities, 159–60; research support, 155–57; School of Medicine, 156, 160; space configurations, 157–59; UCU archive project, 160; writing center, 152
Yee, Sandra, 11

Zieman, Irving Pergament, 163–64, 167–69
Zieman Poetry Library. *See* Suffolk University, Poetry Center

ABOUT THE EDITORS AND CONTRIBUTORS

PETER HERNON is a professor at Simmons College, Boston, where he teaches courses on government information policy and resources, evaluation of information services, research methods, and academic librarianship. He received his Ph.D. from Indiana University and has taught at Simmons College, the University of Arizona, and Victoria University of Wellington (New Zealand). Besides his various activities in New Zealand, he has delivered keynote addresses in seven other countries: Canada, England, France, Finland, Portugal, Spain, and South Africa.

Hernon is the co-editor of *Library & Information Science Research,* founding editor of *Government Information Quarterly,* and past editor of the *Journal of Academic Librarianship.* He is the author of approximately 275 publications, 45 of which are books. Among these are *Improving the Quality of Library Services for Students with Disabilities* (2006), *Comparative Perspectives on E-government* (2006), *Revisiting Outcomes Assessment in Higher Education* (2006), *Outcomes Assessment in Higher Education* (2004), and *Assessing Service Quality* (1998), which received the Highsmith award for outstanding contribution to the literature of library and information science in 1999. He is the 2008 recipient of the Association of College and Research Libraries' (ACRL) award for Academic/Research Librarian of the Year.

RONALD R. POWELL is a professor at Wayne State University, Detroit, Michigan. His teaching and research interests include research methods, academic libraries, education for librarianship, and the measurement and evaluation of library and information resources and services. Among his publications are *Qualitative Research in Information Management* (Libraries Unlimited), *Basic Research Methods for Librarians* (Libraries Unlimited), now in its fourth edition, and *The Next Library Leadership* (Libraries Unlimited).

CARLA WILSON BUSS is the Curriculum Materials and Education Librarian at the University of Georgia, Athens. When the Student Learning Center first opened, she was the Instructional Services Coordinator and a Reference Librarian. She received her Master's in Library Science from Kent State University.

NADINE COHEN is a Reference/Instruction Librarian in the Student Learning Center at the University of Georgia, Athens. She has been in that position since the opening of the building. Her responsibilities include assisting in training the Student Learning Center's student computing staff and coordination of SLC assessment activities. She serves as liaison to the College of Education and is the founding member of CLOC (Community Librarians Outreach and Collaboration), which brings together local area school, public and academic librarians to create a coherent information literacy program that stretches across curricula and grade level. She received her master's degree in library and information science from the University of California, Los Angeles in 1994.

ROBERT E. DUGAN became the Director of the Mildred F. Sawyer Library at Suffolk University in Boston in 1998. During his career he has worked on library services and issues at the local, state, and federal levels, and has worked in public, state, and academic libraries. Article and monograph topics include outcomes assessment, planning, policy implications, and the application of information technologies, financial management, and the federal depository library program. His current interest concerns issues of institutional and organizational accountability, focusing on identifying and considering measures applied by higher education and academic libraries and their presentation to, and usage by, their various stakeholders.

AMY F. FYN earned her Master of Library and Information Science degree in 2007 at Wayne State University in Detroit, Michigan. At Wayne State, she received a Student Travel Award, attended conferences in Eastern Europe, and presented a paper on library collaboration at a conference in Romania. She is interested in academic and special libraries, research methods, and information literacy acquisition. She also holds a Master of English degree from Boston College in Chestnut Hill, Massachusetts, and a Bachelor of Arts in English from The University of Toledo in Toledo, Ohio.

CAROL ANN HUGHES joined the University of California, Irvine Libraries as Associate University Librarian (AUL) for Public Services in March 2002.

She is responsible for the overall planning, budgeting, resource allocation, and administration of the Public Services division, including Web Services and the Grunigen Medical Library. She received her Ph.D. in Information from the University of Michigan, an M.B.A. from the University of California—Los Angeles, and MLS and BA from the University of Illinois, Urbana. Her career has encompassed both the academic and commercial sectors. Hughes currently serves as Chair of the Heads of Public Services for the University of California Libraries and as a feature editor of *portal: Libraries and the Academy*. She is active in the profession and was recently chair of the University Libraries Section of the Association of College and Research Libraries. She currently serves as Chair of the ACRL Advocacy Coordinating Committee. Dr. Hughes is the author of over 40 articles and has made numerous professional and scholarly contributions in the areas of e-books and digital services in academic libraries. She has been awarded the MCB University Press 2001 Award for Excellence and the ALCTS Blackwell North America Scholarship Award 1992 for her publications.

BARBARA S. HUTCHINSON is currently Assistant to the Dean and Director of the Agricultural Experiment Station in the University of Arizona's College of Agriculture and Life Sciences (CALS) in Tucson. In that capacity, she provides grants support to CALS faculty and develops international extramural programs. Dr. Hutchinson has served as President of the U.S. Agricultural Information Network (USAIN), Chair of the AgNIC Executive Board, and is now a Board member of the International Association of Agricultural Information Specialists (IAALD) and a member of the North American Advisory Board for CAB International. She has been involved in the Agriculture Network Information Center (AgNIC) and Western Rangelands initiatives since 1995. She has also provided technical assistance in information management in developing countries throughout the world. Her doctoral studies in Higher Education were focused on organizational change and the role of academic research units. Her current research interests include the development of institutional repositories and the use of Web technologies to facilitate life-long learning and decision making. Hutchinson also holds a Master's in Library Science, a B.A. in History, and is a Professor in the Department of Agricultural Education.

FLORENCE E. KING is the Assistant University Librarian for Human Resources and the Director of the Student Learning Center Electronic Teaching Library at the University of Georgia, Athens. She was part of the Student Learning Center building design team and coordinated the Support Partnership which planned for the opening of the building in 2003. She remains with the SLC as Director of the library portion of the building. Florence received her Master's in Library and Information Science from the Florida State University and has been with the UGA Libraries since 1984.

BARBARA J. KRIIGEL is the Associate Director, Circulation and Technical Services, University of Michigan-Dearborn Mardigian Library. Her experience includes both technical services and reference services in academic, public, and special libraries. She has been active in various professional organizations, such as the Michigan Library Association, the Michigan Library Consortium, the Southeastern Michigan League of Libraries, and OCLC Members Council. Having a passion for authority control, she has given numerous presentations and workshops on the topic for the Michigan Library Consortium and the Innovative Users Group. She holds a Master of Science in Librarianship from Western Michigan University and a B.A. in Mathematics from Andrews University.

FRED MARCHANT is the author of *Tipping Point*, winner of the 1993 Washington Prize in poetry. His second book of poems, *Full Moon Boat*, came out from Graywolf Press in 2000, and *House on Water, House in Air: New and Selected Poems* were released from Dedalus Press, Dublin, Ireland, in 2002. He is also the co-translator (with Nguyen Ba Chung) of *From a Corner of My Yard*, poetry by the Vietnamese poet Tran Dang Khoa. This book was published in 2006 by the Education Publishing House and the Ho Chi Minh Museum in Ha Noi, Viet Nam.

Marchant is a Professor of English and the Director of the Creative Writing Program, and Co-director (with Robert Dugan) of the Poetry Center at Suffolk University, Boston. A graduate of Brown University, he earned his Ph.D. from the University of Chicago's Committee on Social Thought. He is also a long-time teaching affiliate of the William Joiner Center for the Study of War and Social Consequences at the University of Massachusetts-Boston. He has taught creative writing workshops at sites around the country, ranging from the Robert Frost Place in Franconia, NH to the Veterans Writing Group, organized by Maxine Hong Kingston, in the San Francisco Bay Area.

In 1970, Marchant became one of the first officers ever to be honorably discharged as a conscientious objector from the United States Marine Corps. Recently he has edited *Another World Instead: The Early Poems of William Stafford, 1937–1947*. This collection of poems, published by Graywolf Press in April 2008, focuses on Stafford's time as a conscientious objector in Civilian Public Service camps during World War II. Marchant's new collection of his own poetry, *The Looking House*, is forthcoming in January, 2009, also from Graywolf Press.

RICHARD W. MEYER is Dean and Director of Library Services for the Georgia Institute of Technology, Atlanta, Georgia. As dean and director, he represents the interests of the library with the Provost's Office and Academic Council of the University. He received his Masters in Library Science from the University of Illinois in 1970 after having served for two years as a librarian with E. I. DuPont de Nemours. His undergraduate degrees from the University of Missouri were awarded in chemistry (BS) and library science (BA) in 1967. Following several years in the field with the University of Texas at Dallas and Indiana State University, Meyer secured a Masters in Economics from Clemson during a 12-year appointment there as Associate Director. Following nine years at Trinity University in San Antonio as Director, Rich joined Georgia Tech in 2000. Active in the profession with ALA early on, he served as a Trinity's library representative to the advisory board of the Associated Colleges of the South and more recently on the Board of Directors of Solinet. His research and publishing efforts extend to over 50 articles which focus on library management, automation, faculty status, and journal pricing. He marks Georgia Tech's recent receipt in 2007 of the ALA, ACRL *Excellence* in *Academic Libraries* award as a high point in a 40-year career in libraries.

ANNE C. MOORE is now Dean of Libraries at the I.D. Weeks and Lommen Health Sciences Libraries at the University of South Dakota. Until summer 2008, she led public service efforts at the W.E.B. Du Bois Library at the University of Massachusetts–Amherst and coordinated the establishment of collaborations between all the academic support services in the Learning Commons. She joined UMass Amherst Libraries in 2001 and served as Head, Reference Services, until 2004. Her previous experience spanned nearly all aspects of academic librarianship at New Mexico State University, George Mason University, and University of Arizona. She earned her M.S.L.S. at the University of North Carolina at Chapel Hill in 1983 and her Ph.D. in Educational Management and Development, Higher Education Administration in 2001. She is adjunct faculty at Simmons College Graduate School of Library and Information Science. Her research and leadership interests include learning commons, higher education collaborations, information literacy, reference and liaison services, academic libraries, assessment of academic library services, and social science research methods.

JAMES NEAL is Vice President for Information Services and University Librarian at Columbia University, New York, where he is responsible for academic computing services and a network of 25 libraries. Previously, he served as Dean of University Libraries at Indiana and Johns Hopkins. He is active in the areas of scholarly communication, copyright, and digital library development. He has served in key leadership positions in the American Library Association, Association of Research Libraries, Research Libraries Group, Digital Library Federation, National Information Standards Organization, Freedom to Read Foundation, International Federation of Library Associations, and SPARC. He was selected as ACRL Academic Librarian of the Year in 1997 and received ALA's Hugh Atkinson Memorial Award in 2007.

ABOUT THE EDITORS AND CONTRIBUTORS

JEANNE L. PFANDER is Associate Librarian and a specialist for the agricultural and life sciences at the University of Arizona, Tucson. She has a long-term interest in natural resources studies and has been involved in the AgNIC Western Rangelands initiative for the past 10 years. She was involved in the initiation and development of the open access online journal published originally at the University of Arizona Library—the *Journal of Insect Science* (insectscience.org). She is also active on other grant-funded digital projects such as the Arizona Electronic Atlas (atlas.library.arizona.edu) and the Sonoran Desert Knowledge Exchange project (http://www.sdke.org).

ALICE PROCHASKA is University Librarian at Yale University. Prior to assuming this position in 2001, she was the Director of Special Collections at the British Library and librarian at the University of London.

TIMOTHY F. RICHARDS is the Director of the Mardigian Library at the University of Michigan-Dearborn. He provides leadership and direction for the library and represents the library's interests as a member of the Provost's Council of Deans. During his career, he has served in various administrative and public services capacities at the University of Michigan in Ann Arbor, Vanderbilt University, and the University of Michigan–Dearborn. His primary professional interests concern organizational leadership and organizational effectiveness. He has been active in the American Library Association, the Michigan Library Association, and the Michigan Library Consortium. Before becoming a librarian, he served as an officer in the U.S. Army. He earned the Master of Arts in Library Science from the University of Michigan in 1974 and the B.A. in History from the University of New Hampshire in 1968.

GEORGE B. RUYLE is chair of the Rangeland and Forest Resources Program and a Range Management Specialist in the School of Natural Resources, University of Arizona, Tucson. His extension and research areas focus on sustainable livestock production on rangelands with an emphasis on environmental monitoring. For more than 10 years, he has been involved in the initiation and development of the Western Rangelands Partnership, now involving 19 land grant universities to provide a Web portal to rangeland ecology and management information. He served on the National Academy of Sciences Committee on Rangeland Classification and was co-author of the National Research Council book *Rangeland Health: New Methods to Classify, Inventory, and Monitor Rangelands*. He is a Society for Range Management Fellow and Certified Professional in Rangeland Management. Ruyle has a BS from Arizona State University, a Masters from the University of California at Berkeley, and a Ph.D. in Rangeland Science from Utah State University.

ABOUT THE EDITORS AND CONTRIBUTORS

JAY SCHAFER has been Director of Libraries at the University of Massachusetts–Amherst since 2004. He earned his degree in librarianship from the University of Denver and has served in administrative positions at a number of institutions including the University of Colorado at Denver and Bay Path College. In addition to his participation on the Five Colleges Librarians Council, Schafer is currently President of the Boston Library Consortium Board of Directors. He combines his expertise in library collection building, resource sharing, and facilities space planning with a deep dedication to providing innovative, high-quality service to library users. The Learning Commons in the W.E.B. Du Bois Library is one tremendously successful example of his belief that libraries must evolve to meet the needs of today's students while maintaining the high standards expected of a nationally ranked research library.

DEBORAH STANLEY is a reference librarian at the University of Georgia Libraries, Athens, Georgia, and serves as the libraries' Webmaster. She was based in the Student Learning Center Electronic Teaching Library for the first three years of its existence. She received her Masters in Librarianship from the University of Sheffield in the United Kingdom.

TYLER O. WALTERS is the Associate Director, Technology and Resource Services, Georgia Institute of Technology Library and Information Center, Atlanta, Georgia. He provides leadership, vision, and expertise in digital library programs, information technologies, electronic resources management, metadata, and archives and records. Walters is a co-Principal Investigator with the MetaArchive Cooperative, one of the eight original digital preservation partnerships with the Library of Congress' National Digital Information Infrastructure and Preservation Program (http://www.metaarchive.org). His recent committee appointments include the National Science Foundation's National Science Digital Library Sustainability Committee, the Association of College and Research Libraries' Research Committee, and Chair of the DSpace User Group Program Committee for the 2nd International Conference on Open Repositories 2007. Walters was also a member of the ARL/NSF workgroup that produced the report, *To Stand the Test of Time: Long-term Stewardship of Data Sets in Science and Engineering* (http://www.arl.org/bm~doc/digdatarpt.pdf). The author of 20 published articles and presenter at over 50 professional conferences, Walters is a past recipient of the Society of American Archivists' Ernst Posner Award for best article in the *American Archivist* (1998). He holds a Master of Arts in Library and Information Science from the University of Arizona, a Master of Arts in Archival Management from North Carolina State University, and a Bachelors in History from Northern Illinois University.

ABOUT THE EDITORS AND CONTRIBUTORS

DARLENE WARREN is the Associate University Librarian for Client Services in Libraries and Cultural Resources at the University of Calgary in Alberta, Canada. She started her career as a special librarian at Canada Department of Fisheries and Oceans Biological Research Station in St. Andrews, New Brunswick. With the discovery that she most enjoyed working with university students completing summer coursework, she switched to academic librarianship and joined the University of Calgary in the fall of 1988. At Calgary, she has served as a liaison librarian for the sciences, document delivery services librarian in the Health Sciences Library, Head of the Gallagher Library of Geology and Geophysics, and Head of Access Services. She has been in her current position since January 2000. Warren has been active in professional associations and has served The Alberta Library (TAL) (a provincial multi-type library consortium) on numerous committees. She has a Master of Library Service degree from Dalhousie University in Halifax, Nova Scotia, and a Bachelor of Arts in History from Mount Allison University in Sackville, New Brunswick.

ELIZABETH WHITE is a Reference and Instruction Librarian at the University of Georgia Libraries, Athens, Georgia, where she is Libraries Liaison to the School for Public and International Affairs. She also works closely with undergraduate researchers, including the Roosevelt Institution, and trains Endnote and RefWorks users on the campus. White also manages and coordinates the Libraries Virtual Reference service, and has given several talks on the subject. She received her Masters in Library and Information Science from the University of North Carolina at Chapel Hill in 2005.